Prophetic Purposes and the Zeal of the Lord

When Sovereignty and Free Will Meet
By Kenneth L. Birks

Published by Straight Arrow Ministries
First Edition

Cover Design by Hans Bennewitz

www.straitarrow.net
Copyright © 2019

*Dedicated to Richard C. (Dick) Benjamin
Pastor, Teacher, and Apostle who provided
the environment for me and thousands of
others to be taught the Word of God with
authority and integrity.*

~

*Of the increase of His government and peace there
will be no end, upon the throne of David and over His
kingdom, to order it and establish it with judgment
and justice from that time forward, even forever, the
zeal of the Lord of hosts will perform this.*
Isaiah 9:7

*He lays the beams of His upper chambers in the
waters, who makes the clouds His chariot, who walks
on the wings of the wind, who makes his angels
spirits, His ministers a flame of fire.*
Psalm 104:3-4

Foreword

The apostle Paul wrote to young Timothy, *"The things you have heard from me among many witnesses, commit these to faithful men who will be able to teach others also."* I am presenting to you in this book concepts that I have received from those who have been a major inspiration and influence in my life as I've grown and matured in the Lord. The person who has influenced me the most is my spiritual father in the Lord, Dick Benjamin, who provided an environment of learning that was grounded in the authority of the Scriptures.

I am so thankful for the environment and input Dick Benjamin has had in my life through the years. I had the wonderful privilege of attending the Bible College he established in Anchorage, Alaska and sitting under his teaching, along with other teachers such as Jim Feeney and Dick Strutz, who were also products of his teaching ministry. Later, after being sent out, I had the privilege of being under his apostolic ministry as one of the pastors of the many local churches that were established under his ministry. It was during this season that I gained a deeper appreciation and respect for him through the relationship that was established with him.

I'm also grateful for the influence of the late Rev. W. H. Offiler through his book, "God and His Bible or the Harmonies of Divine Revelation." Dick Benjamin is a product of his ministry, who followed the admonition of the apostle Paul to Timothy by committing to faithful men who would be able to teach others the concepts he learned from his pastor, W.H. Offiler.

Even though I may have expanded on the truths I've learned from those who have gone before me, the seedbed for the truths outlined in this book is a direct result of what I've learned from these great teachers of God's Word.

I'm not simply parroting what I've been taught but have thoroughly studied the concepts for myself to make sure what I believe is true and am now presenting them in this book for your consideration. I encourage you to do the same. We should all be like the Bereans who did not believe just because Paul the apostle said it but studied for themselves to see if what he was saying was true.

Table of Contents

Introduction

I believe we are living in a season in which it is of vital importance for us as Christians to know how we should be responding to the times we find ourselves in. There is major spiritual warfare taking place in heavenly places and here on earth. We must be wise and understanding in all that we do, not falling into the traps and snares of the enemy.

God's Holy Word is full of many prophetic promises that have been given for His purposes on earth. They are to be an encouragement to understand His will and purpose for all generations from Adam to the Second Coming of Christ.

By His divine power, God has given to us exceedingly great and precious promises, that through these we may be partakers of His divine nature.[1] With the Father's divine ability working in us, He's called us to be like the sons of Issachar who had an understanding of their times to know how Israel was to respond.[2] We're encouraged to do the same as Paul wrote to the Ephesians church.

Ephesians 5:15-17 See then that you walk circumspectly, not as fools but as wise, [16]redeeming the time, because the days are evil. [17]Therefore do not be unwise but understand what the will of the Lord is.

The promise of the coming of the Messiah was the greatest of all the prophetic purposes God has promised throughout the ages. It is in this promise that we uncover the keys as to how God brings His prophetic purposes to pass. We discover it was the zeal of the Lord that made this happen. Through the study of His word, we also find that in His zeal He continually transforms His ministers into flames of fire to fulfill all that has been prophesied by His Holy prophets.

Isaiah 9:6-7 For unto us a child is born. Unto us, a Son is given, and the government will be upon His shoulder. And His name will be called Wonderful, Counselor, Mighty God, Everlasting Father, Prince of Peace. [7]Of the increase of His government and peace there will be no end, upon the throne of a David and over His kingdom, to order it and establish it with judgment and justice from that time forward, even forever. The zeal of the Lord of Hosts will perform this.

---

[1] 2 Peter1:2-4
[2] 1 Chronicles 12:32

1

This passage speaks of how it's the zeal of the Lord that performs in bringing forth the Messiah, who bears the names of God that express the fullness of the Godhead bodily upon Him. It also speaks of how His zeal will bring forth every prophetic purpose throughout the ages that ushers in the continual increase of His kingdom.

As you open your spirit to the chapters of this book, you will see that it's in His zeal that God has chosen to make those whose hearts are consecrated to His purposes, flames of fire as they go forth fulfilling His word.

Psalm 104:3-4 *He lays the beams of His upper chambers in the waters, who makes the clouds His chariot, who walks on the wings of the wind, who makes His angels spirits,* **His ministers a flame of fire.**

You might ask, "What does it mean when it says, 'He makes His ministers flames of fire?'" I believe it has to do with the zeal of the Lord working in us, as He stirs up our passion, fervency, and destiny to do His will. Paul says it best in his epistle to the Colossians where he said, *"To this end I also labor, striving according to His working in me mightily."*[3] We find out that it's the violent or the energetic ones, filled with His Spirit who will take the kingdom by force.[4]

When baptized in the Holy Spirit, we are also baptized into His fire and zeal. When John the Baptist spoke of Jesus, who would come after him, he said, *"He will baptize you with the Holy Spirit and fire."*[5]

The prophet, Jeremiah, spoke of how God's word was in his heart like a burning fire, shut up in his bones, causing him to be weary of holding it back.[6] The two disciples who encountered Jesus on the road to Emmaus said to one another, *"Did not our hearts burn within us while He talked with us on the road, and while He opened the Scriptures to us?"*[7]

In every generation, God has prophetic purposes to be revealed. The book of Acts records how David served the purposes of God for his generation.[8] A quick look through biblical history shows how many patriarchs, judges, kings, prophets, and apostles served the prophetic purposes for their generations as well. These were people who God chose in His Sovereignty to call forth as His chosen vessels.

---

[3] Colossians 1:29
[4] Matthew 11:12
[5] Matthew 3:11
[6] Jeremiah 20:9
[7] Luke 24:32
[8] Acts 13:36

Introduction

The essence of this book considers that God has sovereign purposes in the earth that are yet to be fulfilled through His sovereignty. Amid performing them, He uses imperfect vessels like you and me to do so. How does our free will work together with God's sovereignty to bring forth His purposes as He fulfills them from one generation to another? This book explores these questions and much more. We discover that one of the Father's most significant traits—His patience combined with our obedience—allows us to be involved with Him.

Just as it was the zeal of the Lord that brought forth the most significant prophetic event of the ages, it will be the Lord in His zeal that executes His plans and purposes that bring an end to this age with the return of Jesus to set up His everlasting kingdom. As we enter into the culmination of all that God's Holy prophets have prophesied through the ages, there are still many prophetic promises or predestinated events that the Father must fulfill before the return of Jesus Christ as seen in the passage below.

*Acts 3:18-21 But those things which God foretold by the mouth of all His prophets, that the Christ would suffer, He has thus fulfilled. [19] Repent therefore and be converted, that your sins may be blotted out, so that times of refreshing may come from the presence of the Lord, [20] and **that He may send Jesus Christ**, who was preached to you before, [21] **whom heaven must receive (retain) until the times of restoration of all things, which God has spoken by the mouth of all His holy prophets since the world began.***

The passage from the book of Acts makes it clear that Jesus will be retained in heaven until all that was spoken by His Holy prophets comes to pass. Just as God in His zeal fulfilled His prophetic purposes concerning the coming of the Messiah through the birth of Christ, He will accomplish all that the prophets foretold concerning the end of the age and the second coming of Christ.

This book has three sections. The first section sets the stage by showing how God has already brought His prophetic purposes into play throughout the history of the Bible. The second section outlines His prophetic objectives for the Church that must be fulfilled before the second coming of Christ. The third section discusses what we must do to prepare ourselves to be useful vessels unto honor as we partner with Him in fulfilling all that was foretold by His prophets.

I do realize some of the thoughts and concepts I am presenting may be different than what some schools of thought would have you to believe. I encourage you to weigh them out carefully, with an open heart and mind, as you allow the Scriptures to interpret themselves. Our loyalty should be to God's word, not schools of thought. Holding on to personal biases will always distort the end result of our thinking. With an understanding that I am just as imperfect as others who have offered their thoughts throughout the centuries, I submit to you, to the best of my abilities, my thoughts, opinions, and conclusions which are based on Paul's second letter to Timothy where he said the following:

> **2 Timothy 3:16** *All Scripture is given by the inspiration of God and is profitable for doctrine, for reproof, for correction, for instruction in righteousness, that the man of God may be complete, thoroughly equipped for every good work.*

As we are faithful to divide the word of truth rightly[9], we must, first, believe that God inspired all Scripture, which is the bottom line of how we interpret God's word. Secondly, if we believe God inspired all Scripture, then we must assume that He has spoken with divine harmony and continuity throughout the Scriptures. If this is so, we must understand that Scripture will interpret Scriptures making them profitable for doctrine.

All doctrines must be in divine harmony with one another. God is not the author of confusion, but instead, all His words are pure, like silver, tried in a furnace of earth, purified seven times, which speaks of the perfection of His word. Therefore, we are to trust in His word, which acts as a shield to those who are trained by it.[10]

We must also understand that God hides some things, which can only be discovered with the aid of the Holy Spirit. It's the Holy Spirit who searches the heart of the Father for the answers as seen in the following passages of Scripture.

> **Proverbs 25:2-3** *It is the glory of God to conceal a matter, but the glory of kings is to search out a matter. ³As the heavens for height and the earth for depth, so the heart of kings is unsearchable.*

> **1 Corinthians 2:10-11,16** *But God has revealed them to us through His Spirit. For the Spirit searches all things, yes, the deep things of God. ¹¹For what man knows the things of a man except the spirit of the man which is in him? Even so, no one knows the things of God except the Spirit of God. ¹⁶For "who has known the mind of the Lord that He May instruct him?" But we have the mind of Christ.*

---

[9] 2 Timothy 2:15
[10] Psalm 119:140, 12:6, Proverbs 30:5

Introduction

We also have an enemy who will use our weaknesses and personal biases to twist the Scriptures.[11]

The principles I have just mentioned are the principles that guide me as I seek to be a workman who does not need to be ashamed, rightly dividing the word of truth. I offer for your consideration the conclusions that I have presented in his book.

It's time for the Church to become the pillar and the ground of all truth. It can only happen as we remain loyal to God's word that came by His inspiration. We must maintain absolute integrity to the inspiration of Scripture; otherwise, what we teach will be in error.

As you read this book, I would encourage you to have your Bible nearby and open so that you can refer to the many footnotes that are at the bottom of each page. My desire, as you read and study this book, is that your hearts will burn as the Scriptures are opened to you in the same manner as it was for the two disciples on the road to Emmaus. As you allow the Holy Spirit to speak to you, He will open the Scriptures so that your hearts burn with newfound passion and fervency. He will set your hearts on fire, filled with zeal and fervency as you go forth as His ministers.

Daniel 11:32b-33a *The people who know their God shall be strong and carry out great exploits. [33]And those of the people who understand shall instruct many;*

Most of the chapters in this book ends with a Biblical enriched poem that either describes or summarizes the chapter. All of the poems were written by me.

May God bless you richly as you read this book and give yourself to the study of His word.

---

[11] 2 Peter 3:16

5

Prophetic Purposes
and the Zeal of the Lord

Setting the Stage

Part 1

*He lays the beams of His upper chambers in
the waters, who makes the clouds His chariot,
who walks on the wings of the wind, who makes
his angels spirits, His ministers a flame of fire.*
Psalm 104:3-4

Prophetic Purposes Patriarchs, Prophets, Judges and Kings

Chapter One

Throughout biblical history, we see that God has specific plans and purposes for the ages, including our present age. It's God who has defined His prophetic objectives for the nation of Israel, the Church, and humanity throughout the ages. When we accept and commit our lives to Jesus Christ, we enter the predestinated purposes of our Lord that are in alignment with His overall intentions and will. We've been saved according to His purposes so that we can be His instruments of righteousness in all that He has foretold and purposed.[12]

Of all that the prophets foretold and came to pass throughout the ages, we see that God has chosen to use human instruments as His means of bringing to pass His prophetic purposes. The Scripture reference below confirms this.

Ephesians 1:11-12 (NIV) In him we were also chosen, having been predestined according to the plan of him who works out everything in conformity with the purpose of his will, [12] in order that we, who were the first to put our hope in Christ, might be for the praise of his glory.

Even though the Father uses us as His instruments of righteousness, it's in His sovereignty and zeal that He performs on our behalf as ministers of flaming fire.

The prophet, Isaiah, speaks of how the zeal of the LORD of hosts performs His prophetic purposes. It was the zeal of the LORD that brought forth the Messiah, whose name was to be called Wonderful, Counselor, Mighty God, Everlasting Father, and Prince of Peace!

---

[12] 2 Timothy 1:9

It's interesting that Jesus, whom the fullness of the Godhead bodily rests upon, takes on all the names that represent the Father, Son, and Holy Spirit; thus, His name: the Lord Jesus Christ.[13]

Isaiah 9:6-7 For unto us a Child is born, unto us a Son is given; and the government will be upon His shoulder. And His name will be called Wonderful, Counselor, Mighty God, Everlasting Father, Prince of peace. *__⁷Of the increase of His government and peace there will be no end__, upon the throne of David and over His kingdom, to order it and establish it with judgment and justice. __From that time forward, even forever the zeal of the LORD of hosts will perform this.__*

The above prophetic passage speaks of the purposes of God from the date of the Messiah coming forth, to the end of this age, and throughout all eternity – a time in which the kingdom of God will continue to expand and grow. The zeal of the LORD will continue to bring it forth through His chosen instruments of grace until the end of this present age. He will perform on their behalf just as He has done since the beginning of time, transforming His ministers into flames of fire as seen in the following passage.

Psalm 104:3-4. He lays the beams of His upper chambers in the waters, who makes the clouds His chariot, ⁴__who walks on the wings of the wind__, who makes His angels spirits, __His ministers a flame of fire.__

This chapter reveals how God, the Father was intimately acquainted and involved with all the ways of the Patriarchs, Judges, Prophets, and Kings mentioned throughout the Bible.[14] We see how God's sovereignty works hand in hand with each one of them as they give themselves to the Lord and His purposes. David saw himself as being fearfully and wonderfully made. He saw his days being formed for him before he was in his mother's womb. We will see how this is true for all of those mentioned in this chapter.[15]

Even though God did shape the lives of the patriarchs, prophets, kings, and others in relation to the His prophetic purposes, they had to submit to Him before He could use them as willing vessels. In His foreknowledge, God, the Father, knew He could trust them to make the right decisions. Therefore, they were His elected, chosen vessels according to His foreknowledge as Peter wrote in his first epistle concerning all of us who have decided to follow the Lord.

---

[13] Colossians 2:9
[14] Psalm 139:3-4
[15] Psalm 139:13-17

1 Peter 1:1-2 Peter, an apostle of Jesus Christ, to the pilgrims of the Dispersion in Pontus, Galatia, Cappadocia, Asia, and Bithynia, elect according to the foreknowledge of God the Father, in sanctification of the Spirit, for obedience and sprinkling of the blood of Jesus.

Patriarchs from the Old Testament

A quick look through the Old Testament reveals to us how God has always used His chosen vessels to bring forth His prophetic purposes.

Abraham, the Father of our Faith

Abraham was sought out by God for His purposes.[16] It was God who chose and called him. As we will see over and over, it's always God who does the seeking and takes the initiative in calling us forth for the intended purposes He has in mind.

In Genesis, God established His covenant with Abraham through a vision, revealing the extent of land that He was giving to him and his descendants. Abraham was told to prepare a sacrifice as his part of the covenant. After the sun went down, and a deep sleep fell upon him, there appeared a **smoking oven** and a **burning torch** that passed between the pieces of the sacrifice Abraham had been told to prepare.[17] The burning torch signifies Abraham's transformation into one of God's ministers, going forth as a minister of flaming fire to execute the Father's will and purpose in the earth.

Even though Abraham was not perfect, God's hand was on Him in a mighty way. On a couple of occasions, he lied concerning Sarah, his wife. Nevertheless, it was because of his obedience to God's plans and purposes that he would become the father of many nations. It was his obedience that enabled God to trust him with His sovereignty. Abraham was willing to sacrifice his son, Isaac, when he knew it was through Isaac that God would fulfill His promises. It was his willingness that caused God the Father to place complete trust in him.[18]

Isaac, the Son of Abraham

Isaac was the chosen child of Abraham to inherit the promises. God had told Abraham, *"My covenant I will establish with Isaac."[19]*

---

[16] Genesis 12:1-3
[17] Genesis 15:1-22, 17:1-8,21,
[18] Romans 4:20-22
[19] Genesis 17:21

Even though Isaac was the chosen one for God's covenant with Abraham to be established through him, he, too, had his faults. He favored his son Esau because he was a skillful hunter who would bring him savory game to eat.[20] Even though God had made it clear to Rebekah and Isaac that Jacob was to be the one who would inherit Abraham's blessing, Isaac wanted to give it to Esau.[21] God had said the older brother Esau would serve his younger brother. Isaac's failure to honor God's intended purposes forced Jacob and Rebekah to revert to deception so that Jacob would inherit the blessing of Abraham.[22]

Isaac also tried to pass his wife off as his sister in the same manner that his father Abraham had done, only to have his folly discovered. God had spoken very clearly to Isaac that He would be with him to perform the oath which He had sworn to Abraham. He did this when He reaffirmed His promise to Isaac saying, *"I will make your descendants multiply as the stars of heaven; I will give to your descendants all these lands, and in your seed, all the nations of the earth shall be blessed."* In spite of this promise, Isaac's heart was filled with fear, when he went to dwell with the Philistines in Gear because of a famine. When the men of the place asked about his wife, he said, "She is my sister." He was afraid the men would kill him because she was beautiful to behold.[23]

It was because of God's grace and mercy that He kept His covenant with Isaac. God, the Father, was able to look beyond Isaac's faults and see the God-fearing man he was in spite of his flaws. As a result, God's sovereignty continued to rule through his life.

Jacob, (Israel) the Son of Isaac

Jacob was the child of Isaac, who God chose to give birth to the twelve tribes of Israel. As with Abraham and Isaac, God was also the initiator of His plans for Jacob. He was to be a crucial figure in the Father's chosen instruments of righteousness in the formation of His plans and purposes throughout the generations of humanity.

Because of Rebekah and Jacob's deception for Jacob to inherit the blessing of Abraham, Jacob was forced to flee for his life. As a result, Isaac sent Jacob to Rebekah's family in Padan Aram to find a wife from the daughters of Laban, Rebekah's brother. Isaac then prayed the

---

[20] Genesis 25:28
[21] Genesis 25:23
[22] Genesis 27:1-29
[23] Genesis 26:1-14

following blessing over Jacob:[24] *"May God Almighty bless you, and make you fruitful and multiply you, that you may be an assembly of people's; and give you the blessing of Abraham, to you and your descendants with you, that you may inherit the land in which you are a stranger, which God gave to Abraham."*[25]

On Jacob's journey to Padan Aram, he encountered the Lord in a dream. In the dream, he saw a ladder set up on the earth with its top reaching to heaven with the angels of God ascending and descending on it. After the dream of the ladder, God renewed with Him the covenant He'd made with Abraham, saying the following: [26]

Genesis 28:13-15 *"I am the Lord God of Abraham your father and the God of Isaac; the land on which you lie I will give to you and your descendants. Also, your descendants shall be as the dust of the earth; you shall spread abroad to the west and the east, to the north and the south; and in you and your seed all the families of the earth shall be blessed. Behold, I am with you and will keep you wherever you go and will bring you back to this land; for I will not leave you until I have done what I have spoken to you."*

Jacob then affirms and comes into agreement with the covenant by acknowledging God as his Lord and makes a promise to give Him a tenth of all that comes his way.[27]

With Abraham, Isaac, and Jacob, we see a clear picture coming forth of how God establishes His sovereign purposes while working with the imperfections of humanity. In the midst of all the trickery and deception, God is not fazed but continues to move forward in His zeal. Through His patience and understanding the weaknesses of man, which He created, He keeps His plans on track by communicating and reminding them that He is the God of the universe who will be with them as they are obedient to Him. It's through His zeal that the Father continually brings forth His prophetic purposes in the earth while making His angels spirits, and His ministers, flames of fire. [28]

Once Jacob arrives in Padan Aram, he encounters the trickery of his uncle Laban who keeps him there while working off the payment for his wives. While there, eleven of his children are born. They're the seeds to

---

[24] Genesis 28:1-2
[25] Genesis 28:3-4
[26] Genesis 28:10-22
[27] Genesis 28:18-22
[28] Psalm 104:3-4

the nation of Israel that would eventually enter the Promised Land given to Abraham and his descendants.

After Jacob is released by the Lord to return to his own country, he has another compelling experience with God, the Father. He wrestles with an angel of God all night, resulting in having his name changed from Jacob to Israel.[29] The nation of Israel is now ready to be formed. On his way back, Rebekah gives birth to his twelfth son but dies giving birth. The seed that would give birth to the twelve tribes of Israel is now complete. The next stage of the Heavenly Father's prophetic purposes is now ready to come forth through Jacob's son, Joseph.

Joseph, the Eleventh Son of Jacob (Israel)

As a young boy, Joseph had received dreams and visions of which God would use to give birth to the nation of Israel.[30] Joseph would be God's instrument of righteousness to bring the Israelites to Egypt where God would then mold and shape them into the nation of Israel.

The dreams Joseph was having would shape not only his future but also the future of his entire family. Even though he was foolish in flaunting his dreams to his brothers, his dreams were from God. God was preparing him for the next season of his life when he would be instrumental in bringing the sovereign purposes of God into the next phase.

Because of jealousy, his brothers sold Joseph to a company of Ishmaelite's, who were on their way to Egypt from Gilead, bearing spices, balm, and myrrh.[31] The Ishmaelite's then sold him to Potiphar, an officer of Pharaoh in Egypt.[32] While serving in Potiphar's house as the overseer of all that he had, Potiphar's wife tried to seduce him. When she realized her attempts had failed, she accused him of trying to rape her. As a result, Potiphar had Joseph put in prison.[33]

While in prison, the Lord was with Joseph showing him mercy and giving him favor. As a result, the Egyptian authorities put Joseph in charge of all the prisoners. Because the Lord was with him, Joseph prospered in his darkest moments while God in His zeal was busy setting the stage for him to be His vessel of righteousness. Joseph would be the one who would bring the next phase of God's prophetic purposes into

---

[29] Genesis 32:28
[30] Genesis 37:5-11
[31] Genesis 37:25-26
[32] Genesis 37:20, 25; 39:1
[33] Genesis 39:7-20

play. The key to Joseph's success was that he continued to fear and honor God in all that he did.

As the story evolves, Joseph is called to interpret dreams that Pharaoh was having concerning the immediate future of Egypt and the surrounding countries. Joseph explains the dreams as seven good years in which Pharaoh is to store food for seven years of famine to be followed by seven good years. As a result, Joseph is released from prison and becomes Pharaoh's right-hand over all of Egypt and is put in charge of storing the food.

> **Genesis 41:39-41** *Then Pharaoh said to Joseph, "Inasmuch as God has shown you all this, there is no one as discerning and wise as you. [40]You shall be over my house, and all my people shall be ruled according to your word; only in regard to the throne will I be greater than you." [41]And Pharaoh said to Joseph, "See I have set you over all the land of Egypt."*

Because of the famine, Joseph's brothers, who sold him into slavery, travel to Egypt for food that had been stored up for the seven years of famine. Upon arrival, Joseph recognizes them and puts them through some harrowing experiences, before they can settle in the land of Goshen with their children and their father, Jacob, whose name is now Israel.

The children of Israel would dwell in Egypt for 430 years while being formed into a nation that would eventually enter the Promised Land given to Abraham. It would be under extreme pressure and hardships that they would be molded together to form the nation of Israel before God could fulfill the next stage of His prophetic purposes.

Moses, God's Servant

Moses was God's chosen instrument to lead the children of Israel out of bondage from the Egyptians.[34] God had big plans for Moses, plans that would require a supernatural display of His power not seen since the flood.

God had been molding Moses' life since his birth when he was hidden away and discovered by Pharaoh's daughter, who then raised him as her son. Later in life, wanting to see what kind of burdens his people were under, he visited them. As a result, Moses ends up murdering an Egyptian, who he caught mistreating one of his brethren and then fled for his life to Midian, where he has his first encounter with God.[35] He

---

[34] Exodus 3:1-8
[35] Exodus 2:11-15

would spend forty years in the desert before his encounter with the Lord.[36]

*Exodus 3:2-3 And the Angel of the Lord appeared to him in a **flame of fire** from the midst of a bush. So he looked, and behold, the bush was burned with fire, but the bush was not consumed. ³Then Moses said, "I will now turn aside and see this great sight, why the bush does not burn."*

God uses the vision of Him appearing to Moses in a flame of fire, which transforms him from a sheep-herder to a minister who would now go forth as a flame of fire.

God has a conversation with Moses, calling him out by name saying, "Moses, Moses!" He then goes on to reveal Himself as the God of Abraham, the God of Isaac, and the God of Jacob. During the conversation, God is very persuasive to Moses as He reveals the purpose of this extraordinary visit.

Exodus 3:10-11 "Come now. Therefore, I will send you to Pharaoh that you may bring My people, the children of Israel, out of Egypt." ¹¹But Moses said to God, "Who am I that I should go to Pharaoh, and that I should bring the children of Israel out of Egypt."

Feeling inadequate for such a mission, Moses finds himself offering one excuse after another. After God shows Moses several miracles, He convinces Him with the promise that his older brother, Aaron would be his mouthpiece.

After 430 years of living in Egypt and crying out for deliverance, from the cruel slavery they were currently under, God was about to deliver them and set them free. Through the hands of Moses and Aaron, God began to pour one plague after another on the land of Egypt until the final one, in which the death angel went through the land smiting the firstborn of every creature and person. Pharaoh's own son died during this plague, which finally prompted him to let the children of Israel go.

Moses was now free to fulfill the prophetic purpose of leading the children of Israel to the Promised Land. God, in His zeal towards His purpose for the children of Israel, made this happen. Because of His sovereignty and patience, He was able to bring His chosen servant into His plan despite Moses' reluctance to be used for such an important assignment.

---

[36] Acts 7:23, 30, Exodus 7:7

The display of God's power in delivering the nation of Israel from their Egyptian bondage is a premier example of God's omnipotence at work in bringing His sovereign purposes to pass. There is nothing too difficult for Him.[37] He is all powerful in His sovereignty and will continue to shape the Nations of the world according to His prophetic purposes until the end of time as we know it. According to His sovereign power and prophetic purposes, He will continue to interact with mankind until the second coming of Jesus Christ. At the second coming, the mystery of God will be finished, and all that His holy prophets have foretold will have come to pass.[38]

It's important to understand in all that Moses went through; his free will was always put into play. He had to agree to go along with God's prophetic purposes. By faith, Moses refused to be called the son of Pharaoh's daughter. By faith he chose to suffer affliction, esteeming the reproaches of Christ greater riches than the treasures in Egypt. By faith he forsook Egypt, enduring as seeing Him who is invisible. By faith, he kept the Passover. By faith, they passed through the Red Sea. In all of these things, Moses chose to exert faith to enter into the prophetic purposes God had in store for him and the nation of Israel.[39]

Joshua, Successor of Moses

Joshua is next in line to be used in fulfilling the next phase of the Father's prophetic purposes. He was the one who was chosen to lead the children of Israel into the Promised Land after the death of Moses. Like Moses, God had been molding and shaping his life for this moment. We should ask ourselves, "What is the purpose God has been busy molding and shaping our lives for?"

Joshua is first mentioned at the battle with the Amalekites. He was the one chosen by Moses to select those who would go to war while Aaron and Hur stood on the top of the hill holding Moses' hands up as the battle raged on.[40]

When God gave the Ten Commandments, it was Joshua, who accompanied Moses part way up Mt Sinai and where He's first mentioned as Moses' assistant. Joshua spent his entire time during Israel's season in the wilderness doing menial tasks as Moses' assistant in preparation of the monumental task of leading the children of Israel

---

[37] Jeremiah 32:17
[38] Acts 3:19-21
[39] Hebrews 11:23-29
[40] Exodus 17:9-14

into the Promised Land that God had covenanted to them through the promise given to Abraham.

Exodus 26:12-13 Then the Lord said to Moses, "Come up to Me on the mountain and be there; and I will give you the tablets of stone, and the law and the commandments which I have written, that you may teach them." [13] So Moses arose with his assistant Joshua, and Moses went up to the mountain of God.

Joshua was also with Moses whenever he would enter into the tabernacle of meeting where God would speak to him face to face.

Exodus 33:11 so the Lord spoke to Moses face to face, as a man speaks to his friend. And he would return to the camp, but his servant Joshua the son of Nun, a young man did not depart from the tabernacle.

Joshua was also among the twelve spies who were sent into the Promised Land by Moses to spy out the land. He and Caleb were the only ones who came back with an excellent report to encourage the children of Israel to take the Land. Unfortunately, the other ten spies discouraged the people with their bad report. As a result, Joshua and Caleb would be the only ones allowed to go into the Promised Land of all who came out of Egypt. Only those who were born during the 40 years in the wilderness, along with Joshua and Caleb, were allowed to enter the Promised Land given to Abraham's descendants.

Because of Moses' sin of striking the rock twice, he was not allowed to enter the Promised Land and was among those who died in the wilderness.[41] Before his death, he had anointed Joshua to be the leader, who had been chosen by God to lead the children of Israel—all those who were born after they came out of Egypt—to conquer the Promised Land. According to Thompson's Chain Reference Bible, this happened at least a year before he leads the children of Israel into the Promised Land.

Numbers 27:18-20 And the Lord said to Moses: "Take Joshua the son of Nun with you, a man in whom is the Spirit, and lay your hand on him; set him before Eleanor, the priest and before all the congregation, inaugurate him in their sight. [20] And you shall give some of your authority to him, that all the congregation of the children of Israel may be obedient."

God had been grooming Joshua for this moment in time before his birth when he was being fashioned in his mother's womb. God had foreordained him to lead the children of Israel into the Promised Land.

---

[41] Numbers 20:7-13

As Moses' assistant, he had seen and heard things that others didn't. These were the seeds of faith imparted to him at a young age to believe in God's extraordinary ability to lead the people of God into the Promised Land. God knew what He was doing with Joshua from the beginning. In His sovereignty, He planned each step of Joshua's life to be the leader who would conquer the Promised Land. God, in His zeal, made it happen for Joshua as He equipped him for this monumental task. As Joshua was obedient in the various stages of his life, God was able to prepare him adequately for this great mission and conquest.

After the death of Moses, God spoke to Joshua and gave him his marching orders. He told him that no man would be able to stand before him and that He would be with him just as he had been with Moses. Joshua was told to be strong and of good courage, as he meditated day and night and observed to do all that Moses had commanded concerning the Law. If he did this, he would have good success.[42]

Joshua 1:2 *Moses, My servant, is dead. Now, therefore, arise, go over this Jordan, you and all these people, to the land which I am giving to them—the children of Israel.*

Before Joshua could begin his first great conquest, he would meet the commander of the Lord's army, whom he must submit to before receiving instructions for the next phase of God's plans and purposes. God revealed to Joshua that He was the One in charge. Before God could rule through His sovereignty, He had to make sure His servant, Joshua, understood and was consecrated to His purposes. He was told to take off his sandals because the place he was standing on was Holy ground.[43] We should ask ourselves, "How consecrated are we to God's Purposes?"

Summary of the Patriarchs

All of the patriarchs just mentioned were not only used to influence their generations but were also used to alter the course of history, moving the people of God forward in the plans and purposes of God. They were all consecrated to God's purposes in the way He had chosen for each of them before they could fulfill their destinies. As a result, they came forth as the zeal of the Lord of Hosts moved with flaming fire to accomplish His prophetic purposes, using them as His chosen instruments of righteousness to do so.

---

[42] Joshua 1:1-9
[43] Joshua 5:13-15

With all the Patriarchs, we see how God was patient and long-suffering in His communication with them. He was very specific in the instructions given. It's important to note that each of the Patriarchs had their faults, but God, who is rich in mercy and sympathetic with the weaknesses of humankind along with His patience was still able to use them. The Father, in His zeal, made His prophetic purposes for their generations come to pass. Their imperfections did not limit God nor do ours. Because God, the Father, can do all things, He works with us in spite of our faults with His sovereignty intact for His own good pleasure.

Philippians 2:12-13 Therefore, my beloved, as you have always obeyed, not in my presence only, but now much more in my absence, work out your own salvation in fear and trembling; [13]for it is God who works in you both to will and to do for His good pleasure.

For example, when God called Moses to deliver Israel, Moses argued with Him, saying he wasn't adequate because he couldn't speak well enough. God's response was, He would give him Aaron as His mouthpiece. Between God, Moses, and Aaron, the prophetic purposes for Moses' generation were all fulfilled.

Old Testament Judges, Prophets, and Kings

During Joshua's reign, he conquered much of the Promised Land, but there were still portions needed to be conquered. It was during this period that God raised up judges to lead the nation of Israel. The era of the Judges was a time in which the people of God were without strong unifying voices like Moses and Joshua to keep them in line with His prophetic purposes. They would often backslide and fall back into the worship of other idols and god's, resulting in losing some of the Promised Land that had been conquered through Joshua. It was known as an era in which everyone did what was right in their own eyes.

Judges 17:6 In those days there was no king in Israel; everyone did what was right in his own eyes.

In the same way, God spoke and directed the Patriarchs of old; He continued to communicate with judges, kings, and prophets throughout the Old Testament, giving them direction for His plans to shape the nation of Israel and other countries.

Amos 3:7 Surely the Lord God does nothing unless He reveals His secret to His servants the prophets.

People like Gideon, Deborah, Samuel, David, Solomon, Elijah, Elisha, Isaiah, Jeremiah, Ezekiel, Daniel, Hosea, Joel, and others were all used in God's divine plans and purposes. The zeal of the Lord continued to perform on their behalf to speak and bring forth His prophetic purposes in the earth.

The Era of the Judges

After Joshua's generation died off, the next generation did not know the Lord nor the work which He had done. As a result, they quickly turned to idols and began serving the Baal's. In God's zeal, He delivered them into the hands of their enemies, who plundered them until they would cry out for deliverance. God would then raise up judges to deliver them.

Judges 2:16-18 Nevertheless, the Lord raised up judges who delivered them out of the hand of those who plundered them. [17]Yet they would not listen to their judges, but played the harlot with other gods, and bowed down to them. They turned quickly from the way in which their fathers walked, in obeying the commandments of the Lord; they did not do so. [18]And when the Lord raised up judges for them, the Lord was with the judge and delivered them out of the hand of their enemies all the days of the judge; for the Lord was moved to pity by their groaning because of those who oppressed them and harassed them.

Does that sound familiar to the way many of us have responded and then turned back to the Lord? When we find ourselves mired, once again, in all the muck from our poor decisions, we cry out. We discover God in His faithfulness is there to accept us back into His fold with His purposes, once again, established in our lives.

Some of the more notable judges were Othniel, Shamgar, Deborah, Gideon, Jephthah, Samson, Eli and Samuel. Samuel was the last of the judges, who in his old age appointed his sons as judges. His sons, however, were rejected by the people of Israel because of their wickedness.[44] The people then demanded a king like the other nations of the world. Samuel tried to dissuade them, but they wouldn't have anything to do with it.[45] Israel's desire for a king was a rejection of the Lord as seen in the following passage.

1 Samuel 8:7-8 And the Lord said to Samuel, "Heed the voice of people in all that they say to you; for they have not rejected you, but they have rejected Me, that I should not reign over them. [8]According to all the works which they have done since the day I brought them out of Egypt,

---

[44] 1 Samuel 8:1-5
[45] 1 Samuel 8:19-22

even to this day—with which they have forsaken Me and served other god's—so they are doing to you also."

The period of the Judges, once again, shows the Father's patience and long-suffering towards His chosen people as they continually turned their hearts away from Him in exchange for their foolish ways. In all of this, God steadily moved forward in His sovereignty towards His intended purposes. Because He understood and was sympathetic to their weaknesses, He was able to work out His Sovereign purposes despite their foolishness. By allowing the law of sowing and reaping to have its effect, His people would cry out for mercy when they found themselves trapped in the enemy's clutches. In His mercy, He would raise up judges to deliver them.

The Era of Kings and Prophets

The era of the Kings began when the nation of Israel rejected the sons of Samuel as judges. Because his sons were sinning outright, taking bribes, and perverting justice, the people of Israel rejected them as judges and told Samuel they wanted a king.

God's hand was on Samuel in his mother's womb before his conception. Samuel would become an integral figure in the era of the kings. He becomes the one chosen by God to usher in the period. God, in His sovereignty, closed the womb of Hannah, Samuel's mother.[46] She is then forced to cry to the Lord for a male child. In her prayer, she offers the child to the Lord all the days of his life.

1 Samuel 1:11 Then she made a vow and said, "O Lord of hosts, if You will indeed look on the affliction of Your maidservant, but will give Your maidservant a male child, then I will give him to the Lord all the days of his life, and no razor shall come upon his head."

The story of Hannah is another beautiful example of how God's sovereignty works hand in hand with free will. Because God in His sovereignty closed Hannah's womb, she chose to pray and offer the child of her prayer to the Lord. It's a picture of God in His zeal making things happen according to His prophetic purposes.

Eli, who was the current judge and priest of the tabernacle, had observed her as she carried on. He thought she was drunk and began to rebuke her.[47] Hannah responded by saying, *"I am a woman of sorrowful spirit. I have drunk neither wine nor intoxicating drink but have poured*

---

[46] 1 Samuel 1:5
[47] 1 Samuel 1:12-14

out my soul before the Lord."[48] Eli then grants her petition, and she returns home, no longer sad.

After Samuel's birth and being weaned, Hannah presented him to Eli, the priest, just as she'd promised.

1 Samuel 1:26-27 And she said, "O my lord! As your soul lives, my lord, I am the woman who stood by you here, praying to the Lord. [27]For this child I have prayed, and the Lord has granted my petition which I asked of Him. [28]Therefore I also have lent him to the Lord; as long as he lives, he shall be lent to the Lord." So, they worshipped the Lord there.

The young child, Samuel, then became Eli's assistant ministering before the Lord, wearing a linen ephod. At an early age, the Lord began molding and shaping him to be the great prophet and judge he would later become.[49] As he grew in stature, he grew in favor with the Lord and men.[50] His first prophecy was a confirmation of what another prophet had spoken to Eli. God had spoken to Eli concerning what his sons were doing. He spoke through Samuel that He would judge his house forever for the iniquity he knew his sons were involved in. His sons had made themselves vile, and he had not restrained them.[51]

Once God fulfilled the prophecy concerning Eli and his sons, Samuel was looked upon as the prophet and judge to lead Israel. During his reign, he ordained Saul as the first King of Israel after the people rejected Samuel's sons because of their evil ways.

Saul then becomes king, but because of his disobedience in following the strict orders given through the prophet Samuel, God rejected Saul as King. He then had Samuel anoint young David to be the future King— the one of whom all future kings would be measured. During the era of the kings and prophets, there were many kings and prophets, who came and went—some good and some bad.

Some of the more notable prophets were Nathan, Elijah, Elisha, Isaiah, Jeremiah, Ezekiel, Joel, Hosea, Daniel, Haggai, and Zechariah. They were often used to speak God's will and purpose to the Kings and the people of Judah and Israel. Often, as they spoke God's intended purposes for the nation of Israel, their words fell on deaf ears. They not only prophesied about their era but also of the coming of the Messiah, the establishment of the early church, and the latter times — the period

---

[48] 1 Samuel 1:15
[49] 1 Samuel 2:18-21
[50] 1 Samuel 2:26
[51] 1 Samuel 2:29, 3:11-14

we are now living in. As we enter the end of the age, we discover these prophets had much to say about our times.

The prophets mentioned above, and some of the kings and judges went forth fervently with the zeal of the Lord performing His plans and purposes, accordingly. They were like the sons of Issachar who were committed to God's purposes. They understood their times and knew how to respond to His intentions. We are also urged to be like the sons of Issachar who are knowledgeable of our times and know how to react.[52]

Ephesians 5:17 Therefore do not be unwise but understand what the will of the Lord is.

As we set our hearts in agreement with the purposes to which we are saved and called, our lives are consecrated to the prophetic purposes as well. Being wise and understanding of our times helps to equip us to go forth in the fervency and zeal of the Lord as we seek to fulfill our callings and destinies in God.

---

[52] 1 Chronicles 12:32

Prophetic Purposes
The New Testament Era

Chapter Two

Jesus came as the fulfillment of all that the Old Testament Prophets had spoken. He came to do the will of God, His Father, coming as a man, entirely dependent upon the Holy Spirit to perform through Him the Father's will. Even though He never ceased to be God, He gave up His rights to act as God.[53] Having the fullness of the Spirit in Him to perform as a flame of fire, He served the will of God, His Father.[54] He came to show us how to minister as flames of fire as we serve the purposes of God for our generations.[55]

The prophet Joel had much to say concerning the New Testament era. He prophesied that God's Spirit would be poured out upon all flesh, not just a select few as had been under the Old Covenant.

Joel 2:28-29 And it shall come to pass afterward that I will pour out My Spirit on all flesh; your sons and your daughters shall prophesy, your old men shall dream dreams, your young men shall see visions. [29]And also on My menservants and on My maidservants, I will pour out My Spirit in those days.

Prophetic Purposes and the Birth of the Church

The fulfillment of Joel's Prophecy came on the day that the feast of Pentecost was entirely fulfilled, giving birth to the Church. The Holy Spirit came suddenly as a sound from heaven like a mighty rushing wind with tongues of fire.[56] With the baptism of the Holy Spirit and fire, these first disciples of Jesus would now be able to go forth like flames of fire

---

[53] Philippians 2:5-9
[54] John 4:34
[55] Hebrews 1:7-10, 10:7, Philippians 2:5-8, John 3:34
[56] Acts 2:1-4

fulfilling the commission Jesus had given to them to go into all the world with the message of the gospel.

These disciples were immediately caught up in the prophetic purposes of their Lord with Peter shedding light on the prophetic passage from the Book of Joel.[57] As a result, they went everywhere with the zeal of the Lord performing His will through them.

The point is; God the Father has prophetic purposes to be fulfilled in His sovereignty. It's in the Father's zeal that God makes them happen through the chosen vessels who have sanctified and consecrated themselves unto His purposes.[58]

We see over and over in the Book of Acts how these first believers went forth in the power of the Holy Spirit. They healed people, raised the dead and performed miracles just as Jesus did. They were used strategically to bring forth the purposes of God with the zeal of the Lord performing on their behalf as they ministered.

The prophet Joel spoke of visions and dreams that were to be poured out on all flesh as the Holy Spirit was to be released to empower His servants. We see this in both the lives of Peter and Paul as they went forth filled with the Holy Spirit performing great acts of faith through them. The same Spirit that raised Jesus from the dead was now working mightily in them.[59]

Peter's Example

Peter had many extraordinary experiences as he went forth to accomplish the destiny to which the Lord had called him. From people being healed by his shadow to being released from prison by an angel, the zeal of the Lord of Hosts performed in and through him. The passage from Psalms that says, *"He makes the clouds His Chariot, who walks on the wings of the wind, who makes His angels spirits, His ministers a flame of fire,"* speaks of how God was working in Peter's life to make His sovereign purposes come to pass.

One of his most unusual experiences was that of receiving a strategic vision of the Lord of Hosts to execute the prophetic purpose of bringing the Gentiles into the Church. The occurrence of Cornelius, a Gentile, receiving a vision from the Lord to call for Peter, reveals one of the strategic ways in which God transforms His ministers into flames of fire while bringing about His prophetic purposes to pass in the earth.[60]

---

[57] Acts 3:16-21
[58] 2 Timothy 2:20-21
[59] Romans 8:11, Ephesians 1:19-20
[60] Acts 10:1-8

Acts 10:3 About the ninth hour of the day he saw clearly in a vision an angel of God coming in and saying to him, "Cornelius!"

Cornelius was given specific instructions to send men to Joppa for Peter. The next day as they went on their journey to find him, Peter had gone up on his rooftop to pray. While praying, he, too, received a vision from the Lord.[61]

Acts 10:10-13 Then he became hungry and wanted to eat; but while they made ready, he fell into a trance [11]and saw heaven opened and an object like a great sheet bound at the four corners, descending to Him and let down to the earth. [12]In it were all kinds of four-footed animals of the earth, wild beasts, creeping things, and the birds of the air. [13]And a voice came to him, "Rise, Peter; kill and eat."

While Peter pondered the vision and what it meant, the three men, who had been sent by Cornelius, appeared at his door asking for him. As he thought about the vision, the Holy Spirit spoke, "Go with them, doubting nothing."[62]

The next day upon arriving at the house of Cornelius, Peter began to share the message of Christ, and how God had anointed Jesus with the Holy Spirit and power.[63] While Peter was speaking, the Holy Spirit interrupted him and fell upon all those who heard him. As a result, these Gentiles were baptized and brought into the Church after receiving the Holy Spirit in the same manner as Peter and the other disciples did on the Day of Pentecost.[64]

The case in point of Peter and Cornelius is an astonishing example of how the Father in His zeal works with His chosen vessels to bring about His prophetic purposes on the earth. In His intensity, He made His sovereign purposes happen with the vessels He had chosen. Both Peter and Cornelius had prepared themselves by walking in obedience to what they knew at the time and were consecrated to God's purposes.

There are many prophetic passages foretelling of the Gentiles becoming a part of God's purposes.[65] The phenomenon of Cornelius and Peter is a foretaste of what's ahead for all those who are consecrated and committed to the kingdom of God and His purposes. As God prepares to bring His body into the fullness of the stature of Jesus Christ with a remarkable outpouring of His Spirit, strategic alliances such as Peter and

---

[61] Acts 10:9-16

[62] Acts 10:19-20

[63] Acts 10:24-43

[64] Acts 10:47

[65] Prophecies of Gentiles coming to Christ: Gen. 22:18, Psalm 22:27, Isaiah 9:2, 42:1

Cornelius' will be familiar experiences for those who engage in all that God will do through the pouring out of His Spirit during the coming season yet to be experienced by His Church..

Paul's Example

The Apostle Paul's conversion and ministry to the Gentiles is another powerful example of how the zeal of the Lord works with His chosen vessels filling them with fervency and zeal while bringing about His prophetic purposes in the earth.

Before his conversion, Saul was a man of passion committed to eradicating believers from the face of the earth. He had risen above his contemporaries in persecuting believers by putting them in prison and even having some of them killed.[66] While on the road to Damascus to persecute Christians living there, the Lord came to him suddenly in His zeal as a blinding light to get his attention.[67]

> ***Acts 9:3-6*** *As he journeyed, he came near Damascus, and suddenly a light shone around him from heaven. [4]Then he fell to the ground, and heard a voice saying to him, "Saul why are you persecuting Me?" [5]And he said, "Who are you, Lord?" Then the Lord said, "I am Jesus, whom you are persecuting.* **It is hard for you to kick against the goads.**" *[6]So he, trembling and astonished, said, "Lord, what do you want me to do?" Then the Lord said to him, "Arise and go into the city, and you will be told what to do."*

This passage gives a clear understanding of how God chooses to intervene at times to make sure His prophetic plans and sovereign purposes for humanity are on course with His overall will and purpose.

Saul was told, "It is hard for you to kick against the goads."

The following is an article from gotquestions.org: *"It is hard for you to kick against the pricks" was a Greek proverb, but it was also familiar to the Jews and anyone who made a living in agriculture. An ox goad was a stick with a pointed piece of iron on its tip used to prod the oxen when plowing. The farmer would prick the animal to steer it in the right direction. Sometimes the animal would rebel by kicking out at the prick, and this would result in the prick being driven even further into its flesh. In essence, the more an ox rebelled, the more it suffered. Thus,*

---

[66] Acts 8:1-3
[67] Acts 9:1-9

Jesus' words to Saul on the road to Damascus: "It is hard for you to kick against the pricks."[68]

The conversion of Saul was quite significant in that it was the turning point that caused him to surrender his life to Christ and be a primary instrument of righteousness in fulfilling the prophecies of the Gentiles coming to Christ. He later wrote nearly half of the books of the New Testament.

The article continues by saying, *"Jesus took control of Paul and let him know his rebellion against God was a losing battle. Paul's actions were as senseless as an ox kicking "against the goads." Paul had passion and sincerity in his fight against Christianity, but he was not heading in the direction God wanted him to go. Jesus was going to goad ("direct" or "steer") Paul in the right direction."[69]*

The next passage in this chapter of Acts continues to show how God forms strategic alliances to make sure his plans are being carried out. We see how He makes His plans very hard to be deviated from, even though He has chosen imperfect human vessels with a free will to execute them. It's hard to kick against the goads when it comes to God bringing His purposes to fruition. We either fall in line, or He will get us out of the way and find someone else. I wonder what would have happened to Saul if he had not submitted. Who knows? Maybe he would have been blind for the rest of his life.

A man named Ananias then receives a vision from God, telling him to arise and go to the place where Saul is staying so that he can pray for him. At the same time, Saul has a vision of a man named Ananias coming to pray for him so that he would regain his sight.[70] Ananias argues with the Lord over this assignment because of what he's heard concerning how this man has persecuted the church. However, God is persistent and says to him, *"Go, for he is a chosen vessel of Mine to bear My name before Gentiles, kings, and the children of Israel." For I will show him how many things he must suffer for my Name's sake."[71]* Ananias realizes the futility of arguing with God and submits to His plans and purposes. As a result, Saul is baptized in the Holy Spirit and begins to minister mightily in the Spirit as one of the Father's chosen vessels to bring the Gentiles to Christ.

---

[68] Kicking against the goads - gotquestions.org
[69] Kicking against the goads - gotquestions.org
[70] Acts 9:10-12
[71] Acts 9:13-16

After a short season in Damascus, God sends Saul into a desert for a period. After his time in the desert, he goes back to Damascus and then to Jerusalem to visit with Peter and James, the Lord's brother. Afterward, he went into the regions of Syria and Cilicia until Barnabas later sought him out. Barnabus then brought him to Antioch, where a new church of Gentile believers was now in existence.[72]

With Saul now firmly placed in ministry, after he and Barnabas had spent a whole year with the church, teaching many people, the Lord was about to go forth in His zeal to send Barnabas and Saul as His chosen instruments. As the prophet, Joel had prophesied, they went forth. They were sent by the prophets and teachers, who were part of the church in Antioch.[73] Saul then becomes Paul, the great apostle to the Gentiles, who turns his known world upside down with the Gospel as the Lord goes before him in His zeal.

Sovereignty and Free Will Working Together

Paul's testimony was, *"Him we preach, warning every man and teaching every man in all wisdom, that we may present every man perfect in Christ Jesus. To this end I also labor, striving according to his working which works in me mightily."*[74]

Both Peter and Paul's experiences give us vivid examples of how God's sovereignty and our free will work together. When Paul was testifying before King Agrippa, he mentions how he was obedient to the vision. In some cases, as with Paul and Peter, God makes it very difficult to disobey Him. Jonah's story is another example, although his example shows us how God's patience works hand in hand with His sovereignty as well. Thankfully, God is long-suffering towards us as we work out our salvation to fulfill His will and purpose.

Just as God poured His Spirit upon the early believers, He's pouring His Spirit on all who believe in the Lord Jesus Christ, today as Paul wrote in his first letter to the Corinthians. Speaking of the gifts of the Spirit, he says, *"There are diversities of gifts, but the same Spirit. There are differences of ministries, but the same Lord. And there are diversities of activities, but it is the **same God who works all in all**. But the **manifestation of the Spirit** is given to each one for the profit of all."*[75]

---

[72] Acts 11:22-26
73 Acts 13:1-3
74 Colossians 1:29
75 1 Corinthians 12:4-7

The word *"works"* means active operation, effectual, powerful, to be active, efficient, fervent, and to be mighty in showing forth. The word *"manifestation"* means to make visible, clear and known.

With these two definitions in mind, we can see, once again, how God in His sovereignty uses His instruments of righteousness as flames of fire to be fervent and mighty in making His power visible. As members of His body, we are to be zealous, active, effectual, efficient and powerful in manifesting the gifts of the Spirit for the benefit of the body as a whole.

May these examples and how the Holy Spirit works in the lives of believers everywhere be an encouragement to you as you set your hearts to be all that God has purposed for your lives. Allow faith to arise in your hearts as you go forth like flames of fire to do His bidding.

Prophetic Purposes
to be Fulfilled

Chapter Three

As we look back and witness throughout God's word, we discover how He has worked in those to whom He has called. We uncover captivating examples of what God desires to do in believers everywhere. We are now engaged in a season, in which the fulfillment of all that has been written and prophesied concerning the church and the nations are about to be fulfilled. Before Jesus returns for His Church, everything that has been foretold by the prophets must come to pass as seen in the following passages.

> *Matthew 5:18 For assuredly, I say unto you, till heaven and earth pass away, one jot or one tittle will by no means pass from the law till all is fulfilled.*

> *Acts 3:20-21 and that He may send Jesus Christ, who was preached to you before, ²¹whom heaven must receive until the times of restoration of all things, which God has spoken by the mouth of His Holy prophets since the world began.*

The prophecy of Joel was only partially fulfilled on the Day of Pentecost as it was a prophecy intended for the whole of the Church age, which doesn't end until the Second Coming of Christ.[76] Believers everywhere will have remarkable opportunities to be strategically involved in all that the Lord is about to do. Now is the time to prepare and be ready for this coming season by putting on the garments that belong to the Lord Jesus Christ. We must put on the new nature while making no provision for the flesh. The Father is looking for vessels entirely consecrated to His purposes in the earth. Will you be one of them? They that know their Lord will be strong and do great exploits.[77]

---

76 Acts 2:16-21
77 Daniel 11:32b-33a

There is still much to be fulfilled. I realize there are many events concerning Israel and other end-time events that the Old Testament prophets, Jesus, Paul, and John spoke about, but what I want to focus on are the prophetic purposes concerning the Church as listed below:

Prophetic Purposes Involving the Church

1. God's people are filled with the fullness of His Spirit, with dreams, visions, and prophecies, while being led into the strategic prophetic purposes of God.[78]
2. The authority of hell will not be able to prevail against the Church.
3. The Church comes to a unity that was prayed for and prophesied by Jesus, who had perfect faith.[79]
4. The Church becomes a mighty fortress.[80]
5. The Church enters the fullness of the stature of Christ.[81]
6. The Church performs exploits doing more magnificent works than Jesus.[82]
7. The bride of Christ is revealed without spot or blemish.[83]
8. The revealing and coming of the Antichrist take place.[84]
9. The "Great Falling Away" happens.[85]
10. God unleashes His final wrath before the Coming of Jesus Christ
11. Jesus returns and binds Satan in the bottomless pit for 1000 years
12. The New Heaven and earth appear after the 1000 years.

Just as the zeal of the Lord has performed throughout history to fulfill His prophetic purposes, He will continue to do so until we receive the new heavens and earth. The Lord of Hosts shall continue to make His ministers flames of fire as they go forth as Paul and others did, serving the purpose of God for their generations.[86]

---

[78] Ephesians 1:17-19, Joel 2:28-29, Acts 10:1-16
[79] John 17:11,20-22, Ephesians 4:13
[80] Matthew 16:18
[81] Ephesians 4:13
[82] John 14:12
[83] Ephesians 5:27
[84] 2 Thessalonians 2:3-4
[85] 2 Thessalonians 2:3
[86] Acts 13:36

Sovereign Acts of the Lord Throughout History

As seen through the patriarchs, prophets, judges, and kings, the zeal of the Lord has been sovereignly active throughout history in bringing His prophetic purposes to pass.

Israel Released from Egyptian Bondage

After the 430 prophetic years of Israel being in Egypt, the Father used mighty signs and wonders to bring the children of Israel, out of Egypt into the Promised Land to form them into the nation He had promised to Abraham.[87]

Israel Enters the Promised Land

As seen in a previous chapter, the nation of Israel entered the Promised land just as it was foretold to them. God was with them every step of the way as they were obedient unto Him.

Rebuilding the Temple after the Babylonian Bondage

Ezra 1:1 *In the first year of Cyrus king of Persia, in order to fulfill the word of the Lord spoken by Jeremiah, the Lord moved the heart of Cyrus king of Persia to make a proclamation throughout his realm and also to put it in writing.*

After the seventy years prophesied by the prophet, Jeremiah came to pass; God in His sovereignty moved upon Cyrus, to release the children of Israel from their Babylonian captivity. Through the zeal of the Lord, an unbeliever named Cyrus was raised up to set them free[88]

Zerubbabel, who was the head of the tribe of Judah during this time, was the chosen instrument of God's righteousness and zeal to be the primary builder of the second Temple. He led the first group of captives back to Jerusalem and began rebuilding the Temple on the old site.[89]

God, knowing Zerubbabel would need plenty of encouragement during the rebuilding, ordained the prophets, Haggai and Zechariah to prophesy while the building was going on.[90]

The Birth of the Church

We've also seen how God used mighty signs and wonders to give birth to His church. The apostles and others went everywhere filled with

---

[87] Genesis 25:13, Exodus 12:41-42
[88] Ezra 1:1-4, Jeremiah 25:11-12, 29:10, Daniel 9:2
[89] Ezra 3:8
[90] Ezra 5:1-2

the zeal of the Lord preaching the gospel with signs following. Multitudes upon multitudes were saved and filled with the Spirit as the Lord opened their eyes to the kingdom perspective.

In all of this, we see how God always takes the initiative in moving His people into His prophetic purposes. The Father in His zeal raises up His instruments of righteousness as flames of fire to make it happen.

The End of the Age

Of all the events that have happened throughout the ages, the season we are about to enter is probably the greatest of all seasons. All that was prophesied by the prophets is about to be fulfilled.

We are now coming to the end of this present age as we await the second coming of the Lord Jesus Christ. Much has been written and prophesied about this era through prophets like Isaiah, Ezekiel, Daniel, Hosea, Joel, Haggai, Zechariah, Jesus, Paul the apostle, and John, one of the original apostles of Jesus Christ.

As God has always taken the initiative in the past, He continues to do so in this present age. Those who are consecrated and committed to His prophetic purposes will find themselves caught up in His prophetic zeal as flames of fire going forth from the positions, they've been ordained to perform in. The zeal of the Lord of Hosts makes this happen.

The Time of Preparation is Now!

The prophetic period we're about to enter requires preparation for what God's about to do. Throughout history, when God moved, it was suddenly without prior notice. He used those who were ready and willing as His vessels unto honor. He's now getting ready to send his ministers as flames of fire in His zeal to complete what He's started. The true laborers are few.[91] Will you be prepared and ready? You won't want to be caught sleeping when the Lord decides to move suddenly.

The authority of hell will not be able to succeed against the beautiful and glorious Church Jesus is building. Satan and all his cohorts can kick against the goads all they want, but it will be a fruitless effort. Those standing by will be used to defeat all the schemes of the enemy.

Now is the time to prepare and get ready! Will you be ready, or will you be caught sleeping?

Romans 13:12 "The night is far spent; the day is at hand. Therefore, let us cast off the works of darkness, and let us put on the armor of light."

---

[91] Luke 10:2

Prophetic Purposes Fulfilled
By Ken L. Birks © 2018 Straight Arrow Ministries

With prophetic purposes to fulfill, the Father moves to infuse.
Through the ages, Patriarchs, Prophets, and Kings, He uses.
In those whose hearts are aflame with His desires, He pursues.
With not one promise failed, He continues in His zeal to perform.
With the night far spent, the time draws near with much to inform.

In His zeal, the Father rains on those whom He delights.
With prophetic purposes in full view, they set their sights.
As the mighty wind blows, all is fulfilled that's declared.
With tongues of fire, He makes us flames of fire, prepared.
With prophetic purposes to fulfill, His vessels, He ignites.

With passion ignited, His vessels stand ready to fulfill.
Armed and ready, they stand waiting for His command.
In battle array, they stand building according to His plan.
With pillars of truth in place, they stand secure in His will.
As the command comes suddenly, they go forth to fulfill.

As the trumpet sounds the alarm, revival fires ignite everywhere.
Saints everywhere rise in the stature of His fullness to declare.
He empowers as His voice thunders to those who have ears to hear.
With great exploits, He performs through His faithful instruments.
As His mighty army marches forward in perfect step, He implements.

In every nook and cranny, His presence and sovereignty are felt.
With the earth filled with His presence, multitudes are helped.
Standing before Him, in judgment, no one is without excuse.
For all who come to Him in repentance, He gives final opportunity.
In the end, all will witness signs and wonders with importunity.

As the final trumpet sounds, all that the prophets spoke, comes to pass.
With the beast fully released, Satan comes in power to destroy in mass.
With the mystery of God finished, the trumpet sounds to be heard.
The earth is scorched as the fullness of God's wrath is released.
As the Son of God sets up His throne, Satan is bound and leashed.

Caught Up in The Zeal of the Lord

Chapter Four

God is looking for vessels of honor—those who have prepared and made themselves ready for what He is about to do. His desire is to fill our hearts with His zeal so that we can fulfill the purposes He's called each of us to do. We've been saved and called according to His purposes, not our own.[92] As we approach each new season in the Lord, it's our opportunity to shine as bright lights. However, we must first prepare ourselves to be used by Him in a manner that brings glory and honor to His name. We must allow Him to cleanse us from all ungodliness.

2 Timothy 2:20-21 But in a great house there are not only vessels of gold and silver, but also of wood and clay, some for honor and some for dishonor. [21] Therefore if anyone cleanses himself from the latter, he will be a vessel for honor, sanctified and useful for the master, prepared for every good work.

We are coming into the final season before the Second Coming of Christ—a season in which everything that's been prophesied, but still unfulfilled, comes to pass. All that God's Holy prophets have spoken, through the ages, must come to pass before the coming of Jesus.[93] This final season will be a time in which a double portion of God's Spirit comes forth suddenly to all those who have prepared their hearts to be sanctified and useful for the master to use them for every good work.

God will have people at the end of the age, who will be fully committed and abandoned to Him and His prophetic purposes.[94] He will have a volunteer army that will walk in step with one another in the positions and callings to which they've been called.[95] They will hear the Lord together as His voice thunders before His great army. They will be

---

[92] 2 Timothy 1:9
[93] Acts 3:19-22
[94] Psalm 110:3 Your people shall be volunteers in the day of Your power;
[95] Joel 2:7-8

full of the Holy Spirit as He leads them into strategic alliances just as He did with Cornelius and Peter. His body will come together, knitted and framed to fulfill His prophetic purposes.[96] His glory will fill all in all as it rests upon them.[97] With signs following, the gospel will be preached to every tribe and nation as they abandon themselves wholeheartedly to the prophetic purposes of the Lord. The zeal of the Lord will catapult them forward as they go forth fulfilling His sovereign plans and predestinated purposes.

Not all Christians will be Involved

The truth of the matter is; all of God's people will not be engaged in these exciting times. Many in the Church will be found sleeping.[98] Those who are of the five foolish virgin class will not have taken the time to fill their vessels with the precious anointing of the Holy Spirit as spoken of in Matthew's gospel.[99] They continually push the default button in ignorance, unbelief, disobedience, and fear rather than filling themselves with the oil of His Spirit. His anointing gets quenched as they continually press their default buttons.

Those of the foolish virgin class are the unworthy vessels spoken of in the previous passage of Scripture, whom the Master doesn't find useful.[100] They're the ones the apostle Paul speaks of, who are saved so as by fire, but their works get burned.[101] They're the outer court that doesn't get measured in Revelation 11.They're more interested in living in the permissible realm of God's grace than the beneficial. Because of their self-centered rather than God-centered ways they will standby in bewilderment while others enjoy the freedom and excitement of being filled with the fullness of God's Spirit.

On the other hand, there will be those of the wise virgin category, who will have their lamps lit and ready to move as the Lord's voice thunders before His great army. These are the ones who will have cast off the works of darkness and put on the armor of light.[102] They're the vessels unto honor, who will have prepared themselves and are filled with the fullness of His Spirit as they go forth as flames of fire with the

---

[96] Ephesians 4:16
[97] Ephesians 1:22-23, Isaiah 60:1-5
[98] Matthew 25:5
[99] Matthew 25:1-13
[100] The wise and foolish virgins will be discussed in detail in a later chapter.
[101] 1 Corinthians 3:11-15
[102] Romans 13:12

zeal of the Lord, working in and through them. They're the ones who sow in righteousness and break up the fallow ground of their hearts until the Lord comes and rains righteousness on them.[103]

Hosea 10:12 *Sow to yourselves righteousness; reap in mercy; break up your fallow ground, for it is time to seek the Lord, till He comes and rains righteousness on you.*

Elements of Preparation

In this section, I am merely introducing the critical elements needed for preparation as we sow in righteousness. Each of them will be elaborated on in full detail in the ensuing chapters. Now is the time to prepare to be used as vessels unto honor. The elements of preparation are listed as follows:

Baptism of the Holy Spirit and Fire is Needed

The Baptism of the Holy Spirit is essential to all that God has in store for us. John the Baptist described it as coming with fire. When the Baptism of the Holy Spirit came to the early disciples, it came with tongues of fire. Jesus said, *"But you shall receive power when the Holy Spirit comes upon you."*[104] Jesus also said, *"He who believes in Me, as the Scripture has said, out of his heart will flow rivers of living water."* He was referring to the Holy Spirit when He spoke this.[105] His anointing will flow through us as believers. As conduits for His anointing, He continually fills the earth with His glory as expressed by the prophet, Isaiah.[106]

Understanding the Sanctifying Process of the Lord

When John the Baptist spoke of the Baptism of the Holy Spirit, he referred to the fire that comes along with it. He said, *"He will burn up the chaff with unquenchable fire."*[107] As we give ourselves to God purposes and are caught up in what His Spirit is doing, the Holy Spirit burns the sinful chaff in our lives. As a result, we lose the desire to feed our fleshly desires,[108] resulting in the sanctifying process of the Lord as He changes us from glory to glory into the image of Christ.

---

[103] Hosea 10:12
[104] Matthew 3:11-12, Acts 2:4-6, 1:8
[105] John 7:37-39
[106] Isaiah 60:1-5
[107] Matthew 3:12
[108] Galatians 5:16

2 Corinthians 3:18 But we all, with unveiled face, beholding as in a mirror the glory of the Lord, are being transformed into the same image from glory to glory, just as by the Spirit of the Lord.

There is a sensitivity to the convicting power of the Holy Spirit as He convicts us of our sin. His job is to convict; our responsibility is to obey and yield by putting off all that was a part of our old nature and putting on that which is part of our new life.[109]

Hearts Fully Committed to God and His Purposes

These believers understand they have been saved and called according to God's purposes while entirely giving themselves to serve their generation just as David did.[110] Their lives are consecrated to God as they acknowledge what it means to take up the cross and follow Jesus by denying self. They're unafraid of losing their lives to gain all that the Holy Spirit desires to do in and through them. They're like the sons of Issachar who understood their times. They continually seek God because of the knowledge and understanding that is quickened to them. They know what it means to seek and find God with hearts wholly devoted to Him.

Psalm 53:2 God looks down from heaven upon the children of men, to see if there are any who understand, who seek God.

Knowing what it Means to Wait on the Lord

These believers recognize their strength and ability comes from God's divine ability working in them. They have an in-depth understanding of what it means to wait on God so that they're walking in step with Him rather than being led by their own will and desires. They understand how the grace of God involves much more than unmerited favor. They realize God's grace is multi-faceted and includes every aspect of our salvation experience, which leads to all that God has purposed for our lives. Understanding God's supernatural strength and divine ability are what enables them to mount on the wings of eagles as spoken by the prophet, Isaiah. They are also men and women of prayer who read and meditate upon God's Word. As the Holy Spirit interacts with them through His Word and prayer, He imparts faith to their spirits.

Isaiah 40:31 But those who wait on the Lord shall renew their strength; they shall mount up on the wings like eagles, they shall run and not be weary, they shall walk and not faint.

---

[109] Ephesians 4:22-24, Colossians 3:5-14
[110] 2 Timothy 1:9, Acts 13:36

To mount up with the *"wings of an eagle"* implies walking in the supernatural or divine ability of God. When Israel came out of Egypt, God reminded Moses of how He brought them out. He said, *"You have seen what I did to the Egyptians, and how I bore you on eagles' wings and brought you to Myself."*[111]

Waiting on the Lord involves being in tune with how God is working in your life. You understand His gentle promptings as He leads you along in His purposes. It comes from having a heart that stays tuned to the Lord's voice. Your heart and mind will have been trained to hear His voice as Jesus said, *"His sheep know His voice."*[112] They know the voice of the Holy Spirit as He speaks of things to come and guides them into all truth.

Knowing Places of Ministry and Function

One of the strategic keys for God's prophetic purposes to be fulfilled concerning the body of Christ coming into the fullness of the stature of Christ is for individual members to know their places of ministry and how to function in them.

The prophecy of a Joel eludes to the fact that everyone marches in step with one another, with no one pushing or shoving. They do not break ranks as they go forth set in battle array as flames of fire, while the Lord gives voice to His great army.[113] Paul, in his letters to the Corinthians and the Ephesians, expresses this thought when he mentions the need for the members of the body to be linked together for God's purposes.[114]

1 Corinthians 12:18 But now God has set the members, each one of them, in the body just as He has pleased.

Ephesians 4:16 from whom the whole body, joined and knit together by what every joint supplies, according to the effective working by which every part does its share, causes growth of the body for the edifying of itself in love.

As individual members who are desiring to be a part of those whom the Lord considers useful vessels, knowing how to function in our designated places of ministry is paramount. It's the Lord who places us in our positions of ministry, not ourselves.[115]

---

[111] Exodus 19:4
[112] John 10:4, 14:26, 16:13
[113] Joel 2:1-11
[114] Ephesians 4:16
[115] Psalm 68:6

Now is time to discover our gifts, talents, and purposes in life that help us to identify our places of ministry, which are necessary for what the zeal of the Lord is about to do. We all have destinies to fulfill.

Walking in The Fear of the Lord

They not only understand what it means to walk in the goodness of God, but they also realize there's a severe side to God's nature.

Psalm 112:1-2 (NIV) Praise the Lord. Blessed is the man who fears the Lord, who finds great delight in His commands. ²His children will be mighty in the land; the generation of the upright will be blessed.

Romans 11:22 Therefore consider the goodness and severity of God: on those who fell, severity; but toward you, goodness, if you continue in His goodness. Otherwise, you also will be cut off.

They understand the only way forward is to continue in God's goodness. There is no turning back once you place your hand on the plow.

Luke 9:62 (NIV) Jesus replied, "No one who puts a hand to the plow and looks back is fit for service in the kingdom of God."

Rightly Divide the Word of Truth – Discernment

2 Timothy 2:15 Be diligent to present yourselves approved to God, a worker who does not need to be ashamed, rightly dividing the word of truth.

To rightly divide the word of truth, we must, first, believe that God divinely inspires all Scripture, which is profitable for doctrine and instruction in righteousness.

2 Timothy 3:16-17 All Scripture is given by inspiration of God and is profitable for doctrine, for reproof, for correction, for instruction in righteousness, ¹⁷that the man of God may be complete, thoroughly equipped for every good work.

Notice that it says, *"thoroughly equipped for every good work."* Believing that God inspired Holy Men to write the scriptures must be the basis of how we interpret and divide His Word of truth. Believing in the Scriptures is what helps us to become useful vessels of honor as we go forth like flames of fire performing the will of the Lord. We do not have the right to pick and choose which Scriptures may be of God and which are not.

Secondly, if we believe all Scripture is divinely inspired, we must also exhibit faith in the divine harmony of Scripture, meaning that

Scripture will interpret Scripture. No Scripture is of private interpretation. All Scripture must be in harmony with the whole.

These people are not babes in Christ, who exist on the milk of His Word. They thrive on the meat of His Word and as a result, have significant discernment in how God operates in their lives.

Hebrews 5:12-14 For though by this time you ought to be teachers, you need someone to teach you again the first principles of the oracles of God, and you have come to need milk and not solid food. ¹³For everyone who partakes only of milk is unskilled in the Word of righteousness, for he is a babe. ¹⁴But solid food belongs to those who are of full age, that is those who because of use have their senses exercised to discern both good and evil.

The Church is called to be the pillar and ground of all truth. When the Church takes seriously the charge to divide the word of truth rightly,[116] it will overflow into the streets with people filled with the truth of God's Word, rather than the lies of the enemy.

In all that has been discussed thus far with the people God has chosen to be instruments of His will and purpose, it was always about God and not so much the person. For example, God chose Abraham to plant the seed of His promise that would one day fill the earth with His glory. He chose Moses to be the instrument to bring His purposes into fruition. The signs and miracles were for moving His plans and objectives into existence as He formed His people to be a conduit for all that He desired to do.

In the next section, we will see the final prophetic purposes that God will fulfill as the culmination of all God's purposes for humanity come to completion before His kingdom is fully established on earth as it is in heaven. We will see that it is God in His sovereignty working with humanity in their free will that He makes everything happen in His zeal. He will, once again, use signs and wonders to bring all that has been foretold by the prophets in bringing His prophetic purposes to pass. As friends of the bridegroom, the Father has made known His business to us.

John 15:15 I no longer call you servants, because a servant does not know his master's business. Instead, I have called you friends, for everything that I learned from my Father I have made known to you. ¹⁶ You did not choose me, but I chose you and appointed you so that you might go and bear fruit-fruit that will last—and so that whatever you ask in my name the Father will give you.

---

[116] 1 Timothy 3:15

Wings of the Wind and Flames of Fire

By Ken L. Birks © 2017 Straight Arrow Ministries

He comes on the wings of the wind, filling our vessels.
With clouds as His chariot, He comes to set us aflame.
With rushing winds, He comes with tongues of fire to ignite.
Filled with flaming fire, His vessels go forth in His Name.
With great expectancy, His name is proclaimed with might.

With passion ignited, transforming power produces purity.
As the chaff begins to burn; the old disappears into ashes.
With His gentle breeze blowing, newness comes with surety.
With each new day, there's an expectation of what's ahead.
As the chaff continues to burn, old strongholds disintegrate.

Made anew by His Spirit, vision and purpose are awakened.
Divine abilities and gifts are birthed, giving sail to the wind.
Flames ignited with explosive power, give birth to ministry.
With the mind of Christ, confidence explodes with desire.
Clothed with splendor, He makes His ministers flames of fire.

As the zeal of the Lord performs, His prophetic Word is fulfilled.
With flaming fire, He goes forth on behalf of His Church, the bride.
From the wings of the wind, He breathes on the dry bones to awaken.
With explosive power, saints are infused with authority from on high.
With His mighty wind, He gives sail to all who watch and standby.

Clothed with the sun, moon, and stars, His bride is fully dressed.
As a chaste virgin, she stands in the fullness of the stature of Christ.
Wedding garments in place, she's made ready for her day, now near.
As the Bridegroom comes in the clouds of heaven, He receives her.
Joined together, she'll be known as He's known, now consummated.

Prophetic Purposes
and the Zeal of the Lord

Prophetic Purposes
to be Fulfilled

Part 2

*Repent therefore and be converted, that your sins
may be blotted out, so that times of refreshing may
come from the presence of the Lord, and that He may
send Jesus Christ, who was preached to you before,
whom heaven must receive until the times of restoration
of all things, which God has spoken by the mouth of all
His holy prophets since the world began.*
Acts 3:19-21

The Great Revival and
The Fullness of the Spirit

Chapter 5

God has great things in store for His Church in the coming days before Christ returns to set up His eternal kingdom. We have seen or heard of many revivals that have come and gone. There's yet one last revival that shall come which will be greater than anything the world has ever experienced. It will be a worldwide revival that comes in many waves before the final outpouring of the Spirit comes that fills all in all with the glory of God. What the disciples of Jesus experienced was just a foretaste of what will be experienced in this coming revival.

The seed of Jesus which the Father planted in the earth will come to full maturity as the many membered body of Christ manifests the fullness of the stature of Christ.[117] All that Christ did and accomplished in His three and one-half years of ministry will pale in comparison to what's ahead. Because His body will fully manifest as the many membered body of Christ, we will do more magnificent works.[118] The manifestation of His seed will be multiplied as His servants go forth in the fullness of His power in every corner of the world proclaiming the message of the gospel of Jesus Christ.

The revival I'm referring to in this chapter is in conjunction with the prophetic promise of the fullness of the Spirit that is to come forth in His Church. This revival will demand the anointing within us to be fully expressed as we go forth with powerful manifestations of the gifts of the Holy Spirit. It will be a revival that results with the church showing the same fullness that was in Christ. When Jesus ministered in the flesh for three and one-half years, He ministered in the fullness of the Spirit that resulted from the Spirit given to Him without measure. It's evident throughout Scripture that the Father's plans and purposes are for His Church to come into the full measure and stature of the fullness of Christ.

---

[117] John 12:23-26
[118] John 14:12

49

Prophetic Purposes and the Zeal of the Lord

The Book of Ephesians speaks of how apostles, prophets, pastors, teachers, and evangelists were given as gifts to the Church so that His many membered body can come into the full measure of the stature of Christ that will express the fullness of the Spirit without measure just as Jesus did.

*Ephesians 4:11-13 And He Himself gave some to be apostles, some prophets, some evangelists, and some pastors and teachers [12]for the equipping of the saints for the work of the ministry, for the edifying of the body of Christ, [13]till we all come to the unity of the faith and of the knowledge of the Son of God, to a perfect man, to the **measure of the stature of the fullness of Christ.***

The above Scripture is a prophetic promise that states God's will and purpose for His Church. The Church is to represent the Father in the same way His Son, Jesus Christ did in His incarnation. The zeal of the Lord will bring this to pass, just as He's done with other prophetic purposes since the beginning of time. He will continue to make His ministers flames of fire, who will go forth to fulfill His prophetic objectives as the culmination of this present age comes to a close. This thought is also expressed in the first chapter of Ephesians, where it says, *"And He put all things under His feet, and gave Him to be head over all things to the church, which is His body, the fullness of Him who fills all in all."* [119]

The Prophet, Isaiah also speaks of this fullness, when he says, *"Arise, shine; for your light has come! And the glory of Lord is risen upon you. For behold, the darkness shall cover the earth, and deep darkness the people; but the Lord will arise over you, and His glory will be seen upon you. Then you shall see and become radiant, and your heart shall swell with joy; because the abundance of the sea shall be turned to you. The wealth of the Gentiles shall come to you."* [120]

Our world is getting darker and darker as Satan preys on those lost in darkness. Deep spiritual darkness has begun to cover the earth as the sinful ways of humankind are running rampant and accepted as normal behavior, everywhere.

As Christians, who are walking in the Spirit, these are exciting times because when sin abounds, grace will much more abound.[121] Now is the season to rise and shine by getting ready to experience a more significant deposit of anointing in our lives as God gets ready to move in His zeal. God's plans and purposes for His Church, the body of Christ, are to be a

---

[119] Ephesians 1:22-33
[120] Isaiah 60:1-2, 5
[121] Romans 6:20

perfect representation of Him in the same way, His son, Jesus was when He walked the earth.

Jesus was given the Spirit without measure, representing the Father's fullness. We, however, as individual members of the body of Christ, have been given a measure of Christ's gift.[122] When each of us adds our part to what God is doing in the Church, we will express the same fullness that Jesus showed when He was on earth over 2000 years ago. We see this in the book of Ephesians as well.

Ephesians 4:16 from whom the whole body, joined and knit together by what every joint supplies, according to the effective working by which every part does its share causes growth of the body for edifying of itself in love.

Jesus, Given the Full Measure of God's Spirit

When Jesus walked the earth, in His incarnation, over 2,000 years ago, He was the perfect representative of God, the Father—the manifestation of God in the flesh. He came in the express image of God the Father with the brightness of the Father's glory indelibly stamped upon His personage.[123] He was given the Spirit without measure to adequately express the Father's image and beauty to all who witnessed His coming. He is quoted telling Philip, one of His disciples, *"to see Me is to see the Father."*

The following Scriptures bear these thoughts out:

Hebrews 10:5 Therefore, when He came into the world, He said: "Sacrifice and offering You did not desire, but a body You have prepared for Me."

John 3:34-35 (NIV) For the one whom God has sent speaks the words of God, for God gives the Spirit without limit. [35]The Father loves the Son and has placed everything in his hands.

John 1:14 And the Word became flesh and dwelt among us, and we beheld His glory, the glory as of the only-begotten of the Father, full of grace and truth.

Jesus was the Anointed One sent to reveal God in all His majesty, power, and grace. He showed us the real character of God, and what it meant to love, care and minister to others as the fruit of the Spirit poured forth from His life. Jesus also showed us the awesome power and majesty

---

[122] Ephesians 4:7, Romans 12:3-4
[123] Hebrews 1:2-3

of God through the gifts of the Spirit manifested through Him. He revealed to us what it is to operate in the authority of God through His anointed teaching, casting out demons and speaking with wisdom to those who opposed Him. He was a man wholly submitted to the fullness of the Spirit working in Him.

The world needs to see the Father in the Church in the same way they saw the Father in Jesus. The Church is also the body that has been prepared by God, the Father. In the same way, God made Jesus' body a vehicle for His presence; His desire is for those same attributes to be in His Church as it becomes a vehicle for His presence. When His body becomes the full manifestation of Christ's presence, it will bring forth the Father's power, glory, and character to the nations of the world without the limitations of space and time. We are now the body of Christ. We are His body which God, the Father, prepared before time existed—eternity with Jesus as the head.

> ***Philippians 2:5-7*** *Let this mind (attitude—NASB) be in you which was also in Christ Jesus, ⁶who, being in the form of God, did not consider it robbery to be equal with God, ⁷but made Himself of no reputation, taking the form of a servant, and coming in the likeness of men.*

Before God, the Father, could initiate His ultimate plan for the many-membered body to express the full measure of His Spirit, in the same way, Jesus did, It was absolutely necessary for the Father to plant the seed of His Son in the earth by giving His life a ransom for many.

The Divine Seed Planted in the Earth

When the fullness of time came, the divine seed of God, which had come to fruition in the life of Jesus, had to be buried in the earth. It was to bring forth a more glorious expression of God's fullness. We see this again in the following passage.

> ***Ephesians 1:22-23*** *And He put all things under His feet and gave Him to be head over all things to the church, ²³which is His body, the **fullness of Him** who fills all in all.*

God needed a vehicle, or an expression of His image not restricted by space and time. It was for this reason, among others, that Jesus had to die—so that the divine seed could multiply and bring forth a more substantial harvest of sons and daughters. His purpose was to bring forth a many-membered body that would be far more glorious than the single expression of His body in the incarnation of His only begotten Son.

Jesus said, *"He who believes in Me, the works that I do he will also do, and greater works than these he will do because I go to My Father.*

And whatever you ask in My name, that I will do, that the Father may be glorified in the Son. "[124] He was speaking here of the many-membered body of Christ. Thus, it was necessary for the Father to plant the divine seed as Jesus said.

> **John 12:23-24** *But Jesus answered them, saying, "The hour has come that the Son of Man should be glorified.* [24]*"Most assuredly, I say to you unless a grain of wheat falls into the ground and dies, it remains alone; but if it dies, it produces much grain."*

What happens when you plant a grain of wheat or a kernel of corn in the ground? It reproduces itself, only now it's multiplied. The problem is; when we look at the fruit that's come forth, it doesn't necessarily resemble the seed the Father planted. What happened? The enemy has been at work sowing tares.[125] Unfortunately, the same problem that existed in the early church continues to prevail in the Church today. The fullness God desires is not happening because the Church is so full of self-will and carnality. The tares of self-will, sensuality, and lust have distorted the harvest of the seed that God so carefully planted. Paul dealt with this problem when he addressed his first letter to the Corinthian Church.

> **1 Corinthians 3:1-3** *And I, brethren, could not speak to you as to spiritual people but as to carnal, as to babes in Christ. [2]I fed you with milk and not with solid food; for until now you were not able to receive it, and even now you are still not able; [3]for you are still carnal. For where there are envy, strife and divisions among you, are you not carnal and behaving like mere men?*

Until we can chew on the meat of God's word, we will not experience the fullness He desires for our lives. Feeding on the meat of the word entails, first, becoming obedient to what we know. If we are to replenish our supply of oil, we must be like the five wise virgins spoken of in Matthew's gospel. It will entail digesting or meditating on the milk and the meat of God's word.

The prophetic purposes and promises God has for this age will surely come to pass, just as they have for past generations. The question is; will you be a part of them, or will you sit by as others join the company of those who are pressing forward in obedience to the fullness that God? The choice is yours!

---

[124] John 14:12-14
[125] Matthew 13:24-30

How the Church Should Look

By looking at the early Church in the book of Acts and the life and ministry of Jesus as He ministered for three and one-half years, we can catch glimpses of what the Church will look like as it ministers in the fullness of God's Spirit.

It's important to keep in mind; there have been many waves of the outpouring of the Holy Spirit in every generation that have manifested signs and wonders throughout the ages. There will most likely be many more waves of revival fires before the final one that ushers us into all that God has for His Church in the last days before the Antichrist comes with lying signs and wonders.

The purpose of this section is to draw our attention to the final harvest that Jesus prophesied and prayed for that gathers the people of God together in perfect unity. This revival will be worldwide, not just in pockets here and there. There are many prophetic passages of Scripture that describe this outpouring in various ways. It's a season in which the Church shall be manifested as the glorious branch of the Lord as His fullness fills all in all.

Isaiah 4:2 in that day the Branch of the Lord shall be beautiful and glorious, and the fruit of the earth shall be excellent and appealing for those of Israel who have escaped.

The Example of the Life and Ministry of Jesus

With this in mind, let's take a quick look at the ministry of Jesus to see what we can expect from this great outpouring of God's Spirit in the final harvest before the return of Christ.

Jesus came as the anointed Son of God to turn the hearts of God's people towards the righteousness that comes from the heart of the Father. Through many miracles, wisdom, and teaching with authority, He astounded His hearers. The demons trembled at His presence. He healed all who came to Him, raised the dead, and performed miracles that went against nature itself. He caused the blind to see, the deaf to hear and healed those with incurable diseases such as leprosy. He was the pure light sent from God the Father to bring light into a dark world.

Jesus had many notable miracles. He fed thousands with a few fish and loaves of bread, raised Lazarus from the dead, walked on water, turned water into wine, cast demons out of the possessed, and more. There were significant catches of fish, calming storms, causing the lame to walk and all kinds of infirmities healed.

As extravagant as these signs and wonders were, what the body of Christ will accomplish when it comes to the fullness of the stature of Christ will be much more significant. Jesus, Himself said, we would do greater works than what He did. Because His body is a many-membered body that stretches across the world and over every continent and country, it will not be limited by space and time as He was in His incarnation.

Try to imagine what it will be like when the Church rises in the glory spoken of by Isaiah, the prophet. God's people, whom He has planted in every city, village, town, and countryside throughout the world will stand up as the vast army. As the Lord breathes on the dry bones prophesied by the prophet, Ezekiel, His glory will fill all in all just as Paul prophesied to the Ephesians. Ezekiel's vision will produce a worldwide revival that is yet to come as the Lord in His zeal sends His ministers forth like flames of fire to fulfill His prophetic purposes during this period. Try to imagine those with the gift of an evangelist going forth as Philip did, preaching the gospel with signs following—people who are entirely abandoned and consecrated to the purposes of God. [126] Watch out! God often decides to act suddenly. It could happen without notice. We must already be busily involved in the work of the kingdom and not found sleeping.

The Example of the Early Church

The early Church that came forth on the Day of Pentecost is an example of what is yet to come. The Bible refers to its time as the early rain. The terms, *"Early and Latter Rain"* are biblical terms used to describe both the natural and spiritual rains that are necessary for natural and spiritual harvests. In the natural, the early rain was used to water the new seed planted so the plants could spring forth. The latter rain was needed to bring the plants into maturity to harvest. In a spiritual sense, they both speak of the outpouring of the Holy Spirit.[127]

God poured the early rain moderately, which was used to plant the seeds of the gospel of Jesus Christ on the earth. As the early disciples went forth in the power of the Holy Spirit, their known world heard the gospel message. On some occasions, thousands upon thousands received salvation in one day. Whole cities got saved as signs and wonders were commonplace. God healed people by being exposed to Peter's shadow.

---

[126] Acts 8:39-40
[127] Deuteronomy 11:14, Proverbs 16:15, Joel 2:23, Hosea 6:3, 10:12, James 5:7

The dead were raised, the lame were healed, devils were cast out, and the Church was set in order through the hands of these early disciples. The seed of God's word was sown into the hearts of the nations with the whole world becoming the Lord's vineyard.[128]

Pastor and author, W.W. Offiler is quoted as saying, *"The early rain ran true to the promise. Righteousness was literally rained from heaven upon them. They were instantly transformed into Spirit-filled men and women capable of ministering in the Spirit, in demonstration and power! For one hundred and fifty years this wonderful outpouring of the Spirit continued. Long after the apostles had gone to their rest, the fruits of their labors were in evidence in the Church."*

Now is the time for the saints of God *(that's you if you're wondering)* to discover who they are in God and what their positions and callings are so that they're in position when God breathes on His Body. For those who have prepared themselves sufficiently, He will come upon them suddenly as the latter rain to bring His sons and daughters to complete maturity. Paul referred to this when he said, *"Till we all come to the unity of the faith and the knowledge of the Son of God, to a perfect man, to the measure of the stature of the fullness of Christ."*[129]

> **Hosea 6:3** *Let us know, let us pursue the knowledge of the Lord. His going forth is established as the morning; He will come to us like the rain, like the latter and the former rain to the earth.*

> **Zechariah 10:1** *Ask of the Lord for rain in the time of the latter rain. He will give them showers of rain, grass in the field for everyone.*

> **James 4:7-8** *Therefore be patient, brethren, until the coming of the Lord. See how the farmer waits for the precious fruit of the earth, waiting patiently for it until it receives the early and latter rain. ⁸You also establish your hearts; for the coming of the Lord is at hand.*

With this in mind, let's turn our attention to Ezekiel's great prophecy of the valley of dry bones and see how the zeal of the Lord comes suddenly to bring His prophetic purposes into play.

The Dry Bones Live

> **Ezekiel 37:1-10** *The hand of the Lord came upon me and brought me out in the Spirit of the Lord and set me down in the midst of the valley, and it was full of bones. ²Then He caused me to pass by them all around, and behold, there were very many in the open valley, and indeed they*

---

[128] "God and His Bible or the Harmonies of Divine Revelation," Rev. W.H. Offiiler.
[129] Ephesians 4:13

*were very dry. ³And He said to me, "Son of man, can these bones live?" So, I answered, "O Lord God, You know." ⁴Again He said to me, "Prophesy to these bones, and say to them, 'O dry bones, hear the word of the Lord! ⁵Thus says the Lord God to these bones: "Surely I will cause breath to enter into you, and you shall live. ⁶I will put sinews on you and bring flesh upon you, cover you with skin and put breath in you; and you shall live. Then you shall know that I am the Lord."'" ⁷So I prophesied as I was commanded; and as I prophesied, there was a noise, and **suddenly** a rattling; and the bones came together, bone to bone. ⁸Indeed, as I looked, the sinews and the flesh came upon them, and the skin covered them over; but there was no breath in them. ⁹Also, He said to me, "Prophesy to the breath, prophesy, son of man, and say to the breath, 'Thus says the Lord God: "Come from the four winds, O breath, and breathe on these slain, that they may live."'" ¹⁰So I prophesied as He commanded me, and breath came into them, and they lived and stood upon their feet, an exceedingly great army.*

The above passage is a prophetic picture of the church coming together as the whole body, joined and knit together by what every joint supplies, according to the effectual working by which every part does its share. We are lively stones who are being built together as a holy temple for a habitation of God's Spirit. As a result, the fullness of Christ will fill the earth with the glory of God.[130] It will be even more significant than the glory that filled Solomon's temple and more excellent than the former as the prophet Haggai prophesies.

Haggai 2:6-9 "For thus says the Lord of Hosts; 'Once more (It is a little while) I will shake all shake heaven and earth, the sea and dry land; ⁷and I will shake all nations, and they will come to the Desire of All Nation's, and I will fill the temple with glory,' says the Lord of Hosts. ⁸'The silver is Mine, and the gold is Mine,' says the Lord of Hosts. ⁹'The glory of this latter temple shall be greater than the former,' says the Lord of hosts. 'And in this place, I will give peace,' says the Lord of hosts."

With the fulfillment of Ezekiel and Haggai's Prophecies, the full force of the latter rain is released to bring the harvest into full maturity with sons and daughters coming into the fullness of the stature of Jesus Christ. The Church then goes forth in the fullness of the Spirit as flames of fire during the trumpet judgments, gathering in the final harvest before the great and awesome day of the Lord. The blindness lifts from Israel

---

[130] Ephesians 4:16, 1:22-23

with the fullness of the Gentiles complete as they, too, are gathered in as part of the harvest.[131]

Come, Lord Jesus! Pour your latter rain upon us as we labor in Your harvest field!

---

[131] Romans 11:25

The Mighty Wind

By Ken L. Birks © 2017 Straight Arrow Ministries

You came as a mighty wind giving birth to Your Church.
As the wind continued to blow, others came, in search.
Your people went forth in the power of Your Spirit in battle array.
With revelation, You breathed Your Word into Scripture.
With Your Word now defined, all could taste, see, and hear.

With the kingdom birthed, hope comes to those lost in darkness.
historically, prophetic winds blew strategically in fierceness.
With the mighty wind of Your Spirit, movements were birthed.
With each movement, truth came forth to further establish.
With the wind, freshness came to those once lost in blindness.

Waiting in anticipation, the enemy comes with counterfeit winds.
Coming to confuse, he deceives from that which is genuine.
Testing the wind with God's Word, we're free from all deception.
Though Satan comes as an angel of light, his works will be shown.
Warned in Scripture, we don't participate in his deceptive winds.

With mighty winds giving breath, the dry bones live and reign.
As He breathes upon His Church, it stands as a mighty army to gain.
With every joint and ligament connected, they go forth in battle array.
As His glory settles, the Church becomes a powerful light to sway.
Being drawn to the light amid darkness, many come, far and near.

Multitudes saved, as the mighty wind blows across land and sea.
With the fullness of His Spirit filling all in all, it spills out everywhere.
With many touched, by His presence, they stand united in prayer.
As the Church is touched, the fullness of the stature of Christ results.
With the fullness of the Gentiles, blindness lifts as they exult.

Come, Lord Jesus, receive your bride as Heaven waits in silence.
With the sounding of the last trumpet, the dead rise in incorruption.
Those alive and remaining, He catches up to the clouds of Heaven.
Coming in the clouds of Heaven, He gathers all that wait for Him.
In wonder we wait, Come, Lord Jesus, blow Your mighty wind.

The Church, a Mighty Fortress

Chapter Six

Jesus has a glorious vision for the Church He's building. He's in the process of building a Church that will withstand anything Satan tries to use to come against it. Because Jesus is the One in whom God created all things, He's the most significant architect that has ever existed. He's now in the process of building something perfect and beautiful out of our lives as we are knitted and framed together for His purpose and glory. We are the living stones He is using to build with. We must allow the master architect to have His way as He builds according to His plans and purposes.

> *1 Peter 2:4-5 Coming to Him as a living stone, rejected indeed by men, but chosen by God and precious, ⁵you also as living stones, are being built up a spiritual house, a holy priesthood, to offer up spiritual sacrifices acceptable to God through Jesus Christ.*

When you examine your life, how do you see yourself being fitted and framed into all that Jesus is building? Are you an observer or a significant part of all that's being built and framed together for a habitation of His presence?

Jesus is Building His Church

The Church Jesus is building is intended to be a place of safety and refuge – a mighty fortress for God's people, especially as we get closer and closer to the fulfillment of all that the prophets have prophesied. Having a place of safety to gather may be why the writer of the book of Hebrews warned us not to forsake our assembling as we see the Day approaching.[132]

> *Proverbs 18:10 The name of the Lord is a strong tower; the righteous run into it and are safe.*

---

[132] Hebrews 10:25

The church is very close to the heart of Jesus. When God allowed the divine seed of His Son to be planted in the earth, He gave birth to the Church as Paul writes to the church at Ephesus. He tells them, Jesus died for it so that it could become a glorious church without spot or wrinkle.

Ephesians 5:25-27 Husbands, love your wives, just as Christ also loved the church and gave Himself for her, ²⁶that He might sanctify and cleanse her with the washing of water by the Word, ²⁷that He might present to Himself a glorious church, not having spot or wrinkle or any such thing, but that she should be Holy without blemish.

The above passage is the prophetic vision of the church, which also includes the prophetic vision Jesus gave for it according to Matthew's gospel.

Matthew 16:18 And I also say that you are Peter, and on this rock, I will build My church, and the gates of Hades shall not prevail against it.

The vision of Jesus is for the church to become a mighty fortress where the sons and daughters of God can dwell in safety from the enemy and have a place to launch their missions throughout the world. Jesus, the great architect, has designed His Church to be a spiritual force. He has created it to be an entity that Satan has no power or authority over.

When Jesus spoke of the gates of Hell not being able to prevail against the Church, He was referring to the authority of hell and Satan. Vines Greek Dictionary refers to the term *"gates"* as the strength of authority where those in power render justice and decisions. In other words, the church is designed to be a fortress or a pillar where truth prevails. The church is to be the pillar and ground of all truth as Paul exhorted Timothy.

1 Timothy 3:15 I write so that you may know how to conduct yourself in the house of God, which is the church of the living God, the pillar, and ground of the truth.

Today's Church in Need of Many Repairs

Looking at the state of the Church today, we can see that it's not what Jesus intended it to be. It's a laughing stock and not a force to be reckoned with in the eyes of the world. The Church has lost her voice and influence amid compromise and being intimidated by the enemies of her faith. As the prophet, Isaiah wrote, *"Justice is turned back, and righteousness stands afar off; for truth is fallen in the street, and equity cannot enter."*[133] She is no longer the city set on a hill. She has abdicated

---

[133] Isaiah 59:14-20

her authority in favor of being relevant for the sake of drawing more people into it. As a result, she has compromised the truth of God's Word with diminished light and influence in the world.

Here's part of a poem that expresses the thought.

No longer relevant in our world, the Church cries out in disbelief.
Pleasing the whims of our cultures, she stands weakened without voice.
No longer preaching sound doctrine, she stands in fear, intimidated.
Compromising truth for the sake of being relevant, the enemy laughs.
Caught in a web of deceit and mistrust, she cries out for relief.

Without truth, Satan comes with a vengeance to carry out his ploys.
Filling the Church with lies, those with itching ears give ear to his voice.
Truth no longer boldly proclaimed; people do what's right in their eyes.
Satan laughs as he readily fills the vacuum, the Church abdicates.
As his cohorts march forward in deceit, multitudes join their war cries.[134]

The stanzas from the above poem speak to the conditions of the Church in today's world; the people love it so just as the prophet, Jeremiah spoke to the people in his day.

__Jeremiah 5:30-31__ An astonishing and horrible thing has been committed in the land: [31]The prophets prophesy falsely, and the priests rule by their own power, and my people love to have it so. But what will you do in the end?

If the Church is to be the mighty fortress in which the authority of hell cannot prevail against it, God's authority must rule completely. His authority can only rule as the Church today adopts the pattern revealed to the early church that was put in place by Paul, the wise master builder. Instead of coming up with our versions of the blueprint, we must return to the design given to Paul. We must build on the foundation of the Lordship of Jesus Christ as the chief cornerstone as Paul wrote to the churches at Corinth and Ephesus.

1 Corinthians 2:10-11 According to the grace of God, which was given to me, as a wise master builder I have laid the foundation, and another builds on it. [11]For no other foundation can anyone lay than that which is laid, which is Jesus Christ.

Ephesians 2:19-22 Now, therefore, you are no longer strangers and foreigners, but fellow citizens with the saints and members of the

---

[134] www.straitarrow.net/devotional-poetry/truth

household of God, [20] having been built on the foundation of the apostles and prophets, Jesus Christ Himself being the chief cornerstone, [21] in whom the whole building, being fitted together, groves into a holy temple in the Lord, [22] in whom you also are being built together for a dwelling place of God in the Spirit.

When we build according to our ways rather than the pattern shown in the word of God, we create structures that cannot contain the outpouring of the Holy Spirit—something God considers as evil. Building a structure that cannot hold His anointing is something the prophet, Jeremiah warned us about as well.

Jeremiah 2:13 *For my people have committed two evils: They have forsaken Me, the fountain of living waters, and hewn themselves cisterns—broken cisterns that can hold no water.*

In addition to crying out for revival, we should be crying out for the Holy Spirit to help us build according to the blueprint, which came forth with the early rain. When the Holy Spirit was poured out on the Church on the day of Pentecost, the first disciples went forth with signs and wonders preaching and teaching the gospel of the kingdom everywhere. If we are to walk in the same anointing as they did, now is the time to repent of the self-will that holds back His precious anointing from being poured out in abundance so that the seasons of refreshing will come.[135]

Proper Authority Structure Must Be Implemented

Today, in many quarters of the Church, the proper authority structure is missing. God's authority must rule in the Church before He can breathe upon the dry bones.[136] Creating the appropriate structure is something we must partner together with the Lord to do. It's not something we can fabricate on our own. It must be the Lord who builds His house as we labor together with Him.[137] He will do it in His zeal. Our part is to die to self-will and allow Him to place the members of His body as He pleases. Until we repair the cracks in the foundation, God will withhold the outpouring of the Holy Spirit that produces the revival we all desire.

---

[135] Acts 3:19
[136] Ezekiel 37:1-10
[137] Psalm 127:1

A Shaking is Coming

There's a shaking coming to the church before it comes to the world.[138] Before God releases His final judgments on the earth, He must begin with the household of God.[139] There must be a Holy fear that comes upon the Church in the same way as it was in the early church which resulted in the death of Ananias and Saphira.[140] The judgment of God not only struck fear into the disciples but caused unbelievers to look upon them favorably. It resulted in a dramatic shifting in the Spirit realm as signs and wonders increased markedly with multitudes of believers added to the Church at an alarming rate.[141]

Our vision for the Church must be the same as it was for Jesus. As we labor together with Him to build His Church, the gates or authority of hell will not be able to prevail against it. Building according to the pattern will cause us to experience the peace and security that comes from dwelling in a mighty fortress, where His name is exalted. It will be the strong tower the Psalmist spoke of—a place where the righteous can live in safety.[142]

We're Lively Stones being Built Together

When Jesus spoke of building His church, He was talking about building our lives together for a habitation of the Spirit. We know the Holy Spirit dwells in each one of us individually, but He was referring to a much more considerable infilling that inhabits His body, the Church. As we allow the Holy Spirit to connect our parts in the way He's placed them; we will be ready for the final outpouring of His Spirit. His living water will continue to flow into sturdy cisterns, without cracks containing the anointing emanating from Him.

There's a mighty outpouring coming, and the Church He's building will be the only entity on earth that will be able to contain it. The question is; will your part be connected to the whole or will you, with an independent spirit, hit the default button through fear and unbelief? The choice is yours!

I'm more concerned about the leaders in His Church because they have a higher responsibility to be in their designated positions, operating

---

[138] Hebrews 12:26
[139] 1 Peter 4:17
[140] Acts 5:1-11, Hebrews 12:27-28, Isaiah 4:4, 1 Peter 4:17
[141] Acts 5:12-16
[142] Matthew 16:18, Proverbs 18:10

in the measure of grace that God has granted to them. The anointing flows from the head down. As the Psalmist so adequately illustrates, *"It's like the precious oil upon the head, running down on the beard, the beard of Aaron, running down on the edge of his garments, where the Lord commands His blessing."*[143]

Paul mentions the importance of remaining connected to the head as well in his letter to the Church at Colosse. He says, *"Let no one cheat you of your reward… by not holding fast to the Head, from whom all the body, nourished and knit together by joints and ligaments grows with the increase that is from God."*[144] If the leaders of His Church are not holding fast to the head, there will be missing links interfering with the anointing as it flows through the body, resulting in an interrupted flow of His blessing. Our nourishment and well-being in the Lord are vitally dependent on being firmly connected to the other members of the body of a Christ.

Remember! It's God, the Father who sets the members of the body just as He has pleased. It's our responsibility to discover who we are in Christ, what our gifts are, and how we fit into the scheme of the whole. As we ultimately surrender our lives to His will and purpose in humility, we'll find and know our positions and purpose. Discovering our areas of responsibility and operating in them with the gifts He has given to us is how Jesus is building His Church as a mighty fortress.

The Five-Fold Ministry

The Five-fold ministry gifts mentioned in Ephesians 4:11 are essential in relation to how Jesus is building His Church. These are the gifts He gave to the Church for it to become a mighty fortress. Without the impartation from all five gifts Jesus gave to His Church, it will be undernourished. Some of the main ingredients in the diet will be left out. It takes a regular impartation from all five of these ministries, coined as the five-fold ministry, for the church to be healthy and strong—a fortress of security and safety.

True Biblical leadership is essential as it relates to the five-fold ministry. The saints of God need to hear from all five of the ministry gifts that Paul mentioned to the Church at Ephesus. They include apostles, prophets, evangelists, pastors, and teachers. Churches today are very one dimensional, meaning whichever gift the lead pastor operates in the most is the primary way in which a particular church is fed. For

[143] Psalm 133
[144] Colossians 2:19

instance, if the lead pastor's gifting is primarily an evangelist, the people will be inspired but not shepherded or taught very well. They will also need the input that is necessary from the apostolic and prophetic gifts.

The Apostolic Voice

The Church needs to hear the apostolic voices, who stir the hearts of God's people with vision that goes beyond their local churches. Many of God's people have apostolic vision lying dormant that must be awakened before they can adequately go forth to fulfill their callings in God. Without the voice of the apostolic grace challenging them, they're stuck in the form of mundane Christianity without fully realizing their purpose.

As I ponder what God wants to do in the Church, I'm reminded of some of the great apostolic voices of the 70s and 80s. People like Jim Durkin, Dick Benjamin, Dick Iverson, John Wimber, Chuck Smith, Jack Hayford, Bob Mumford, Derek Prince, Ern Baxter, Charles Simpson, Don Basham, and others who challenged thousands upon thousands of young people throughout to go into the harvest fields. They left the comforts of their homes, to go forth on church planting teams spreading the gospel of Jesus Christ, fulfilling the great commission, and serving the purposes of God for their generation.

The Prophetic Voice

The prophet is needed as well. The voice of the prophet speaks to the global vision of the Church and the individual callings of God's people to help confirm His will and purpose in their lives and the Church. God's will has been proved over and over in my life as I have had those with prophetic voices speak into my life. Hearing their prophetic voices have always been an encouragement to me as I have gone through the various seasons of my life.

The Evangelistic Voice

The voice of the evangelist is much needed in the Church in this hour as we are about to engage in the greatest harvest of souls known to humanity. God's people need to be trained and stirred to share the gospel of Jesus Christ effectively. There are people everywhere caught up in the chains of darkness just waiting for the light of the gospel to penetrate the darkness of their hearts. If our lights are hidden, how will they see? The voice of the evangelist must be released so that the saints of God can be equipped for evangelistic ministry.

Romans 10:14-15 How then shall they call on Him in whom they have not believed? And how shall they believe in Him of whom they have not heard? And how shall they hear without a preacher? [15]*And how shall they preach unless they are sent? As it is written: "How beautiful are the feet of those who preach the gospel of peace, who bring glad tidings of good things!"*

The Voice of the Teacher

The teacher's voice should be much in demand during an era in which truth has fallen in the streets. The Church is to be the pillar and ground of truth to the world that is caught up in the lies and deception of the enemy. In a day when the truth is watered down for the sake of relevance, teachers need to be received who know how to divide the word of truth rightly. I believe God is raising up godly teachers throughout the world who will be able to instruct multitudes upon multitudes in the purity of God's word so that a strong biblical foundation is built in the lives of believers everywhere.

The Pastor's (Shepherd's) Voice

Shepherds or pastors are essential to all that God is doing in His Church. God is in the midst of raising up godly leaders who will not be afraid to speak forth the full counsel of His word. We are presently in an era that is very similar to the time of the Judges when everyone was doing what seemed right in their own eyes. The Church needs godly pastors who will use their authority in a godly way, without abusing those under their care. They're required to protect the people of God from all the schemes of the devil.[145] They must shepherd the people of God through His word, which is sharper than any two-edged sword piercing the division of soul and spirit so that the thoughts and intents of their hearts get discerned.[146]

Assimilating the Five-Fold Ministry

I believe God is calling for an integration of the five-fold ministry to come forth so that His Church can be the mighty fortress that He's called it to be. The five-fold ministry is as an integral part of the blueprint the apostle Paul received from the Holy Spirit on how Jesus is building His Church. Incorporating the five-fold ministry is a big part of what enables a church to be a cistern that contains the living water that flows from the

---

[145] Acts 20:28-29
[146] Hebrews 4:12

throne of God. The Church must be able to handle the outpouring of the latter rain. Otherwise, God's precious anointing is wasted.[147]

Assimilating the five-fold ministry may seem overwhelming to those who are pastoring small churches. They may be thinking, "How can my church afford to have all these ministries?" Instead of being overwhelmed, they could connect with other ministries in their stream of churches and local regions. When you relate to others, it forces you to let go of self-will and insecurity. Leaders have a responsibility before God to build relationships with other leaders either in their streams of fellowship or their regions. They need to be able to draw from one another's ministries where they are lacking. After building relationships based on trust and mutual respect, they could then invite them to share from their pulpits.

Another more practical way to incorporate all five ministries into the pulpit ministry is for leaders to stretch themselves. It's easy for them to get into a groove of preaching out of their wheelhouse. The problem with this is that they become very one dimensional in their preaching. As they prepare messages, they could begin to think like an apostle, prophet or evangelist, and what their churches need to hear from those perspectives. What does a church need to understand from a teacher or pastor's perspective? Stretching may require more study and preparation on their parts, but it will be helpful as they attempt to preach and teach the whole counsel of God rather than being one dimensional.

Elders, Shepherds, Deacons, and Saints

If the Church is to become the mighty fortress that Jesus envisioned, it will need to have elders and deacons who are commissioned to take care of the needs of the flock as the saints of God are busy doing the work of the ministry.[148] Elders are to take care of spiritual needs, while deacons tend to natural needs.[149] Elders could be divided into two classifications; those who rule and those who shepherd.

Ruling and Shepherding Elders

1 Timothy 5:17 Let the elders who rule well be counted worthy of double honor, especially those who labor in Word and doctrine.

1 Peter 5:1-2 The elders who are among you I exhort, I who am a fellow elder and a witness of the sufferings of Christ, and also a partaker of the

---

[147] Jeremiah 2:13
[148] Ephesians 4:12
[149] Philippians 1:1

69

glory that will be revealed: [2]Shepherd the flock of God which is among you, serving as overseers, not by compulsion but willingly, not for dishonest gain, but eagerly; [3]nor as being lords over those entrusted to you, but being examples to the flock.

In any given local church, there's both a need for shepherding elders and ruling elders. The need for ruling elders is less as too many muddy the waters. Ruling elders should tend to vision, doctrine, preaching, teaching and financial matters while shepherding elders concentrate on meeting the spiritual needs of the flock.

When Paul spoke to the Ephesian elders, he encouraged them to feed the flock, knowing that wolves would try to destroy them.

Acts 20:27-28 *For I have not shunned to declare to you the whole counsel of God. [28]Therefore take heed to yourselves and to all the flock, among which the Holy Spirit has made you overseers, to shepherd the church of God, which He purchased with His own blood.*

In the past, the term "shepherding" was widely abused in the Church. Nevertheless, it's a necessary part of the Church Jesus is building. Satan has tried to destroy the flock of God through the abuse of ungodly, demanding shepherds or pastors. The enemy tricks them into lording over those entrusted to their care, rather than the godly examples they should have been. One of the primary qualities of elders is that they are not to be self-willed.[150] A self-willed elder can cause a lot of damage to the flock as they are more susceptible to the enemy's devices.

The Church seems to swing from one pendulum to another. In today's world, it seems as though the contemporary Church is allowing too much of what happened during the period of the Judges to be normal Christian behavior. During the period of the Judges, everyone did what was right in their own eyes. There's a real lack of authority and discipline in the modern Church because elders have abdicated the authority that was given to them by the Lord. Oh, but the people love to have it so, just as they did in Jeremiah's rebuke to the leaders during his day.

Jeremiah 5:30-31 *An astonishing and horrible thing has been committed in the land: [31]The prophets prophesy falsely, and the priests rule by their own power, and the people love to have it so, **but what will you do in the end.***

The Importance of Deacons

Deacons are very much needed in the church as well. We see in the early Church how the apostles were getting so bogged down by tending

---

[150] Titus 1:7

to the natural needs of the church; they were unable to focus on what they were called to do. Their solution was to ordain deacons to oversee the physical demands. As a result, the word of God spread as the disciples multiplied greatly.[151]

> **Acts 6:2-4** *Then the twelve summoned the multitude of the disciples and said, "It is not desirable that we should leave the word of God and serve tables, [3]Therefore brethren, seek out from among you seven men of good reputation, full of the Holy Spirit and wisdom, whom we may appoint over this business; [4]but we will give ourselves continually to prayer and to the ministry of the word."*

Saints and the Work of the Ministry

We are all called to serve the purposes of God no matter who we are or what our station in life is. We have been saved and called according to God's purpose and grace rather than our works.[152] Everyone is to be involved in ministry in one degree or another. Jesus gave the five-fold ministry for the equipping of the saints for the work of the ministry, for the edifying of the body of Christ.[153] Disciples are very much involved in the building process. In Paul's letter to the church at Ephesus, he gave much insight into the structure of the Church. He showed us that it's the saints of God who are called to do the work of the ministry.[154] The elders and deacons are overseers of these wonderful volunteers who are to do the bulk of the ministry.

Incorporating, elders, deacons, and the five-fold ministers is a significant part of the blueprint for the Church Jesus is building. It's His Church, and we are His co-laborers. His Church is to be a mighty fortress where His name is a strong tower for the righteous to run into and be safe from the storms that are brewing in the world. The question is; will you be a vessel of honor, who dedicates your life to the purposes of God in this hour of the Church's destiny or will you sit by while others labor in the Lord's harvest.[155] Will you be among the few who respond to the call?

---

[151] Acts 6:7
[152] 2 Timothy 1:9
[153] Ephesians 4:12
[154] Ephesians 4:12
[155] Luke 10:2

Prophetic Picture of the Last Days Church

The book of Joel gives us a powerful prophetic picture of what the church will look like as all that was foretold by the prophets comes to pass before the second coming of the Lord.[156] He sees the Church with everyone marching in perfect step with no one breaking rank as they leave a world that is being consumed with the horrors of tribulation.

Joel 2:7-8 They run like mighty men; they climb the wall like men of war; every one marches in formation, and they do not break ranks. [8]They do not push one another; Everyone marches in his own column. Though they lunge between the weapons, they are not cut down.

The prophecy of Joel is a prophetic picture of the church coming together in perfect unity. Everyone knows their position and calling in God. Self-will and insecurity are replaced with a desire to be wholly consecrated to God's will and purpose. They're not only in sync with God but are in sync with one another as they go forth like flames of fire fulfilling His Word. No one pushes or shoves as they're content with who they are in Christ. As Paul and Titus were in step with each other,[157] so are they as they march towards the ultimate destiny for all of God's people.

Joel's prophecy is the fulfillment of what Paul spoke to the Church at Ephesus.

Ephesians 4:16 from whom the whole body, joined and knit together by what every joint supplies, according to the effective working by which every part does its share, causes the growth of the body for the edifying of itself in love.

Whether we find ourselves as elders, deacons or saints doing the work of the ministry, whatever our hands find to do, we must do with all our might; for there is no work or devise in the grave where we are going.[158]

In God's sovereignty, the zeal of the Lord will bring Joel's prophecy to pass. As we are consecrated to our Lord's purposes as vessels of honor, this is what awaits us.[159]

The prophet Isaiah speaks of how the zeal of the Lord will intervene with His glory filling the earth like the rising of the sun when the enemy comes in like a flood. God will lift a standard against him when He sees

---

[156] Acts 3:19-21
[157] 2 Corinthians 12:18
[158] Ecclesiastes 9:10
[159] 2 Timothy 2:19-26

how truth has fallen in the streets and wonders at the lack of intercessors. God's righteousness will sustain Him as He puts on righteousness as a breastplate and garments of vengeance for clothing while cladding Himself with His zeal as a cloak.[160]

When the Church is clothed in these same garments, she arises in His magnificent glory that fills all and all. The glory of the Lord is then seen in every corner of the earth as His bride, who has now made herself ready, rises in the beauty of her wedding garments. She goes forth with signs and wonders with the message of the gospel as multitudes upon multitudes are led into the mighty fortress of the Church from the onslaught of the enemy.

I close this chapter with a stanza from a poem I recently wrote

In the end, the gates of Hell will not prevail as Jesus builds His Church.
Let us purpose in our hearts to be a part of all that Jesus is building.
Let's join hearts together in unity, seeking to silence the enemy's voice.
As the glory of the Lord rises upon us, let us bask in His love and power.
For God Omnipotent reigns overall! Nothing's difficult for Him.[161]

---

[160] Isaiah 59:14-20, 60:1-12
[161] www.straitarrow.net/devotional-poetry/truth

The Bride of Christ Revealed

Chapter Seven

One of the most precious prophetic events yet to take place, aside from the second coming of Christ, is the revealing of the bride of Christ. Throughout the Scriptures, a beautiful picture is painted in our imaginations of the relationship between Christ and His bride. A bride will be prepared for the Father's only begotten Son, who will appear in the glory and splendor of her Lord as she waits for His Coming.

The revealing of the bride of Christ plays a significant role in all that God desires to do before the coming of the great day of the Lord. It's a remarkable part of His prophetic purposes. It's the centerpiece of the end time scenario. Therefore, we need to know our role and what the Lord's expectations of us are.

Throughout the Bible, there are many prophetic pictures of the bride of Christ in both the Old and New Testaments. The truth concerning the bride of Christ is one of the great mysteries of the Bible. In Paul's letter to the church at Ephesus, he compares the relationship of Jesus to the Church in the same manner of a husband to his wife and then sums it by saying, this is a great mystery.

***Ephesians 5:32** This is a great mystery, but I speak concerning Christ and the church.*

The mystery concerning Christ and the Church is one of the prophetic purposes of God that will be revealed in its fullness before Christ returns for His Church. Because it's a great mystery, there are many hidden facets to it in the Scriptures that must be searched out to bring forth the complete picture. As kings and priests unto God, we are told to search out the hidden truths that are locked away.

***Proverbs 25:2** It is the glory of God to conceal a matter, but the glory of kings is to search out a matter.*

God's desire towards us is to give us the spirit of wisdom and revelation to unlock the mysteries He's hidden throughout the ages.[162]

---

[162] Ephesians 1:17-18, Matthew 13:16-17,

Jesus often spoke to His disciples in parables that were somewhat mysterious so that only those who had ears to hear could understand what He was saying. The Father has designed us in such a way that it takes a relationship with the Holy Spirit for His word to come alive in our spirits. As we are diligent to search matters out, the Holy Spirit gives us greater revelation and understanding of His word.[163]

Jesus is the Bridegroom

As with all truths, they're based on the reality of the New Testament. Types and shadows are worthless unless they point clearly to New Testament realities.[164] As we begin to look at some of the New Testament realities, we will see that Jesus looked upon Himself as the bridegroom. When the disciples of John the Baptist questioned Jesus as to why His disciples didn't fast, His reply to them was, *"While the bridegroom is with them, the attendants of the bridegroom cannot fast, can they?"*[165] Again, when sharing with His disciples the parable concerning the *"Ten Virgins,"* He referred to Himself as the bridegroom.[166] Paul also mentions this in a couple of his epistles where he speaks of believers who are betrothed to one husband and are to be presented to Christ as a chaste virgin.[167]

We've already seen in Paul's letter to the church at Ephesus, that he compared the church and its relationship to Jesus as a bride in the same way a husband relates to his wife. Again, in his letter to the Romans, Paul writes, *"Therefore, my brethren, you also have become dead to the law through the body of Christ, that you may be married to another—to Him who was raised from the dead, that we should bear fruit to God."*[168] From the Old Testament, we have the passage from the prophet Isaiah among others.

Isaiah 62:3-5 You shall also be a crown of glory in the hand of the Lord and a royal diadem in the hand of your God. ⁴You shall no longer be termed Forsaken, nor shall your land any more be termed Desolate; but you shall be called Hephzibah, (My delight is in her) and your land Beulah; (Married) for the Lord delights in you, and your land shall be married. ⁵ For as a young man marries a virgin, so shall your sons marry

---

[163] Matthew 13:10-17
[164] Hebrews 10:1
[165] Mark 2:18-20
[166] Matthew 25:1-12
[167] 2 Corinthians 11:2
[168] Romans 7:4

you, and as the bridegroom rejoices over the bride, so shall your God rejoice over you.

The Church, throughout Scripture, is referred to many things, including the bride of Christ. These Scriptures and others make it quite clear that the Church is called to be the bride of Christ. She will be commensurate with the stature of Jesus in every aspect when He comes out of His room to receive His bride from her chamber as seen in the following passages.

Joel 2:16 *Gather the people, sanctify the congregation, assemble the elders, gather the children and the nursing infants. Let the bridegroom come out of his room and the bride out of her bridal chamber.*

While the bridegroom waits, the bride is busy making herself ready for the grand wedding day. The bride has much to do as she waits for her bridegroom.

Revelation 19:7 *Let us be glad and rejoice and give Him glory, for the marriage of the Lamb has come, and His wife has made herself ready.*

We are given vivid pictures in types and shadows throughout the Old Testament that help paint a picture of the Bride of Christ. The Song of Solomon, the Virtuous Woman of Proverbs 31, the servant going to pick a bride for Isaac in Genesis 24, and the books of Ruth and Esther are all types and shadows of this beautiful relationship between Christ and His bride.

The Song of Solomon describes the intimacy between the bride of Christ and her groom. It's as we grow more and more into the intimate relationship Christ desires from us that we become more like Him in every way. His ultimate desire is for us to conform to His image completely. Conformity takes place from glory to glory until the fullness of His glory rests upon us. Our lamps are continually filled when we purpose to walk in the anointing that comes from our relationship with the Holy Spirit. It's the oil that makes us ready to be His bride.

In Matthew's Gospel, we find one of the most astounding passages of Scripture concerning the bride of Christ. It describes how vital the anointing of the Holy Spirit is in our relationship with Christ. In the parable of the ten virgins, the mystery of her role in the end time scenario begins to emerge as part of God's prophetic picture at the end of the age. As we break this parable open, we will see how it fits perfectly with other portions of Scripture creating a divine harmony of revelation and understanding of who she is and the role she plays.

Keep in mind, the parable of the ten virgins follows the discourse Jesus had with His followers when they asked a Him the question, *"What shall be the sign of your coming and the end of the age?"*[169] Jesus shares this parable with them to teach them how to prepare for His second coming. He begins with the adverb of time, *"then,"* which connects it to the end time scenario he had just explained to them.

The Parable of the Ten Virgins

Matthew 25:1-13 Then the kingdom of heaven shall be likened to ten virgins who took their lamps and went out to meet the bridegroom. ²Now five of them were wise, and five were foolish. ³Those who were foolish took their lamps and took no oil with them, ⁴but the wise took oil in their vessels with their lamps. ⁵But while the bridegroom was delayed, they all slumbered and slept. ⁶"And at midnight a cry was heard: 'Behold, the bridegroom is coming; go out to meet him!' ⁷Then all those virgins arose and trimmed their lamps. And the foolish said to the wise, 'Give us some of your oil, for our lamps are going out.' ⁹But the wise answered, saying, 'No, lest there should not be enough for us and you; but go rather to those who sell, and buy for yourselves.' ¹⁰And while they went to buy, the bridegroom came, and those who were ready went in with him to the wedding; and the door was shut. ¹¹"Afterward the other virgins came also, saying, 'Lord, Lord, open to us!' ¹²But he answered and said, 'Assuredly, I say to you, I do not know you.' ¹³"Watch therefore, for you know neither the day nor the hour in which the Son of Man is coming.

There are keywords contained in this parable that are relevant and very helpful in interpreting and understanding the message Jesus was teaching His disciples. Let's not forget, the truth between Christ and His bride is one of the great mysteries of the Bible. I believe the word of God contains many clues that help to unravel this great mystery as we are diligent to search them out. The key words or phrases in this parable are: virgins, lamps, oil, the door was shut, "I don't know you," and the midnight hour.

They're all Virgins

The Parable of the Ten Virgins illustrates to us the relationship between Christ and His bride, while she waits for His second coming. The fact that they are all virgins confirms they're all Christians who claim to know Christ, but only the wise are allowed to go into the bridal chamber.

---

[169] Matthew 24:2

The word *"virgin"* means clean, pure and holy, and applies to all Christians who have come to believe in Jesus Christ. God doesn't use words like purity, holiness, or righteousness to describe unbelievers. In Paul's letter to the Church at Thessalonica, we are given an explicit definition of what the word, *"virgin."* means as it relates to being espoused to Christ.

> **2 Corinthians 11:2** *For I am jealous for you with godly jealousy. For I have betrothed you to one husband, that I may present you as a chaste virgin to Christ.*

The "New Thayer's Greek English Lexicon" defines *"chaste"* in this passage as being pure from carnality, chaste, modest, pure from every fault, and immaculate. The word *"chaste"* is illustrated further by the fact that Jesus is returning for a Church that is spotless and without blemish.[170]

God's desire is for all of us to be chaste virgins who are vessels unto honor, rather than dishonor. This parable is in sync and harmony with what Paul said about some vessels being for celebrated recognition while others are dishonorable. The difference between the two vessels shows there will be a separation in the last hour of the Church. As we look at other passages of Scripture that are in harmony with this one, we will see more evidence of this separation.

They all had Lamps

All ten virgins had lamps, which represent the unfolding of God's word in our lives to direct our steps unto Him in a perfect way. Because lamps represent God's word, this, once again, reveals to us that all ten virgins are Christians. As seen in the following Scripture, lamps represent God's word in our lives.

> **Psalm 119:105** *Your Word is a lamp to my feet and a light to my path.*

They All had Oil

All ten virgins had oil in their lamps, which once again reveals they're all born again Christians. Oil in the Scriptures almost always represents the anointing of the Holy Spirit. Oil is one of the symbols used in scriptures to signify the Holy Spirit. All ten virgins had some oil, but the five wise virgins had an extra supply. The parable reveals that there is an additional supply of oil added when we become fully immersed in the

---

[170] Ephesians 5:25-27

Spirit through Spirit baptism. Then, by continually walking in His Spirit, the oil or the anointing is continuously refilled.

From the following passages of Scripture, we see that oil is synonymous with the anointing of the Holy Spirit.

1 Samuel 16:13 Then Samuel took the horn of oil and anointed him in the midst of his brothers, and the Spirit of the LORD came upon David from that day forward. So, Samuel arose and went to Ramah.

All who have been born again receive a supply of oil. It's when we're baptized in the Holy Spirit that we get the additional amount.[171] The word *"anointing"* in the following passages means to smear or rub with oil, which shows the anointing of the Holy Spirit is synonymous with oil

1 John 2:20 But you have an anointing from the Holy One.

1 John 2:27 But the anointing which you have received from Him abides in you, and you do not need that anyone teach you.

The word "anointing" from these two Scriptures indicates that this anointing renders them holy, separating them to God. The passage teaches that the gift of the Holy Spirit is the all-efficient means of enabling believers to possess a knowledge of truth.in the Septuagint it is used of oil for "anointing" the high priest, e.g., Exodus 29:7, lit., "Thou shalt take of the oil of the anointing." In Exodus 30:25, etc., it is spoken of as "a holy anointing oil."[172]

The deciding factor in this parable that makes the difference between the wise and the foolish virgins was the extra preparation to obtain a more substantial proportion of oil, which comes by being baptized in the Holy Spirit. It then continues by walking in the Spirit and stirring up His gifts. Those who were ready went into the marriage, and those unprepared didn't go in.

The Door Shuts

As the door shuts, the foolish virgins came to say, *"Let us in."* Jesus' reply to them was, *"I don't know you."*

In the Greek language, there are two words for the word "know" – ginosko and oida. Ginosko suggests progress in knowledge, while oida suggests fullness of knowledge of knowing perfectly. In the parable, the word *"oida"* is used. It's also used to convey the thought of connection

---

[171] In chapter 12, there will be more discussion on the baptism of the Holy Spirit.

[172] Anointing – (Strong's #5545 — Noun Neuter — chrisma — khris'-mah) Paragraph is a quote from Vines Expository Dictionary.

or union, as between man and woman.[173] Jesus is saying to them, "I don't know you intimately in a way that a husband loves his wife."

The five foolish virgins did not measure up to His fullness. By choosing to walk in the permissive realm of His grace rather than the beneficial sphere, they settled for a life that didn't bring them into the fullness of all that the Father was offering. Therefore, they didn't have the oil in their lamps when He came for them.

Just because the five foolish virgins weren't ready doesn't mean they miss out on the second coming. Jesus goes on to say, *"Watch, therefore, for you know neither the day nor the hour in which the Son of Man is coming."[174]* As we will see, in other passages of Scripture, God has a bridal chamber where He takes the bride. She will be taken to a place of refuge during the great tribulation to await His second coming. The prophet, Isaiah confirms this thought along with Zephaniah and Jesus.

*Isaiah 26:20-21 Come, my people, **enter your chambers, and shut your doors** behind you; hide yourself, as it were, for a little moment, until the **indignation** is past. [21]For behold, the Lord comes out of His place to punish the inhabitants of the earth for their iniquity; the earth will also disclose her blood and will no more cover her slain.*

Zephaniah 2:3 Seek the Lord, all you meek of the earth, who have upheld His justice. Seek righteousness, seek humility. It may be you will be hidden in the day of the Lord's anger.

Luke 21:36 Watch therefore, and pray always that you may be counted worthy to escape all these things that will come to pass, and to stand before the Son of Man.

The Scriptures above show that there are some who will be hidden and taken into the bridal chambers while others will not. The fact that it says we may be hidden and must be counted worthy to escape shows there will be a separation of Christians in the last days. The critical thought to explain the difference separating the wise from the foolish virgins is preparation. The bride must prepare herself to be ready.

---

[173] From Vines Expository Dictionary: the differences between ginosko (No. 1) and oida demand consideration: (a) ginosko, frequently suggests inception or progress in "knowledge," while oida suggests fullness of "knowledge," e.g., John 8:55 , "ye have not known Him" (ginosko), i.e., begun to "know," "but know Him" (oida), i.e., "know Him perfectly;" In Matthew 25:12 , "I know you not" (oida) suggests "you stand in no relation to Me.

[174] Matthew 25:13

Revelation 19:7 Let us be glad and rejoice and give Him glory, for the marriage of the Lamb has come, and His wife has made herself ready.

There is a preparation that must happen if we are to be a part of the bride of Christ, whom the Father counts worthy to escape the "Great Tribulation."[175]

2 Timothy 2:20-21 But in a great house there are not only vessels of gold and silver, but also of wood and clay, some for honor and some for dishonor. [21]Therefore if anyone cleanses himself from the latter, he will be a vessel for honor, sanctified and useful for the Master, prepared for every good work.

It says, *"If we purge ourselves from the works of carnality, then we will be a vessel of honor."* We all have the choice of changing from a seldom-used vessel to one that is greatly valued and often used as a vessel of honor. Who has the prerogative? Is it God's sovereignty concerning who is a part of the bride of Christ? No! It says, *"If a man, therefore, purges himself from these, he shall be a vessel unto honor."*

The Midnight Hour

The midnight hour speaks of the dark hour at the end of the age. Let us not wait until *"the midnight hour"* is upon us before we start to do our preparing. Now is the time to get that extra supply of oil into our vessels.

The Woman Clothed with the Sun, Moon, and Stars

The next area of revelation and insight concerning the bride of Christ comes from the book of Revelation concerning the woman clothed with the sun, moon, and stars.

Revelation 12:1 Now a great sign appeared in heaven: a woman clothed with the sun, with the moon under her feet, and on her head a garland of twelve stars.

In the book of Revelation, we discover this woman clothed with the sun, moon, and stars is a vital clue that breaks open this great mystery between Christ and His Church. This woman is none other than the bride of Christ.

This great sign appears during the sounding of the seventh trumpet. As the temple of God opens in heaven, God reveals the bride of Christ in all her glory. The prophetic vision of the woman with the twelve stars and the moon under her feet comes after she has attained to the fullness of the stature of Christ. She has been ministering in her glory during the

---

[175] Luke 21:36

other trumpet judgments as the earth was filled with the fullness of God's glory. Multitudes upon multitudes will come to know Christ with the final harvest completed. This passage reveals she is ready to be taken to her bridal chamber to await her Lord's second coming.

Keywords: Sun, Moon, and Stars

There are several keywords in this passage that help to reveal who she is. We find the first set of keywords in the first verse—the sun, moon, and the stars. The sun, moon, and stars are created symbols of the eternal Godhead revealed through the creation of the world. She is wearing her wedding garments, clothed with the Lord Jesus Christ, the triune name that represents the fullness of the Godhead bodily.[176] She has fully immersed herself in the Lord Jesus Christ, making no provision for the flesh.[177]

Romans 1:20 For since the creation of the world His invisible attributes are clearly seen, being understood by the things that are made, even His eternal power and Godhead, so that they are without excuse.

The passage from the book of Revelation gives us a clear picture of the bride of Christ. The sun, moon, and stars represent the created symbols of the triune God showing that she is fully immersed in the Father, Son, and Holy Spirit. The prophetic picture in this passage reveals that the bride of Christ is entirely covered with the divine glory of the Father, standing securely on the atonement of the Son of God, and crowned with the full power and beauty of the Holy Spirit.

The sun represents the Father in that all energy comes from the sun in the same manner that all life comes from the Father.[178] As the Scripture says, *"For the LORD God is a sun and shield; The LORD will give grace and glory."[179]*

The moon reflects the glory of the sun, just as Jesus reflected the glory of the Father. Notice that it says, *"the moon under the woman's feet."* The bride of Christ stands securely upon her Chief Cornerstone, who is the Lord Jesus Christ.

Ephesians 2:20-22 having been built on the foundation of the apostles and prophets, Jesus Christ Himself being the chief cornerstone, in whom

---

[176] Colossians 2:9
[177] Romans 13;14
[178] Acts 17:28
[179] Psalm 84:11

the whole building, being joined together, grows into a holy temple in the Lord.

As the stars are everywhere, they represent the omnipresence of the Holy Spirit, who is in the lives of believers everywhere. When God made a covenant with Abraham, He said His descendants would be as the stars of heaven.[180]

The bride is, therefore, wholly immersed into the Father, Son, and Holy Spirit—the Triune God—the fullness of God. Just as Jesus represented the Father in all His glory, she does as well—a bride commensurate to her groom.

The Holy Spirit Impregnates Her

Revelation 12:2 Then being with child, she cried out in labor and in pain to give birth.

In the same manner that Mary, the mother of Jesus, was impregnated by the Holy Spirit, before her marriage, to give birth to her male child, so it with the bride of Christ. The question is, "Who is this male child?" There are theories about this, with the most popular one being the Lord Jesus. The problem with that theory is that Revelation 4:1 makes it clear that everything in the book of Revelation that happens after chapter four is all future. One of the reasons many believe that the male child is Jesus is because verse five says, *"She bore a male child who was to rule all nations with a rod of iron."* However, the promise of ruling with power over the nations with a rod of iron, Jesus gives to all those who overcome. [181]

My purpose here is not to get into vague theories as to who the male child is, but to merely point out that in all probability he is not Jesus. The weight of Scriptures that are in harmony with one another reveals the woman to be the bride of Christ, which makes it impossible for this male child to be Jesus. My guess is, they're the 144,000 Jews, who are mentioned twice in the book of Revelation. The first mention of them is when the Father seals them while still on earth. The second time is when they're in heaven as the first fruits redeemed from among men to God and the Lamb.[182] The question is; when did they get caught up to heaven. The man-child answers the question. I could be wrong about this. It's just a thought to consider, although it makes perfect sense to me. Natural Jews go first because they are the Lord's first fruits. What could be more

---

[180] Genesis 15:5, 22:17
[181] Revelation 2:26-27
[182] Revelation 7:3-8, 14:1-5

glorious in the Father's eyes than natural Jews who have come into the perfection of the bride of Christ in all her glory, clothed with the Lord Jesus Christ?

The Male Child Caught up to Heaven

As the bride prepares to give birth to her male child, Satan is cast out from the second level of heaven where all spiritual warfare takes place, of which he's had access to since the fall. He tries to destroy the male child just as he attempted with Moses and Jesus upon their births. His tactics don't seem to change. God intercedes and catches him up to heaven. Satan then makes war with Christ's bride after her male child is caught up to heaven as the first fruits of those who will soon follow at the second coming.

Revelation 12:5-6 She bore a male child who was to rule all nations with a rod of iron. And her child was caught up to God and His throne. Then the woman fled into the wilderness, where she has a place prepared by God, that they should feed her there one thousand two hundred and sixty days.

The Bride Escapes on the Wings of a Great Eagle

Once the male child is caught up to heaven, Satan goes after the bride with a vengeance. As war breaks out in heaven, God then casts Satan and all his angels, who followed him in the rebellion to the earth. Satan, knowing his time is short, goes forth to cause as much havoc as he can. He knows that if he can destroy Christ's bride, he will have thwarted a primary prophetic purpose God has in mind. As Satan comes after the bride of Christ, he has one objective – to utterly annihilate her. He sends a flood after her, but God has already seen his ploys and knows what Satan is going to do and intervenes in His zeal to see His prophetic purposes fulfilled. Another Exodus is about to take place.

Revelation 12:13-14 Now when the dragon saw that he had been cast to the earth, he persecuted the woman who gave birth to the male Child. But the woman was given two wings of a great eagle, that she might fly into the wilderness to her place, where she is nourished for a time and times and half a time, from the presence of the serpent.

The woman or the bride of Christ flees into the wilderness, where she has a place prepared by God. She stays there for 1,260 days, or 3 1/2 years of the great tribulation which occurs as the seven vials of God's wrath are poured out during the sounding of the seventh trumpet. The wilderness is a place where she is nurtured and provided for by God, the

Father, during this terrible time that is yet to come upon the face of the earth. The place where she is nurtured and cared for during the great tribulation is her wedding chamber.

*Isaiah 26:20-21 **Come, my people, enter your chambers,** and shut your doors behind you; hide yourself, as it were, for a little moment, **until the indignation** is past. [21] For behold, the Lord comes out of His place to punish the inhabitants of the earth for their iniquity; the earth will also disclose her blood and will no more cover her slain.*

The Keyword Phrase – Wings of a Great Eagle

To those who keep His commandments, God's promise is, they will be saved or rescued from the final outpouring of His wrath which occurs during the "Great Tribulation."

*Revelation 3:10 "Because you have kept My command to persevere, **I also will keep you from the hour of trial which shall come upon the whole world**, to test those who dwell on the earth.*

The word *"kept"* is the Greek word *"terro,"* which means to guard against loss or injury, to cause one to escape in safety out of the power and assaults of the enemy. It implies a fortress or full military lines of apparatus.[183]

The meaning of the word *"terro"* is what's happening with the bride as she escapes on the wings of the great eagle.

The passage in Revelation concerning the bride of Christ isn't the first time God has used the term, *"wings of a great eagle,"* to help His people escape the tyranny of ungodly leadership. The first time was with the children of Israel when they left Egypt under Moses' leadership. Eagle wings speak of the supernatural deliverance of God in His zeal to bring about His prophetic purposes.

Exodus 19:4 You have seen what I did to the Egyptians, and how I bore you on eagle's wings and brought you to Myself.

The supernatural deliverance of God brought forth a healthy people as the children of Israel left Egypt.[184]

The prophecy of Joel mentions this present company of believers as a people who come, great and strong, the like of whom has never been.[185] This second Exodus will bring forth an even stronger group of people,

---

[183] Strong's Concordance #5083, Thayer's Greek Lexicon #5083
[184] Psalm 105:37
[185] Joel 2:2

which will be discussed more thoroughly in the next chapter. The passage below reveals how Israel left Egypt on the wings of an eagle.

Psalms 105:37-41 *He also brought them out with silver and gold, and there was none feeble among His tribes.* *[38]Egypt was glad when they departed, for the fear of them had fallen upon them.* *[39]He spread a cloud for a covering, and fire to give light in the night.* *[40]The people asked, and He brought quail and satisfied them with the bread of heaven.* *[41]He opened the rock, and water gushed out; It ran in the dry places like a river.*

Isaiah 40:31 *They that wait upon the Lord shall renew their strength; they shall mount up with wings as eagles, they shall run, and not be weary, and they shall walk, and not faint.*

The passage below is a prophetic picture of the bride of Christ being taken out on the wings of a great eagle as she makes her exodus from the fiery red dragon, the serpent of old, called the Devil and Satan.[186]

Isaiah 5:26-30 *He will lift up a banner to the nations from afar and will whistle to them from the end of the earth; surely, they shall come with speed, swiftly.* *[27]No one will be weary or stumble among them, No one will slumber or sleep; nor will the belt on their loins be loosed, nor the strap of their sandals be broken;* *[28]whose arrows are sharp, and all their bows bent; their horses' hooves will seem like flint and their wheels like a whirlwind.* *[29]Their roaring will be like a lion; they will roar like young lions; yes, they will roar and lay hold of the prey; they will carry it away safely, and no one will deliver.* *[30]In that day they will roar against them like the roaring of the sea. And if one looks to the land, behold, darkness and sorrow; and the light is darkened by the clouds.*[187]

The above prophetic passage of scripture is speaking of the bride being called by God to the wilderness. Verse 30 speaks of the "Great Tribulation" where it says, *"Behold, darkness, and sorrow; and the light is darkened by the clouds."* It also says in verse 27, *"no one is weary or stumbles,"* which is the terminology used for eagle wing deliverance.

The Bride's Place of Refuge

Revelation 12:6 *Then the woman fled into the wilderness, where she has a place prepared by God, that they should feed her there one thousand two hundred and sixty days.*

This great event takes place during the blowing of the seventh trumpet as the seven vials of wrath are about to be poured out on the

---

[186] Revelation 12:3, 9, 13
[187] See Joel 2:3-11 for a parallel passage of Scripture.

inhabitants of the earth. The great tribulation will take place for three and one-half years. During this time the bride will be tucked away in an area of security and refuge from the storm unleashed on the inhabitants of the earth. The sounding of the seventh trumpet is also known as the time when the Antichrist arises in the fullness of the power of Satan. In fact, he will be Satan incarnate, just as Jesus was the incarnation of God, the Father.

Just as the first Exodus delivered the nation of Israel from the judgments upon the Egyptians and brought them into the wilderness on the wings of a great eagle to be nurtured and cared for by God, the Father, so shall the bride of Christ be nurtured and cared for in her place of refuge, free from the final judgments that will be poured out on the earth prior to the second coming of Christ.

The prophet, Isaiah gives us another prophetic picture of this significant event in the following Scripture passage.

*Isaiah 4:1-5 And in that day **seven women** shall take hold of one man, saying, "We will eat our own food and wear our own apparel; **only let us be called by your name, to take away our reproach."* ²*In that day the Branch of the Lord shall be beautiful and glorious, and the fruit of the earth shall be excellent and appealing for those of Israel who have escaped.* ³*And it shall come to pass that he who is left in Zion and remains in Jerusalem will be called holy—everyone who is recorded among the living in Jerusalem.* ⁴*When the Lord has washed away the filth of the daughters of Zion, and purged the blood of Jerusalem from her midst, by the spirit of judgment and by the spirit of burning,* **⁵then the Lord will create above every dwelling place of Mount Zion, and above her assemblies, a cloud and smoke by day and the shining of a flaming fire by night. For over all the glory there will be a covering.** **⁶And there will be a tabernacle for shade in the daytime** *from the heat, for a place of refuge, and for a shelter from storm and rain.*

The biblical imagery in this passage speaks of the bride of Christ and the cleansing she goes through to be made beautiful and glorious. It also speaks of the protection she receives in her place of refuge.

Notice, that it says, *"Seven women shall take hold of one man, to be called by His name to take away her reproach."* The number seven is the number of perfection and completion, which describes the bride, now perfect, without spots or blemishes. The one man is her bridegroom, who is the only one in the universe, who can remove her reproach.

This passage of Scripture is another clue to the unraveling of the great mystery of Christ and His bride. It's also the fulfillment of the Day of Atonement and the Feast of Tabernacles for those who have ears to hear.

The divine harmony of the revelation of Christ and His bride is unfolding as the Scriptures interpret themselves.

In the same way that Israel was protected from all the plagues when God unleashed His wrath upon the Egyptians, so shall the bride of Christ be safeguarded during the outpouring of His anger during the "Great Tribulation." Verse five speaks of a cloud of smoke by day and the flaming fire by night – the same terminology that was used for the children of Israel while God fed, nurtured, and protected them in the wilderness for forty years.

The Fate of the Foolish Virgins

Once the bride makes her gray escape, Satan is granted to make war with the saints, who are left behind and to overcome them.[188] The foolish virgins are those who are left behind when the bride escapes. They are those who were not counted worthy to escape the great tribulation. They are the outer court of the temple of God that doesn't get measured in chapter eleven of the book of Revelation, but instead gets trampled on.[189] They are the little sister with no breasts mentioned in the Song of Solomon.[190] They are the ones who get cast into the outer darkness that Jesus spoke of in two of His parables.[191]

After Satan realizes the bride has been swept away on the wings of a great eagle, he is enraged with her and goes to make war with the remnant that is left behind, who have the testimony of Jesus Christ.[192] At this juncture in time, the Antichrist is granted to make war and receives authority over every tribe, tongue, and nation.

This period is also known as the outer darkness. The light of the gospel is now gone from the earth as the bride gets swept away. Up until now, the Antichrist has been restrained by the abiding sense of the Holy Spirit in the bride of Christ.[193] With her now gone, the Antichrist is no longer restrained and seeks to kill all those believers who are cast into the outer darkness. These are the foolish virgins who didn't have the necessary oil in their lamps to go out and meet the bridegroom.

---

[188] Revelation 12:9, 13:7
[189] Revelation 11:1-2
[190] Song of Solomon 8:8
[191] Matthew 22:13, 25:30
[192] Revelation 12:17
[193] 2 Thessalonians 2:6-7

2 Thessalonians 2:7 For the mystery of lawlessness is already at work; only He who now restrains will do so until He is taken out of the way.

The foolish Virgins have two choices as they find themselves in this outer darkness that is now entirely under the control of the Antichrist. They must either accept his mark or experience martyrdom by being beheaded. If they receive the mark of the beast, they blaspheme the Holy Spirit and are eternally damned to hell.[194] Those who get martyred will be a part of the dead in Christ who rise to meet Jesus at the second coming. Many will deny Christ by taking the mark, thus the great falling away that must occur before the second coming.

2 Thessalonians 2:2 Let no one deceive you by any means; for that Day will not come unless the falling away comes first, and the man of sin is revealed, the Son of perdition.

Revelation 13:15 He was granted power to give breath in the image of the beast, that the image of the beast should both speak and cause as many as would not worship the image of the beast to be killed.

Revelation 20:4 And I saw thrones, and they sat on them, and judgment was committed to them. Then I saw the souls of those who had been beheaded for their witness to Jesus and for the Word of God, who had not worshipped the beast or his image and had not received his mark on their foreheads or on their hands. And they lived and reigned with Christ for a thousand years.

It's during this time that the Antichrist and the false prophet perform extraordinary miracles, even calling fire down from heaven.[195] The Antichrist sits as God in the temple of God, showing himself as God.[196] A great deception falls upon humanity as he is entirely unrestrained. His goal is to deceive the remnant of God's people into taking the mark of the beast.[197] As a result, many who are a part of the remnant that was left behind fall away and receive the beast's mark. Those who receive the mark become part of the great falling away Paul spoke of to the church of the Thessalonians.[198] Those who do not accept the mark are beheaded and become part of the dead in Christ, who rise first at the second coming of Christ.

The revealing of the bride of Christ and her role in the end time scenario is a remarkable testimony of God. By making His ministers

---

[194] Revelation 14:9-13
[195] Revelation 13:13-14
[196] 2 Thessalonians 2:4
[197] Revelation 13:15-17
[198] 2 Thessalonians 2:3

flames of fire while He executes His zeal towards His Church, the bride, God fulfills one of His most significant prophetic purposes as this age ends with the second coming of His Beloved Son on the horizon.

The Bride of Christ

By Ken L. Birks © 2017 Straight Arrow Ministries

Clothed in the beauty and splendor of her Lord, she arrives.
She leaves behind her, the fragrance of the One she loves.
Crowned with twelve stars like a royal diadem, she shines brightly.
Espoused as a chaste virgin to the One she loves, she waits nightly.
The angels above rejoice as she awaits her chariot.

In faithfulness, she takes hold of Him, who takes away her shame.
So that she can stand in His righteousness, she takes on His name.
By the spirit of judgment and burning, she is purged and now waiting.
With all her filth washed away, she's made excellent and appealing.
Without spot, blemish or wrinkle, she awaits her bridegroom.

Toiling day and night as a virtuous woman, she makes herself prepared.
Standing firmly on her foundation radiating, His presence is declared.
As the moon reflects the sun's glory, she radiates her Father's grandeur.
Multitudes upon multitudes await this day as others mock or ignore.
As the wedding day approaches, the Spirit and the bride say, come.

Impregnated by the Holy Spirit, she awaits the birth of her male child.
Gathering herself together, the great decree is about to be unveiled.
In hopes of being hidden in the time of the Master's wrath, she waits.
Representing the wise virgins, she waits with her lamps filled with oil.
Measuring her inner temple, the Master finds her measure full.

Giving birth to her male child, the enemy tries to snatch him.
Before Satan can capture him, he's caught up to heaven above.
Now angry, he makes war with this beautiful bride as his prey.
Rescued, she escapes as a tide of violence tries to sweep her away.
In the form of two wings of a great eagle, her chariot suddenly arrives.

Taken to her bridal chambers, a place is prepared especially for her.
Allured into place in the wilderness, she awaits her bridegroom.
The Father's fury comes, unleashed on the inhabitants of the earth.
Safely hidden away, she rests in her shelter from the storm.
She wonders, "What happens to her little sister, the foolish virgins?"

Caught up to her Bridegroom, the Father's fury is now ended.
Received and known as He is, her marriage is consummated.

The Bride of Christ Revealed

Her groom, riding on a white horse, gathers His saints to encounter.
From the four winds, they gather for the great battle, now prepared.
With the brightness of His coming, those left on earth are scorched.

With earth purged of evil, the banquet is prepared for all caught up.
Saints from every generation along with the Patriarchs come to sup.
A thousand years of peace, they build, plant, and rule the nations.
As Satan is loosed for a season, he deceives as the great pretender.
With the new earth and heavens, the bride appears in glorious splendor.

The Bride in Army Boots

Chapter Eight

In the previous chapter, we saw a beautiful prophetic picture of the bride of Christ revealed in all her glory before escaping on the wings of an eagle from the serpent, the devil. In this section, we will see another prophetic picture of the bride transformed into a mighty army as she makes her way to this site, where she will be fed and nurtured by the Lord for three and one-half years.

The question that comes to mind is, how is God going to sweep down like a great eagle to transport millions or even billions of people to a secret place of refuge? First of all, nothing is too difficult for God, who can speak things into existence. His ways and means are beyond our comprehension. The same God who transported Philip, the evangelist from one place to another, can just as quickly move a whole company of people.[199] He is also the same God who swooped down and gave Elijah a ride into the heavens above in His magnificent chariot of fire with horses of flaming fire.[200] As we have seen, time and time again throughout the ages, God is able, in His sovereignty, to make His prophetic purposes come to pass. God can transform His ministers, through His zeal into flames of fire as He brings His intentions to pass.

All that I have and will be sharing in this section of the book are the final events that will culminate as the mystery of God concludes. It's during the sounding of the seventh trumpet that everything comes to a grand finale. It's at this time that the bride escapes to her place of refuge, the Antichrist shows his true colors, and the last seven bowls of wrath are released. Then finally, at the end of the sounding of this trumpet with the mystery of God finished, Jesus is released from heaven to come and set up His kingdom on earth as it is in heaven.

The display of fireworks from the heavens above will be much more magnificent than anything the earth has ever experienced since the creation of the world. What God did with Moses in bringing the children of Israel out of their Egyptian bondage will pale in comparison to the

---

[199] Acts 8:39-40
[200] 2 Kings 2:11

grand finale. The question remains, "Is God in His zeal able to make this happen?" Absolutely! Nothing is too difficult for Him. We may have seen shock and awe in the natural as one country goes to war with another, but it will be nothing in comparison to the shock and awe that will happen at the end of this age.

The Blowing of the Trumpet

The trumpet is blowing, and the alarm is sounding. Now is the time to be spiritually alert to all that is about to happen, lest we are caught sleeping.

Joel 2:1 Blow the trumpet in Zion and sound the alarm in my holy mountain! Let all the inhabitants of the land tremble for the day of the Lord is coming, for it is at hand.

*Joel 3:14-16 Multitudes, multitudes in the valley of decision! For the day of the Lord is near in the valley of decision. ¹⁵The sun and the moon will grow dark, and the stars will diminish their brightness. ¹⁶The Lord will roar from Zion and utter His voice from Jerusalem; the heavens and earth will shake, but the Lord will be a **shelter** for a His people, and the strength of the children of Israel.*

The second chapter of the book of Joel along with Isaiah's prophecies gives us another fascinating picture of the Church with fire devouring before them and a flame of fire burning behind them in the day of darkness and gloom. As the Lord blows His trumpet, sounding the alarm, God's people come, excellent and strong. The land is like the garden of Eden before them.

Joel 2:3 A fire devours before them, and behind them, a fire burns; the land is like the Garden of Eden before them.

The ensuing passages of Scripture give us is a final picture of what the Church looks like as she goes forth before the coming of the great and notable day of the Lord. It shows the sovereignty of God in action as He makes His ministers flames of fire in His zeal, performing on their behalf. She has already come into her fullness as she awaits her entrance into the Garden of Eden during the millennial age.

Joel gives us some prophetic insights as a result of the Church coming into the stature of the fullness of Christ.[201]

---

[201] Joel 2:3-11

Prophetic Insights from Joel

The land is a desolate wilderness behind them – Joel 2:3

As the fire devours behind them, it leaves a desolate wilderness in their wake. The bride escapes as the fury of God's wrath, is unleashed in the form of seven bowls upon all unbelievers. During this time, seven angels appear with seven golden bowls full of the wrath of God to pour out on the earth. The seas and rivers will become blood with all the living creatures in them dying. The earth becomes scorched with fire, darkness fills the land, and a mighty earthquake causes islands and mountains to disappear as great hailstorms fall on all humanity.[202] It will be a day of darkness and gloominess, a day of clouds and thick darkness, just as the prophet, Joel prophesied.[203] All of this is what is behind them as the bride flees on the wings of a great eagle.

The prophet, Ezekiel confirms these prophecies as well. His description is identical to the woes being poured out as the angels of God spill their bowls of wrath upon the inhabitants of the land.

Ezekiel 38:19-20 "*For in My jealousy and in the fire of my wrath I have spoken, 'Surely in that day there shall be a great earthquake in the land of Israel, ²⁰so that the fish of the sea, the birds of the heavens, the beasts of the field, all creeping things that creep on the earth and all men who are on the face of the earth shall shake at My presence. The mountains shall be thrown down, the steep places shall fall, and every wall shall fall to the ground.'*"

Their appearance is like swift steeds as they run, leaping over mountaintops in battle array – Joel 2:4-5

Joel, then gives us a picture of the bride in army boots, going forth in battle array while she is ushered to her place of refuge on the wings of a great eagle, fleeing from the presence of the serpent.[204] Ezekiel's prophetic picture shows us the same formidable army that the prophet Joel prophesied about now going forth in the strength of the breath that God breathed into her.[205] The bride is currently encapsulated in the sovereignty of her Lord as God goes forth in His zeal to bring about the culmination of all that has been prophesied by His prophets through the ages.

---

[202] Revelation 15:4-8, 16:1-21
[203] Joel 2:2
[204] Revelation 12:6,14, Isaiah 26:17, 20-21. 4:4-6,
[205] Ezekiel 37: 9-10

As we've already seen, *"eagle wings"* speak of the Lord's supernatural strength and deliverance. The bride's spiritual muscles are pumped and ready for whatever her Lord has in mind. She is now wearing army boots dressed for battle and fully engaged with her spiritual armor in tack. She is in absolute submission to the sovereignty of her Lord as she goes forth in battle array.

Isaiah 40:31 They that wait upon the Lord shall renew their strength; they shall mount up with wings as eagles, they shall run, and not be weary, and they shall walk, and not faint.

Notice the parallel passage from the book of Isaiah

Isaiah 5:26-30 He will lift up a banner to the nations from afar and will whistle to them from the end of the earth; surely, they shall come with speed, swiftly. [27]No one will be weary or stumble among them, no one will slumber or sleep; nor will the belt on their loins be loosed, nor the strap of their sandals be broken; [28]whose arrows are sharp, and all their bows bent; their horses' hooves will seem like flint and their wheels like a whirlwind. [29]Their roaring will be like a lion; they will roar like young lions; yes, they will roar and lay hold of the prey; they will carry it away safely, and no one will deliver. [30]In that day they will roar against them like the roaring of the sea. And if one looks to the land, behold, darkness and sorrow; and the light is darkened by the clouds.

In the above passage, the prophet, Isaiah gives us another prophetic picture, which speaks of the Church being called by God to the wilderness. Verse 30 speaks of the *"Great Tribulation,"* where it says, *"Behold, darkness, and sorrow; and the light is darkened by the clouds."* It also says in verse 27, *"no one is weary or stumbles,"* which is the same terminology used for eagle wing deliverance.

People writhe in pain – Joel 2:6

Joel's prophecy also speaks of the passage in the book of Revelation that references the" Great Tribulation." They curse God because of their pain. As the final bowls of God's wrath are being poured out during the reign of the Antichrist, the people writhe in pain. Again, we see the evidence of people writhing in pain from the bowls of wrath being poured out during the tribulation where it says; *"Loathsome soars came upon all those who had the mark of the beast."* As they're scorched with excessive heat, they gnawed their tongues because of the pain.[206]

---

[206] Revelation 16:2, 9-11

They march in formation not breaking rank – *Joel 2:7-8*

In reference to marching in formation and not breaking rank, another prophetic picture is given of the church coming together in perfect unity. Everyone knows their positions and callings in God. Self-will and insecurity are replaced with a desire to be wholly consecrated to God's will and purpose. They're not only in sync with God but are in sync with one another as they go forth like flames of fire fulfilling His word. No one pushes or shoves as they are content with who they are in Christ. As Paul and Titus were in step with each other,[207] so are they as they march in unity towards the culmination of all that God's Holy prophets have spoken. The prophetic picture of not breaking rank and marching in formation is the fulfillment of what Paul spoke to the Church at Ephesus.

> ***Ephesians 4:16*** *from whom the whole body, joined and knit together by what every joint supplies, according to the effective working by which every part does its share, causes the growth of the body for the edifying of itself in love.*

The bride has come to the perfect unity Jesus prayed for before her great escape. She has learned to walk in an unerring step with her Lord and the other members of His body. They are faultlessly joined together in the same mind and judgment the apostle Paul exhorted them to do.[208] They are not only walking in the unity of the Spirit but also in the unity of the faith. As they march in perfect step with one another, they're in perfect step with the Commander of this vast army. They hear His voice together as He orders their actions and gives them instructions just as He did with Joshua at the battle of Jericho. They enter the same holy ground that Joshua did when he met the Commander of the Lord's army.[209] As a result, they are perfectly submitted to His sovereign rule as He leads this great army—the bride in army boots.

They climb into houses like thieves – *Joel 2:9-11*

The picture of the bride climbing into dwellings like thieves is a prophetic picture of the bride recovering all that was stolen by Satan in the fall of humanity when Adam and Eve sinned. The Lord is leading His great army in His zeal as He executes His word giving them instructions. Just as the children of Israel received all kinds of goods

---

[207] 2 Corinthians 12:18
[208] 1 Corinthians 1:7
[209] Joshua 5:13-15

from the Egyptians upon their Exodus, the bride is now laying claim to all that belongs to the Lord, which Satan stole in the fall.

Just as David recovered all that the Amalekites had stolen from him at Ziklag, we shall recover all that the thief, Satan, took from God and His people.[210] Abraham, our father in the faith, is another example of recovering all when Sodom and Gomorrah along with Lot and his family were captured with all their goods. When Abraham heard about it, he took 300 of his men and brought back all the spoil along with Lot and all the others.[211]

From the time of the bride coming into the fullness of the stature of Jesus, the restoration of all things will have been taking place, but now she's delivering the final blow to Satan as she breaks into his domain and recovers everything that was lost in the fall of humanity.

> ***Joel 2:25*** *"So I will restore to you the years that the swarming locust has eaten, the crawling locust. The chewing locust, My great army which I sent among you."*

> ***Acts 3:20-21*** *and that He May send Jesus Christ, who was preached to you before, [21] whom heaven must receive until the **times of restoration of all things,** which God has spoken by the mouth of all His holy prophets since the world began.*

God, once again, through His sovereignty, brings His prophetic purposes to pass with His bride in army boots. Nothing is too difficult for God. In His omnipotence, He can do all things. Let us put our faith in God's sovereign abilities and not our own. As we do, His omnipotence will pour through our lives as He makes us ministers of flaming fire.

---

[210] 1 Samuel 30:18-19
[211] Genesis 14:10-16

On the Horizon

By Ken L. Birks © 2017 Straight Arrow Ministries

On the horizon, comes flashing storm clouds, dark and grey.
Looking down from heaven above, the Father sees the land so dry.
With vengeance, a storm comes pouring water on thirsty ground.
With His fist, He gathers clouds together sending rain, now found.
The flashing clouds come like a tempest upon this long-awaited day.

On the horizon, God's people wait with hearts filled with anticipation.
Seeing dark storm clouds coming, they stand in the awe as He thunders.
Satan, gathering forces with one mind, insults to wreak provocation.
As darkness covers the earth, God's people rise and shine in wonder.
Is this the beginning of the birth pangs that were foretold so long ago?

With thirst unquenchable, they ask for more for the thirsty ground.
Crying repent, they shout so times of refreshing will be found.
Walking circumspectly, new wineskins are prepared for His anointing?
Knowing it's time to shine, they prepare for His glory to fill the land?
Preparing, they ask for rain in the time of the latter anointing?

Casting spells of hate on followers, Satan comes, lying and destroying.
An army comes great and strong, destroying schemes of darkness.
Waiting on the Lord, they're renewed in preparation for what's coming.
As praise begins to arise upon those who follow, they respond in love.
Without effect, weapons of darkness give way to the light from above.

Linking arms, they march together in step with one purpose, onward.
With their mountains to take, the anointing thrusts them forward.
Like the noise of a mighty army, they advance in step with one another.
An ear to the Father's voice, they march, having found their position.
Looking on with delight, He breathes with fierceness and vision.

On the horizon, anointing increases as the glory of God begins to settle.
The blind and deaf are healed, while multitudes are fed without trouble.
Rain asked for comes with full force as they march, heeding His voice.
With the fullness spoken of evident to all, anointing comes in full force.
Multitudes upon multitudes give heed to the sound of their battle cry.

Like David, losing all and recovering, they're instructed to recover all.
In battle array, they go forth recovering all the enemy stole in the fall.

Prophetic Purposes and the Zeal of the Lord

In hatred, those who cast spells stand defenseless, drained of color.
As the earth quakes before them, they march as the heavens tremble.
Executing God's word, with the day of the Lord at hand, they prevail.

Revealing of the Antichrist

Chapter Nine

Just as every generation since the beginning of the Church age has thought Christ would return in their time, so it's been with the revealing of the Antichrist. Paul's thoughts to the Thessalonica church clarify the issue for us.

2 Thessalonians 2:1-2 Now, brethren, concerning the coming of our Lord Jesus Christ and our gathering together to Him, we ask you, ²not to be shaken in mind or troubled, either by spirit or by word or by letter, as if from us, as though the day of Christ had come.

Paul makes it clear in his second letter to the Thessalonians that the Antichrist must be revealed before the second coming of Christ. His reason for writing the letter was to set them straight concerning the fact that Christ had not already come as some were declaring. He then points out things that must take place before He comes.

2 Thessalonians 2:3-4 Let no one deceive you by any means, for that Day will not come unless the falling away comes first, and the man of sin is revealed, the son of perdition, ⁴who opposes and exalts himself above all that is called God or that is worshipped, so that he sits as God, showing himself that he is God.

Even though people down through the ages have had ideas as to who the Antichrist may be, he hasn't revealed himself yet. Therefore, it's impossible for Jesus to return at any time. The Antichrist must be revealed first. To think that Jesus can return before all that the prophets have foretold, including the revealing of the Antichrist is deception.

Characteristics of the Antichrist

In the above passage, Paul not only warns us about being deceived concerning the coming of Christ but also gives us a glimpse into the characteristics of the Antichrist. The attributes found in the Antichrist are the same ones that caused Satan's expulsion from the third realm of heaven. At one point, Satan was the most beautiful of all the archangels. Unfortunately, he became proud and wanted to be like God.

The Antichrist will be the incarnation of Satan just as Jesus was the incarnation of God, the Father. Just as Satan tried to exalt himself above God, so it is with the man of sin. In the following passages, the prophet, Ezekiel exposes Satan's true colors.

Ezekiel 28:13-14 You were in Eden, the garden of God; every precious stone was your covering: the sardius, topaz, and diamond, beryl, onyx, and jasper, sapphire, turquoise, and emerald with gold. The workmanship of your timbrels and pipes was prepared for you on the day you were created. 14 "You were the anointed cherub who covers; I established you; you were on the holy mountain of God; you walked back and forth in the midst of fiery stones.

Before his fall, Satan was one of the most influential angelic beings in the universe, being of great beauty. His name was Lucifer. He held a high position in heaven before he became Satan. He was perfect in every way but abused his position and beauty, which resulted in bringing destruction upon himself.

Ezekiel 28:15 You were perfect in your ways from the day you were created, till iniquity was found in you.

In the preceding passages and the passage below, we see descriptions of Lucifer's beauty and abilities, and the characteristics that caused him to lose his anointed position. The features found in Lucifer are very similar to those Paul mentions in his letter to the Thessalonians about the man of sin, the Antichrist.

Isaiah 14:13-14 For you have said in your heart: I will ascend into heaven, I will exalt my throne above the stars of God; I will also sit on the mount of the congregation on the farthest sides of the north; 14I will ascend above the heights of the clouds, I will be like the Most High.

Lucifer wanted to sit as God and wanted his throne to be in heaven, not on earth. The name "Most High" in the Bible is the word *"El Elohim"* not only means "Most High," but also means "the possessor of heaven and earth." Lucifer attempted a rebellious mutiny with a third of the angels following him, without realizing how mighty God was.

Imagine, a creature – a created angel, wanted to be the possessor of heaven and earth. His self-will and rebellion are what led to his expulsion from the third realm of heaven, thus becoming the devil. Lucifer did not want to get closer to God because of love. It was the jealousy in his heart that caused his downfall. He was not satisfied with just getting closer; he wanted to sit as God on His throne.

When God cast Lucifer out, He threw him out of the third heaven. The Lord Jesus mentioned this when He said, *"I saw Satan fall from heaven like lightning."*

> **Luke 10:18** *And He said to them, "I saw Satan fall like lightning from heaven."*

What Jesus meant was that He saw Satan fall from the third heaven like lightning. Right now, the devil is still in the heavens. His place, today, is in the second heaven. He dwells there as much as he resides in the earth. He rules from that position of authority. The second place is where we wrestle against spiritual hosts of wickedness in the heavenly places. Eventually, Satan will be thrown out of this realm as well, just before the great tribulation.

> **Revelation 12:7-8** *And war broke out in heaven: Michael and his angels fought against the dragon, and the dragon and his angels fought, ⁸but they did not prevail, nor was a place found for them in heaven any longer.*

Once Lucifer is expelled from all heavenly realms for good, he sets up his throne on earth in the form of the Antichrist to sit amid God's people proclaiming himself as God is his final attempt to be the possessor of heaven and earth. He will come with great deception to deceive all the inhabitants of the planet. The Antichrist will become Satan, incarnate with the power given to him to rule during the great tribulation. Even in the midst this, God, the Father will be in complete control as He fulfills His sovereign and prophetic purposes.

The subject of the Antichrist has been one of considerable speculation throughout the ages. It appears, every generation has had ideas as to who he may be, all of which have come to naught. We shouldn't concern ourselves as to who he is nor what is name is. These speculations are nothing more than diversions to shift our attention away from the real dangers he poses to Christians. Like Satan, he's a great deceiver, who, with his lies, will deceive many. There will be a great falling away because of His deception as he sits as God among God's people. However, there are many clues contained in the word of God as to where he comes from and how it is that he sits as God and showing himself as God.

The Antichrist Spirit is Already Here

> **1 John 2:18-19** *Little children, it is the last hour; and as you have heard that the Antichrist is coming, even now many antichrists have come, by which we know that it is the last hour. ¹⁹**They went out from us,** but they*

were not of us; for if they had been of us, they would have continued with us; but they went out that they might be made manifest, that none of them were of us.

The Antichrist spirit has been among us since the beginning of time in one form or another. It was with Adam and Eve in the garden of Eden in the form of a serpent. It was with the early church with false apostles and prophets.

2 Corinthians 11:13-15 For such are false apostles, deceitful workers, transforming themselves into apostles of Christ. [14]And no wonder! For Satan, himself transforms himself into an angel of light. [15]Therefore it is no great thing if His ministers also transform themselves into ministers, whose end will be according to their works.

Paul writes concerning the mystery of iniquity, *"It is at work until He is taken out of the way,"* speaking of the Holy Spirit's presence in the life of believers. Once the bride of Christ is swept away on the wings of a great eagle, the way is paved for the revealing of the Antichrist in all his demonic powers. With the antichrist spirit already at work in the world, he will be readily accepted as God with his deceptive powers of evil fully released to bring the world under his dominion.

2 Thessalonians 2:7-11 For the mystery of lawlessness is already at work; only He who restrains will do so until He is taken out of the way. [8]And then the lawless one will be revealed whom the Lord will consume with the breath of a His mouth with the brightness of His coming. [9]The coming of the lawless one is according to the working of Satan, with all power, signs, and lying wonders, [10]and with all unrighteous deception among those who perish, because they did not receive the love of truth, that they might be saved. [11]And for this reason, God will send them strong delusion, that they should believe the lie, [12]that they all may be condemned who did not believe the truth but had pleasure in unrighteousness.

Jesus also spoke of false prophets, who would rise to deceive many during a time in which lawlessness abounds. Because of lawlessness abounding, He said, *"The love of many would grow cold."*[212]

The antichrist spirit will become more and more pervasive as this present age comes to an end. We're already experiencing the collective mindset of ungodliness in every corner of our societies. The media, political arenas, educational systems, and entertainment are just some of the areas in which it's obvious the antichrist spirit is gaining momentum.

---

[212] Matthew 24:11-12

The world is more and more falling under the seductive sway of Satan and his devices.[213] People no longer think for themselves but are under the spell of the collective mindset that is full of lies and deception. The way is being paved for the Antichrist to be fully revealed and released in a way that people will believe he is God.

As discussed in earlier chapters, there will be many waves of revival fires before the final outpouring of God's Spirit produces a world-wide revival in every nook and cranny of our planet. There will also be waves of false revivals resulting from the antichrist spirit in the form of lying signs and wonders that pave the way for the revealing of the antichrist and the great falling away. Major discernment is needed now as the time draws near.

Where does the Antichrist Come From?

We must ask ourselves, "How does the Antichrist gain so much influence that he can sit as God in the midst of His people?" In John's first epistle, he gives us a glimpse into this mystery. He mentions, *"They went out from us, but they were not of us."*

> *1 John 2:18-19 Little children, it is the last hour; and as you have heard that the Antichrist is coming, even now many antichrists have come, by which we know that it is the last hour. [19] **They went out from us**, but they were not of us; for if they had been of us, they would have continued with us; but they went out that they might be made manifest, that none of them were of us.*

We've already seen that Paul mentions that there are false apostles, and deceitful workers, who can transform themselves into apostles of Christ.[214] The antichrist spirit is alive and well in the Church today. Satan's deceptive tactics are at work with great swelling words of emptiness that allure through the lusts of the flesh, and sensuality. He once again traps those who've previously escaped the corruption that was in the world with his deceptive tactics.[215]

The antichrist spirit will come with destructive heresies and covetousness as false prophets and teachers fill the pulpits of churches across the globe. Just as apostle John said, *"They went out from us, but they were not of us."* With Satan's false prophets and teachers firmly entrenched in the Church, the antichrist spirit paves the while the perfect

---

[213] 1 John 5:19
[214] 2 Corinthians 11:13-15
[215] 2 Peter 2:18

plan is put in place for him to arise within the ranks of the Church before he's revealed in his time.

The deception in the Church will be world-wide. The vacuum that's left when the bride is taken out on the wings of an eagle creates the perfect storm for the Antichrist to come forth in the fullness of Satan's power.

You might ask, "Is there a precedent for the Antichrist coming forth from the Church?" The answer is an unequivocal, "Yes!" I offer the following thoughts to be considered.

The man of sin or the Antichrist is typified in both the Old and New Testaments. His source can be discovered in the positions that are closest to God. Jesus spoke of twelve legions of heaven, which are governed by twelve Archangels.[216] One of them was Lucifer, who fell.

The late Bible teacher and pastor, W.H. Offiler quotes, *"Satan was once an Archangel, Lucifer, and the angelic realm was next to the Throne of God. There were twelve archangels, and it is among the prophetic twelves of the Bible that this monstrous traitor is discovered. Jacob had twelve sons, from whom all the tribes of Israel came. One of these sons was a traitor to the sanctity of his father's couch and home. Rueben, the firstborn of Jacob, sinned a great sin, a presumptuous sin, and was rejected as far as the inheritance of the Birthright blessing was concerned."*[217]

Continuing in his dialogue, Offiler says, *"The New Testament example is found in the twelve disciples, who later were to become the apostles of our Lord. 'I have chosen you twelve, and one of you is the devil.'*[218] *There can be no question of the antichrist spirit in Judas; he betrayed the Son of God."* He goes on to say, *"The Antichrist comes from one or the other of the twelves of the bible. The shadows we have shown, as they appear in both testaments. The antitypical revelation of this awful being, which is yet future, is discovered in the last book of the Bible, the book of Revelation."*

Offiler then goes on to say, *"In Revelation 12:1-17, is found the revealed mystery of the perfected Church, the Church in the last days. The woman is clothed with the Sun, and with the Moon under her feet, and crowned with a diadem of twelve Stars."*

Offiler then speaks of the meaning of the twelve stars and says, *"At the head of the Woman, the Church are twelve stars. These stars are*

---

[216] Matthew 26:53

[217] From the book, God and His Bible or the Divine Harmonies of Divine Revelation by W.H. Offiler

[218] John 6:70

twelve men—apostles—of our Lord, appointed by him to lead the church to its final ministry, and to its final victory. As one of the first twelve was a devil and betrayed his Lord, so one of this last twelve will likewise fall, betray his Lord, sell out to the devil, and become the recipient of all the power of Satan. The falling star of Revelation 9:1 is this last day traitor, and to him is given all the power of Satan together with the keys to the abyss."

The Beast from the Sea

In John's vision in the book of Revelation, he sees a beast rising out of the sea with all the authority, power and the throne that was possessed by the dragon.

Revelation 13:1-2 *Then I stood on the sand of the sea. And I saw a beast rising up out of the sea, having seven heads and ten horns, and on his horns ten crowns, and on his heads a blasphemous name. ²Now the beast which I saw was like a leopard, his feet were like the feet of a bear, and his mouth like the mouth of a lion. The dragon gave him his power, his throne, and great authority.*

The passage above is a prophetic picture of the Antichrist becoming the incarnation of Satan with all of Satan's power and authority given to him, which happens after he has been mortally wounded and comes back to life. As a result, the whole world marvels and follows him. The falling star becomes a bright star in the eyes of his followers. He receives the power to continue for forty-two months, which is the three and one-half years of the great tribulation.[219]

He Makes War with the Saints

Once he receives power and authority, his next objective is to eradicate the remnant of the saints from the earth, who were left behind when the bride escaped on the wings of a great eagle.

Revelation 13:7 *It was granted to him to make war with the saints and to overcome them. And authority was given him over every tribe, tongue, and nation.*

With power now granted, the Antichrist performs great signs, even making fire come down from heaven. With his great signs and wonders, he deceives those who dwell on the earth. He makes an image of the

---

[219] Revelation 13:3-5

beast who was mortally wounded and now causes everyone to receive a mark on either their right hands or foreheads to buy or sell.[220]

Those who do not accept his mark will be beheaded. Here is the patience of the faith of the saints. Those who were left behind must either take the mark or die. Many of them will fall for his deception, believing his lies and blaspheme the Holy Spirit by receiving his mark. Thus, the great falling away, spoken by Paul now takes place.[221] It's during this season that the hearts of many grow cold. Many will betray one another, even people from their households just as Jesus prophesied.

Matthew 24:12 And because lawlessness will abound, the love of many will grow cold.

Mark 13:12-13 Now brother will betray brother to death, and a father his child; and children will rise up against parents and cause them to be put to death. [13] And you will be hated by all for My name's sake. But he who endures to the end shall be saved.

The Antichrist's Final Destination

After ruling for forty-two months, the Antichrist, the devil, and the false prophet are thrown into a bottomless pit and later cast into the lake of fire, where they're tormented day and night.[222]

Concluding Thoughts

Now is the time to set our hearts towards the Lord and His purposes so that we can be found as vessels unto honor. Those in the five foolish virgin category will find it very difficult to resist the deceptive powers of the antichrist spirit that comes in full force during the reign of the Antichrist. It will take a passionate relationship with the Lord to remain faithful in that day and hour with all the distractions the enemy of our faith throws at them.

May God bless you mightily as you ponder all that God is doing. Allow His sovereignty to have its rule in your lives, and you will sail through these times like flames of fire as He fulfills His prophetic purposes. Don't be caught sleeping or kicking against the goads. Allow the Lord to accomplish His mission in your lives just as He did for Peter and Paul. You will be abundantly blessed throughout eternity.

---

[220] Revelation 13:7-18

[221] Revelation 13:15-16, 20:4, 2 Thessalonians 2:3

[222] Revelation 20:1-3, 7-10

The Beast from the Sea

by Ken L. Birks © 2018 Straight Arrow Ministries

The man of sin comes as the beast from the sea to scheme.
With horns and crowns on his head, he comes to blaspheme.
Like a leopard and feet of a bear, he comes with vengeance.
With a mouth like a lion, he receives power to kill and devour.
With great authority, he's released with Satan's full power.

With hate and deception, he comes to destroy and terminate.
In the full incarnation of evil, he comes to impersonate.
Coming as the man of sin, he sits as God in the temple.
He opposes and is exalted above all that is called God.
With rage, war breaks out in heaven, causing all to tremble.

Cast down from heaven, he wages war against all Christians.
Coming to kill, he strikes those who are to rule the kingdom.
Caught up as first fruits, they escape as God takes possession.
Filled with rage, Satan sends a flood to drown and destroy the bride.
Rescued on the wings of a great eagle, the Father gives ride.

Given power over the remnant left behind, he seeks to destroy.
Strong delusion comes, giving him exceeding power to trap.
With signs and wonders, he deceives those on earth with ploys.
With great power, he causes all to receive his mark or be killed.
As his mark is received, multitudes fall away, being grilled.

With the righteous ones removed, the fury of the Lord is released.
To those who receive his mark, seven angels appear with plagues.
With grievous sores, blood, scorching fire, and earthquakes, He releases.
Kept from the hour of trial upon the whole world, the bride escapes.
For three and a half years they're tormented, while the bride feasts.

Taking vengeance with 10,000s of His saints, Jesus descends.
Those killed by the beast rise in the clouds to meet Him as they ascend.
From her place of refuge, the bride rises to meet them in the air.
Bound for a thousand years, the beast no longer blasphemes or snares.
Tormented day and night, they're cast into the lake of fire with the tares.

Second Coming of Christ

Chapter Ten

Paul writes, *"We shall all be changed—in a moment, in the twinkling of an eye, at the last trumpet. For the trumpet will sound, and the dead will be raised incorruptible, and we shall be changed. For this corruptible must put on incorruption, and this mortal must put on immortality."*[223]

The second coming of Christ is the grand finale of all our expectations and hope in Christ. It's the great hope that acts as an anchor to our soul throughout all our hardships, trials, and tribulations.[224] It's what keeps us going and abounding in the work of the Lord even during pain, sorrow, and difficulties.

Jesus promised that He was going away to prepare a special place for each of us where we would dwell with Him forever and ever. During difficult times and the trials of life, the words of Jesus give us much comfort and hope.

> *John 14:1-3 Let not your heart be troubled; you believe in God, believe also in Me. ²In My Father's house are many mansions; if it were not so, I would have told you. I go to prepare a place for you. ³And if I go and prepare a place for you, I will come again and receive you to Myself; that where I am, there you may be also.*

The second coming of Jesus gives us an essential expectation of the grand and glorious things that will take place at His appearing. It gives us a vibrant faith picture of being completely changed and conformed to His image, which includes total deliverance and freedom from the bondage of this flesh. It also gives us the dramatic faith picture of what it means to reign with God throughout eternity.

> *1 John 3:2-3 Beloved, now we are children of God; and it has not yet been revealed what we shall be, but we know that **when He is revealed, we shall be like Him, for we shall see Him as He is.** ³And*

---

[223] 1 Corinthians 15:51-53
[224] Hebrews 6:19

everyone who has this hope in Him purifies himself, just as He is pure.

The second coming of Christ or the rapture of the Church that has been coined by many is one of the great mysteries of God's Holy Word. About this great event, Paul writes, *"Behold, I tell you a mystery."*[225]

The purpose of this chapter is to unravel the mystery so that we are not confused amid various interpretations and misunderstandings of the second coming of Christ. I know that sounds like a lofty goal, but as we allow Scripture to interpret Scripture, it will unravel before us. To fully engage in this puzzling mystery, it's best to set aside preconceived ideas, momentarily, so that you can see it from a fresh perspective without filters. You can always go back to your former views if you so decide.

As with any doctrinal position, it's essential to start with the most obvious clues that are plainly evident or written which speak for themselves. It's like putting a puzzle together. When you put all the border pieces together first, you begin to see how the other parts fit into the framework. Sometimes, you may have a cluster put together, but it's not ready to be fitted in before you put other pieces in play. The problem many have with doctrinal thoughts is, they try to build from that which is ambiguous or obscure, rather than that which is straight forward and obvious. As a result, they end up with clusters of thought that don't fit together in harmony with one another.

Following the Clues to the Mystery

In Paul's letter to the Thessalonians, he writes that he doesn't want them to be ignorant of this mystery so that we are without hope.[226] We are told to be like the Bereans and search the Scriptures to find the answers to the great puzzles of life.[227] Too many of us believe something just because it's the most popular thought that's being passed around, rather than searching the Scriptures for ourselves. As we examine the Scriptures and follow the clues, we can see for ourselves what the Holy Spirit says on any given subject.

As we begin to explore the clues on the second coming, let's start with the most obvious one from Paul's letter to the Thessalonians.

---

[225] 1 Corinthians 15:51
[226] 1 Thessalonians 4:13-15
[227] Acts 17:11

Clue #1: The Dead in Christ will Rise at the Last Trumpet

*1 Thessalonians 4:15-17 For this we say to you by the word of the Lord that we who are alive and remain until the coming of the Lord will by no means precede those who are asleep. ¹⁶For the Lord will descend from heaven with a shout, with the voice of an archangel, and with the trumpet of God. And **the dead in Christ will rise first.** ¹⁷Then we who are alive and remain shall be caught up (raptured)[228] together with them in the **clouds** to meet the Lord in the air. And thus, we shall always be with the Lord.*

Clues #2: Dead in Christ Must Rise First

There are two apparent clues in this passage. The first clue mentions that we who are alive and remain shall by no means precede the dead in Christ. The dead in Christ must rise first, which points us to the next clue. The question we must ask ourselves is, when do the dead in Christ rise? Paul's letter to the Corinthians answers the question.

*1 Corinthians 15:51-52 Behold, **I tell you a mystery:** We shall not all sleep, but we shall be changed— ⁵²in a moment, in the twinkling of an eye, at the **last trumpet.** For the trumpet will sound, and the **dead will be raised** incorruptible, and we shall be changed.*

We saw in the previous Scripture that the dead in Christ must rise first. Now we see that it's at the last trumpet that the dead are raised. We also saw in the previous chapters; seven trumpets sound at the opening of the seventh seal in the book of Revelation. As the seventh trumpet begins to sound, the bride of Christ gets swept away on the wings of a great eagle as the Antichrist begins his reign of terror for three and one-half years. It is during this time when the seventh trumpet continues to sound that the seven bowls of God's wrath are poured out upon the earth for the next three and one-half years. This is the time of the Antichrist's reign referred to as the great tribulation—the outer darkness.

Clue #3: He's Coming in the Clouds of Heaven

The second clue mentions meeting Jesus in the clouds. If this is true, we should find other Scriptures that specify this description as well. Let's take a look.

---

[228] Parentheses added by me. The word rapture is not in the Bible but is derived from the phrase "caught up," which is the Greek Word, "harpazo."

*Revelation 1:7 Behold, **He is coming with clouds,** and **every eye will see Him**, even they who pierced Him. And all the tribes of the earth will mourn because of Him. Even so, Amen.*

As we look to Matthew's gospel, we will find that these three clues come together in the same passage of Scripture, thus showing the continuity of the Holy Spirit in speaking forth the mind and will of the father as He communicated God's Word through the chosen apostles.[229]

The passage in Matthew's gospel reveals that Jesus is answering the question posed by His disciples, when they asked Him, *"Tell us, when will these things be? And what will be the sign of Your coming, and of the end of the age?"* In the following passage, Jesus gives them a direct answer to their straightforward question. All three clues given so far converge in this passage of Scripture.

Clue #4: After the Tribulation

*Matthew 24:29-31 Immediately **after the tribulation** of those days the sun will be darkened, and the moon will not give its light; the stars will fall from heaven, and the powers of heaven will be shaken. [30] **Then** the sign of the Son of Man will appear in heaven, and then all the tribes of the earth will mourn, and **they will see the Son of Man coming** on the **clouds of heaven** with power and great glory. [31]And He shall send His angels with a **great sound of a trumpet,** and they will gather together His elect from the four winds, from one end of heaven to the other.*

As I write, I can sense the wheels turning in your heads. You're still thinking the rapture and the second coming of Christ are two separate events. The problem with that thinking is that the Scripture from where the word *"rapture"* comes from is speaking of this event only.[230] It very specifically said that the dead in Christ must rise first, and it's here when the last trumpet sounds that the dead in Christ rise.

All clues point to the passage above as the timing of the second coming of Christ. Just as Jesus was taken up into heaven in the clouds, He will return in the clouds of heaven as was told to his disciples when Jesus left.

*Acts 1:9-11 Now when He had spoken these things, while they watched, He was taken up, and a **cloud received Him** out of their sight. [10]And while they looked steadfastly toward heaven as He went up, behold two*

---

[229] 2 Timothy 3:16, 2 Peter 1:21

[230] 1 Thessalonians 4:17 The phrase "caught up" is where the word "rapture" is taken from. It means to be snatched by force. It is the Greek Word, harpazo."

men stood by them in white apparel, (most likely the two witnesses, Moses and Elijah)[231] [11]who also said "Men of Galilee, why do you stand gazing up into heaven? This same Jesus, who was taken up from you into heaven, will **so come in like manner** *as you saw Him go into heaven."*

Clue #5: The Old Testament Confirms the Timing

The Old Testament also confirms the fact that Jesus is coming on the clouds of heaven. For the testimony of Scripture to be so exacting on this description, shows the importance of this clue about the timing or the second coming.

Daniel 7:13-14 *I was watching in the night visions, and behold, One like the Son of Man,* **coming with the clouds of heaven!** *He came to the Ancient of Days, and they brought Him near before Him.* [14]***Then to Him was given dominion and glory and a kingdom,*** *that all peoples, nations, and languages should serve Him. His dominion is an everlasting dominion, which shall not pass away, and His kingdom the one which shall not be destroyed.*

Clue #6: Jesus Only Prepared His Disciples for the One Event

The question to ask is, "If there is to be a separate event of the rapture, why didn't Jesus or the two witnesses prepare the disciples for it." Instead, the event they are preparing them for is the second coming.

Another reason, there are so many who buy into the theory of two separate events is that there are Scriptures that speak of being preserved from the wrath of God, which is right. The bride will be safely tucked away in her place of refuge during the time of the great tribulation, and the remnant or the Christians representing the foolish virgins will be martyred at the beginning. They will be among the dead in Christ who rise first. Those who fall away will be among the unbelievers who get destroyed by the brightness of His coming.[232]

Another passage which seemingly supports two separate events is the passage from Luke's gospel that speaks of one taken and the other left.

Luke 17:33-37 *Whoever seeks to save his life will lose it, and whoever loses his life will preserve it.* [34]*I tell you, in that night there will be two people[233] in one bed: the one will be taken, and the other left.* [35]*Two*

---

[231] Parentheses added by me.

[232] 2 Thessalonians 5:9, Revelation 3:10, 2 Thessalonians 2:8

[233] NIV says two people rather than two men. In the KJV and NKJV it says men; however, the word "men" is in italics which means it was added, not being in the original text.

*women will be grinding together: the one will be taken, and the other left. [36]Two men will be in the field: the one man will be taken, and the other left. [37]And they answered and said to Him, "Where, Lord?" So, He said to them, **Wherever the body is, there the eagles will be gathered together."***

This passage is in perfect harmony with the woman or the bride of Christ mentioned in Revelation 12, who is taken on the wings of a great eagle to her secure place where God preserves her during the reign of the Antichrist. The safe area is where the body of eagle saints gather during the great tribulation. It's from here that she is raptured up to meet the Lord when He comes.

The passage from Luke's gospel is a perfect example of taking a passage of Scripture that is somewhat nebulous and building on it rather than seeing how it fits into the framework of that which gives us a more precise understanding. The thought above and Scripture from Luke's gospel fit perfectly into the context established in this chapter and the two previous chapters. They all form a divine harmony of revelation with all the pieces to the puzzle connected perfectly.

During the Sounding of the 7th Trumpet Jesus is Released from Heaven

Acts 3:20-21 And that He may send Jesus Christ, who was preached to you before, [21]whom heaven must receive until the times of restoration of all things, which God has spoken by the mouth of all His holy prophets since the world began.

It's during the days of the sounding of the seventh trumpet that the mystery of God is finished, and Jesus is finally released for that long-awaited day, the Second Coming of Christ.

Revelation 10:7 But in the days of the sounding of the seventh angel, when he is about to sound, the mystery of God would be finished, as He has declared to His servants the prophets.

Revelation 16:17 Then the seventh angel poured out his bowl into the air, and a loud voice came out of the temple, from the throne, saying, "It is done!"

It's during the sounding of the 7th trumpet that the seven bowls of God's judgment get poured out on all humankind.

At the end of the sixth bowl of wrath being poured out, Jesus announces, *"It is done,"* and He is ready to come. Satan then gathers his forces together for the final battle at Armageddon. This, once again, shows the coming of Christ at the end of the great tribulation—another piece added to the divine harmony of revelation.

> ***Revelation 16:15-18*** *Behold; I am coming quickly as a thief. Blessed is he who watches, and keeps his garments, lest he walk naked and they see his shame. And they gathered them together to a place called in a Hebrew, Armageddon.* [17]*Then the seventh angel poured out his bowl into the air, and a loud voice came out of the temple of heaven, from the throne, saying, "It is done!"* [16]*And there were noises and thunderings and lightnings; and there was a great earthquake, such a mighty and great earthquake as had not occurred since men were on the earth.*

> ***Revelation 19:11-16*** *Now I saw heaven opened, and behold, a white horse. And He who sat on him was called Faithful and True, and in righteousness, He judges and makes war.* [12]*His eyes were like a flame of fire, and on His head were many crowns. He had a name written that no one knew except Himself.* [13]*He was clothed with a robe dipped in blood, and His name is called The Word of God.* [14]*And the armies in heaven, clothed in fine linen, white and clean, followed Him on white horses.* [15]*Now out of His mouth goes a sharp sword that with it He should strike the nations. And He Himself will rule them with a rod of iron. He Himself treads the winepress of the fierceness and wrath of Almighty God.* [16]*And He has on His robe and* on His thigh a name written: KING OF KINGS AND LORD OF LORDS.

The time has come for the final execution of the prophetic purposes of God as all things are fulfilled just as the prophets of old prophesied. With the mystery of God now finished, Jesus comes with eyes of flaming fire, riding on a white horse with all of those whom He gathered from the four winds. He is ready to strike the nations and set up a His rule as the zeal of the Lord performs on His behalf with the armies of heaven following hard after Him.

Come, Lord Jesus! Help us to keep our lamps lit with Your precious oil and not be caught sleeping as we wait for the midnight cry.

The Second Coming of Christ

by Ken L. Birks, 2018 © Straight Arrow Ministries

On His white horse, He prepares to ride with sword in hand.
Prepared to take vengeance, He comes to those who disdain.
As the last trumpet blows, He signals, He's ready to mount up.
Gathering the righteous together, they're caught up.
No longer chained to earthly realities, they're now freed.

From the four winds, they're gathered for the great battle.
With new celestial bodies, His saints are forever changed.
In the twinkling of an eye, they come, meeting Him in the air.
As the corruptible puts on incorruption, they're made anew.
Leaving behind the sting of death, they embrace victory.

Ready to engage in the great battle, they mount up, prepared.
With the seventh angel pouring his bowl, a loud shout is heard.
As the great noise is heard, thunderings and lightnings alert.
A shout from the temple signals. "It is done!" The time is now.
As a great and mighty earthquake shakes the land, He's ready.

As every island and mountain disappear, they ride together.
With Armageddon as their destination, senses fill with expectation.
Riding to the great battle, He who rides the white horse leads.
In flaming fire, they come to punish with everlasting destruction.
Into the bottomless pit, the serpent of old is bound and thrown.

A thousand years, he's bound until loosed again for a short season.
With the kingdoms of this world now His, He sets up His throne.
Dining together, they sit with the patriarchs and prophets of old.
For a thousand years, they dwell in peace in His presence.
Building, planting, and ruling, they wait for the new heavens and earth.

With walls of Jasper, New Jerusalem comes as a city of pure gold.
Beyond comprehension, they see, hear and sense all that's prepared.
Basking in His presence, their hearts continually bring forth praise.
Worshipping Him who was worthy to loose the seals, they exult.
Forever, to the King of Kings who was slain, they honor and praise.

Prophetic Purposes
and the Zeal of the Lord

Bridal Preparations
Part 3

Let us be glad and rejoice and give Him glory, for the marriage of the Lamb has come, and His wife has made herself ready.
Revelation 19:7

We've now been exposed to much that Christ desires to perform in and through His Church as the culmination of all that has been prophesied by His Holy prophets is at hand. We must now consider how to prepare for these significant events. The bride must make herself ready. As we labor together with the Lord, the Holy Spirit conforms us to the image of Christ. It's as we submit to this process that we're made ready as vessels unto honor, sanctified and useful for the Master, prepared for every good work. This section explores all that Christ desires to do in our lives.

Baptism in the Holy Spirit

Chapter Eleven

When we consider the preparation that's needed to have our vessels filled with the oil that is necessary to remain faithful to our calling, the baptism of the Holy Spirit is essential. Without it, our flames will go out. We won't have the spark that's needed to ignite the passion and zeal God has purposed for us to have. When the early disciples of Jesus received the baptism of the Holy Spirit, they received it with tongues of fire with their passion ignited. As a result, they went forth like flames of fire fulfilling the purposes to which God had called them.

I realize, as I share my thoughts on the baptism of the Holy Spirit, there are various interpretations as to how this happens in our individual lives. If you're convinced that your perspective is biblically sound, you should stick to it. However, if your viewpoint is based on experience or you have not really searched the matter out for yourself, I would caution you. Doctrinal positions should never be based on experience, but rather on convictions that are biblically sound.

I once had someone tell me, "I don't believe speaking in tongues is the sign of the baptism of the Holy Spirit because it's not the way it happened to me." Whether tongues are or aren't, is not the point. If we all decided to base our doctrinal positions on personal experiences, there would be a myriad of interpretations. In His sovereignty, God can move upon us in all kinds of ways. However, if they're not clearly defined in the Bible, we don't have the prerogative to promote or try to start movements based on personal experiences. We must teach according to the Bible, not our experiences.

Jesus Allowed Scriptures to Interpret Who He Was

Just as Jesus allowed the Scriptures to interpret who He was, so must we. It is through an understanding of the Scriptures with the aid of the Holy Spirit that we receive our identity and purpose. It was as Jesus opened the Scriptures and began to explain the events concerning Himself that the hearts of His disciples burned within them. He was able to open their understanding in a way that they could comprehend the meaning of Scriptures. [234]

> *Luke 24:32* *And they said to one another, "Did not our heart burn within us while He talked with us on the road, and while He opened the Scriptures to us."*

The Holy Spirit desires to open the Scriptures for us as well. He desires to open them in a way that causes His fire to burn within us, making us flames of fire as we go forth ministering in His zeal. One of the reasons so many Christians in today's Christianity lack passion and intensity towards the Lord is that they haven't had Scriptures opened to them in the way only the Holy Spirit can do through His baptism.

The beautiful thing about God is that He is intimately acquainted with all our ways.[235] When we give reign to the Holy Spirit, He knows how to communicate with us so that we understand the Scriptures in a way that we can understand them. Because He is intimately acquainted with all our ways, He knows how to speak to us according to our levels of understanding.

When I first received the baptism of the Holy Spirit, after being saved for a year and a half, it was an awesome experience. It was as though the windows of heaven had opened before me with the word of God coming alive in my heart in a manner that was entirely new to me. As the eyes of my understanding were exquisitely opened, I fell in love with Him and His word that continues to this day.

I come from a Classic Pentecostal or Charismatic perspective. Before that, I was raised with an Evangelical Holiness perspective. When I first turned my life over to the Lord in the mid-70s, I had just come out of the hippie culture and had mixed up ideas about spiritual beliefs. The one thing that helped me to become established in the faith was that I'd determined not to filter what I was learning through any former beliefs I'd picked up along the way. I put them on a shelf so to speak. Throughout my Christian walk, I have tried to steer away from labels and just be a Bible-believing Christian. I have chosen not to use filters but to allow the Scriptures to interpret themselves in all that I believe and teach. My loyalty is to the word of God, not a school of thought. With that in mind, I ask that you put your convictions aside, momentarily, and allow God's word to speak for itself.

As discussed in a previous chapter, it was the oil that made the difference as to which virgins went on to become the bride of Christ.

---

[234] Luke 24:44-45
[235] Psalm 139:1-4

They all had oil, but the foolish virgins didn't take the time to get the extra supply that was needed. We've seen that oil is symbolic of the Holy Spirit's presence in our lives. Getting the additional portion of the oil is the main ingredient that's needed in our preparation to be ready when the bridegroom comes. Therefore, we need to know how to get it.

The Baptism of the Holy Spirit was Prophesied

The fact that there are prophecies concerning the baptism of the Holy Spirit makes it part of the prophetic purposes that should come to pass in our lives just as it did for the early church. The prophet Joel foretold that the Holy Spirit would be poured out on all flesh, which includes you and me. In this chapter, we'll see that both John the Baptist and Jesus prophesied the baptism of the Holy Spirit as well as the prophet, Joel.

John the Baptist's Prophecy

Matthew 3:11 I indeed baptize you with water unto repentance, but He who is coming after me is mightier than I, whose sandals I am not worthy to carry. He will baptize you with the Holy Spirit and Fire.

John's prophecy is very significant in that Peter identified the passages in Acts 2 and Acts 10 as the baptism of the Holy Spirit spoken by John. Speaking of both events, when questioned by the Jerusalem council of elders as to why he went to the Gentiles, Peter said, *"Then I remembered the word of the Lord, how he said, 'John indeed baptized with water, but you shall be baptized with the Holy Spirit.' If therefore God gave them the gift as He gave us when we believed on the Lord Jesus Christ, who was I that I could withstand God."*[236]

Jesus' Prophecy

John 7:37-39 on the last day, that great day of the feast, Jesus stood and cried out, saying, "If anyone thirsts, let him come to Me and drink. [38]He who believes in Me, out of his heart will flow rivers of living water." [39]But this He spoke concerning the Spirit whom those believing in Him would receive, for the Holy Spirit was not yet given because Jesus was not yet glorified.

According to John's gospel, it's when Jesus ascended back to heaven from where He'd come that He would once again be glorified with the Father. He had told His disciples it was to their advantage for Him to go to the Father, so that the Holy Spirit could come to them. It was when

---

[236] Acts 11:16-17

Pentecost fully came that the Holy Spirit came and baptized them with tongues of fire just as Jesus had prophesied.[237]

It's important to note; it's with the baptism of the Holy Spirit that we receive the fire of the Lord. It not only consumes the chaff in our lives but provides the passion and the zeal of the Lord to go forth in passion and zeal fulfilling the Father's purposes.[238] Because of the passion and intensity that comes with it, is what makes it so crucial to open our hearts to the truth of God's word and receive all that He has for us.

Baptism in the Holy Spirit as a Second Experience

As we look to all that the baptism of the Holy Spirit entails, it's important to understand that there's a difference between the birth of the Spirit and the baptism of the Holy Spirit. The fact that Jesus said we should hunger and thirst for it shows us the importance of knowing the difference between the birth and the baptism.

The Greek Word for baptism is *"baptizo,"* which means to be thoroughly whelmed or immersed. As it relates to Spirit baptism, it means to be fully immersed into God's Spirit or be baptized in the Holy Spirit. When we are born again, we experience the birth of His Spirit just as the disciples did after the resurrection of Jesus from the dead when He breathed on them as told by John, the disciple whom Jesus loved.

The Example of the Original Disciples

John 20:22 And when He had said this, He breathed on them, and said to them, "Receive the Holy Spirit."

Before Jesus breathed the Holy Spirit upon them, the disciples were still under the Old Covenant. Now that Jesus had risen from the dead, the New Covenant was in full force, which meant they needed to be born again by His Spirit, so He breathed on them, and they received. They were then told to wait in Jerusalem until they would receive the promise that would endue them with power from on high.

Luke 24:49 Behold, I send the promise of My Father upon you; but tarry in Jerusalem until you are endued with power from on high.

*Acts 1:8 But you shall receive **power** when the Holy Spirit has come upon you: and you shall be witnesses to Me in Jerusalem, and in all Judea and Samaria, and to the end of the world.*

---

[237] John 17:5, 16:7, Acts 2:2-4, Mark 16:17
[238] Matthew 3:11-12

The Baptism of the Holy Spirit

The passage from the book of Acts is a continuation of Jesus' conversation at the end of the gospel of a Luke. Luke wrote both books. The disciples had already received the birth of the Spirit and were now being told to wait for the baptism of the Holy Spirit.

The Greek word for *"power"* is *"dunamis,"* which has its root meaning in the Greek word for *"dynamite."* What Jesus was saying is, *"You will receive explosive power when you are baptized in the Holy Spirit."* After receiving this explosive power, they went forth in the zeal of the Lord preaching the gospel with signs and wonders.

The Example of Philip's Ministry in Samaria

Another example of the birth of the Spirit coming before the baptism of the Holy Spirit is found in the book of Acts with Philip's ministry in Samaria. Philip was having dramatic results as he ministered in the Spirit. Multitudes with one accord were heeding the things spoken by him as they witnessed the miracles which he did. Demons were screaming as they came out of people, those who were paralyzed and lame were healed, and there was great joy in the city.[239]

When the apostles, who were at Jerusalem, heard what was happening in Samaria, they sent Peter and John to Samaria to authenticate it. Upon arriving and observing all that was happening, Peter and John realized these people had received salvation, been delivered and even water baptized but hadn't received the baptism of the Holy Spirit. They then proceeded to lay hands on them and pray for them to receive the gift of the Holy Spirit. It wasn't enough to be saved, delivered and baptized in water; they still needed the baptism of the Holy Spirit to go forth in the zeal of the Lord.[240]

The Example of the Disciples in Ephesus

Another example, in the book of Acts, which reveals two separate experiences in the Holy Spirit is found when Paul came upon some disciples in Ephesus. He'd discovered they'd only been baptized into John's baptism, not having heard of the Holy Spirit. Paul then proceeded to tell them about Jesus. When they believed Paul's message about Jesus, he then baptized them into Christ. After getting them saved and water baptized, they received the baptism of the Holy Spirit.

In all three of these examples, it's clear there were two experiences in the Holy Spirit—the birth and then full immersion in the Holy Spirit.

---

[239] Acts 8:1-13
[240] Acts 8:14-17

Speaking in Tongues

Probably, the most significant and controversial question concerning the baptism of the Holy Spirit is the issue of speaking in tongues as the evidence of having received it. There are various views and interpretations throughout Christendom, even amongst Charismatics. I am a tongues talking Christian, who believes it to be the evidence of having received it. Though I understand this, I would not say to someone, who doesn't speak in tongues that they're not baptized in the Holy Spirit. That's between them and God. If God chose to move upon them in His sovereignty, who am I to question their experience. However, when establishing doctrine, our commitment must be to how it plays out in God's Word. It's from this perspective that I share my thoughts.

As stated earlier, with any doctrinal position, there must be a divine harmony of revelation. In the New Testament, we often find a truth introduced in the gospels, the experience of its reality in the book of Acts, and in the epistles, further elaboration. These three must be in divine harmony without contradicting the others. For example, Jesus started the tongues movement when He stated, *"And these signs will follow those who believe; in My name, they will cast out demons; they will speak with new tongues."* That's all He said about it. He didn't explain how or when. But He did say, "When the Holy Spirit comes; He would teach us all things."[241] He was trusting the Holy Spirit to instruct and guide us into the full revelation of all truths.[242] In the book of Acts, we see how the apostles and other believers received tongues. In the epistles, Paul gives much instruction about speaking in tongues.

Tongues in the Book of Acts

In the second chapter of the book of Acts, we have the account of the early disciples. In this report, they received the baptism of the Holy Spirit, evidenced with tongues of fire.

Acts 2:1-4 *When the Day of Pentecost had fully come, they were all with one accord in one place. [2]And suddenly there came a sound from heaven, as of a mighty rushing wind, and it filled the whole house where they were sitting. [3]**Then there appeared to them divided tongues, as of fire, and one sat upon each of them. [4]And they were all filled with the Holy Spirit and began to speak with other tongues as the Spirit gave them utterance.***

---

[241] John 14:26
[242] John 16:13

The Baptism of the Holy Spirit

Just as Jesus promised them, the Holy Spirit came upon these early disciples and apostles of Jesus. They were baptized in the Holy Spirit just as a John the Baptist had prophesied.[243] Jesus had told them; they would speak with other tongues but did not mention how or when this would happen. Now we see that it happens with the baptism of the Holy Spirit. Peter, later, identified this great event as the baptism of the Holy Spirit as promised by John, Jesus, and the prophet, Joel.[244] Peter not only defines this event as the promise for these believers but for as many as the Lord calls in the days and years ahead.

Acts 2:39 For this promise is for you and your children, and to all who are afar off, as the Lord our God will call.

Another dramatic event in which the baptism of the Holy Spirit, evidenced by speaking in tongues is found in the book of Acts is when Peter was commissioned to the house of Cornelius. The event of Peter being called to the home of Cornelius is the prophetic fulfillment of God bringing the Gentiles into the salvation of Jesus Christ for the first time. Just as this prophetic purpose was fulfilled on the Day of Pentecost with the early believers, so it was with these first Gentile believers. God was now calling the Gentiles into the family of God, which resulted in them receiving the baptism of the Holy Spirit in the same manner as Peter and the others did.

God calling Peter to the house of Cornelius is an excellent example of God, in His zeal making His prophetic purposes come to pass. While Peter was still speaking, God interrupted Him and broke in with the power of the Holy Spirit. Because of the cultural barriers that had been formed in both parties, God had to break through the strongholds of their thinking processes. God in His sovereignty knows how to break through in spite of our archaic forms of thinking. This should bring hope and vision to us as all as we look to the future in all that God desires to do.

*Acts 10:44-47 While Peter was still speaking these words, the Holy Spirit fell upon all those who heard the word. [45]And those of the circumcised who believed were astonished, as many as came with Peter, because the gift of the Holy Spirit had been poured out on the Gentiles also. [46]**For they heard them speak with tongues and magnify God.** Then Peter answered, [47]"Can anyone forbid water, that these should not be baptized who have received the Holy Spirit just as we have?"*

It's important to note; the reason Peter and the other Jews knew that the Gentiles had received the baptism of the Holy Spirit was they heard

---

[243] Matthew 3:11, Acts 11:16
[244] Acts 11:15-16

them speak in tongues. Hearing them speak in tongues was the evidence that they had received it. Jesus said all believers would speak in tongues. We now see the most significant barrier fulfilled as the Gentile believers are filled as well. This event is also further fulfillment to what Peter spoke when he said the baptism of the Holy Spirit is available to as many as the Lord calls.

Another great example of speaking in tongues as the evidence of the baptism of the Holy Spirit is when Paul came upon some disciples in Ephesus. He discovered they'd only been baptized under John's baptism.

Acts 19:1-6 And it happened, while Apollos was at Corinth, that Paul having passed through the upper regions, came to Ephesus. And finding some disciples, [2]he said to them, "Did you receive the Holy Spirit when you believed?" So, they said to him, "We have not so much as heard whether there is a Holy Spirit." [3]And He said to them, "Into what then were you baptized." So, they said, "Into John's Baptism." [4]Then Paul said, "John indeed baptized with a baptism of repentance, saying to the people that they should believe on Him who come after Him, that is, on Christ Jesus." [5]When they heard this; they were baptized in the name of the Lord Jesus. [6]And when Paul had laid hands on them, the Holy Spirit came upon them, and they spoke in tongues and prophesied.

There are couple points in the above passage that are worth pointing out: The first is that Paul recognized these people were believers in God, so he asks them the question, "Did you receive the Holy Spirit since you believed?" At this point, Paul doesn't know they don't know about Jesus. He assumes they do and asks the question about Spirit baptism, meaning he recognizes it as a second experience following salvation by believing in Jesus. For Paul to ask if they had received the baptism in the Holy Spirit is an appropriate question to ask a believer. Secondly, once Paul shares the gospel with them, and they believe, he baptizes them into Christ and then proceeds to lay hands on them so that they can receive the baptism of the Holy Spirit. Once they receive, they begin to speak in tongues, which, once again, shows speaking in tongues as the evidence of having received the baptism of the Holy Spirit.

We now have three actual examples of speaking in tongues as the evidence of having received the baptism of the Holy Spirit. There are two other examples, but they don't explicitly say that speaking in tongues was involved. However, there is a strong implication they were. The first is with the revival at Samaria with Philip and Peter involved. As discussed earlier, these people were saved and baptized but hadn't received the baptism of the Holy Spirit.

Upon Peter's arrival, he discovers they haven't received the Holy Spirit and proceeds to get them baptized in the Holy Spirit. The passage doesn't say they received tongues, but Simon the sorcerer saw something that made him want to offer money to Peter to acquire the ability to administer this extraordinary gift. When Peter rebuked Him, he said, *"Your money perish with you, because you thought that the gift of God could be purchased with your money! You have neither part nor portion in this **matter**, for your heart is not right in the sight of God."*

The Greek word for *"matter"* is *"logos,"* which means *"a word, speech, discourse, or account."*[245] There is a strong possibility Peter was referring to the divine utterance that just came forth as a result of their baptism in the Holy Spirit.

The other example was with Paul when Ananias prayed for him to receive the Holy Spirit. It doesn't say that Paul spoke in tongues, but later it's quoted in his letter to the Corinthians that he speaks in tongues more than anyone.

Acts 8:17 And Ananias went his way and entered the house; and laying hands on him he said, "Brother Saul, the Lord Jesus, who appeared to you on the road as you came, has sent me that you may receive your sight and be filled with the Holy Spirit."

1 Corinthians 14:18 I thank my God I speak in tongues more than you all.

In summary of this section, there are three primary examples of speaking in tongues as the evidence that the disciples received it with the baptism of the Holy Spirit. The two other examples show, in all probability, speaking in tongues was the sign. As Paul said, *"By the mouth of two or three witnesses every word shall be established."*[246]

Is Speaking in Tongues for Today?

Whether or not speaking in tongues is for today is a matter we must discuss because whatever you believe about this will affect you in one way or another.

When the baptism of the Holy Spirit came upon the early disciples on the day of Pentecost, Peter had much to say about it, quoting from Joel's prophecy. As he summed up his message, he said, this same promise of the Holy Spirit is for everyone to whom the Lord calls. To all of us who

[245] Vines Expository Dictionary
[246] 2 Corinthians 13:1

have been drawn by God into this great salvation, the promise is to us throughout all generations. There is no time limit on it.

Acts 2:39 For this promise is to you and your children, and to all who are afar off, as the Lord our God will call.

As we have seen in some passages, the baptism of the Holy Spirit is also referred to as the gift of the Holy Spirit. When Paul was writing to the Corinthians, he mentioned that he didn't want them to come up short in any gift, while they eagerly waited for the second coming of Christ.

*1 Corinthians 1:4-8 I thank a God always concerning you for the grace of God which was given to you by Christ Jesus, [5]that you were enriched in everything by Him in all **utterance** and all knowledge, [6]even as the testimony of Christ was confirmed in you, [7]**so that you come short in no gift,** eagerly waiting for the revelation of our Lord Jesus Christ, [8]who will also confirm you to the end, that you may be blameless in the day of our Lord Jesus Christ.*

The two passages of Scripture just mentioned reveal that the baptism of the Holy Spirit, evidenced with speaking in tongues is for as many as the Lord calls from every generation until the time Christ returns for His Church.

The next passage is the primary one used by those who say speaking in tongues was done away when the Bible was canonized. It mentions that tongues, prophecies, and knowledge will be done away with when that which is perfect comes. The popular interpretation is that the canonization of the Bible is that which is perfect, which means, with its advent, we no longer need tongues and prophecies, but somehow knowledge is still required, even though it says, knowledge will be done away with too. Let's look at the passage and see for ourselves.

1 Corinthians 13:8-10 Love never fails. But whether there are prophecies, they will fail, whether there are tongues, they will cease, whether there is knowledge, it will vanish away. [9]For we know in part, and we prophesy in part. [10]But when that which is perfect has come, then that which is in part will be done away.

The key to this passage is to determine what Paul was referring to when he said, *"But when that which is perfect has come, then that which is in part will be done away."* The problem with the idea that the canonization of the Bible is the interpretation to "that which is perfect," is that neither Paul nor his readers wouldn't have had an idea as to what he was saying. The Bible wasn't canonized until the fifth century. In verse twelve the interpretation is seen.

1 Corinthians 13:12 For now we see in a mirror, dimly, but then face to face. Now I know in part, but then I shall know just as I also am known.

Paul is referring to the second coming of Christ as to when we will see Jesus face to face. We will be like Him in every way as we are changed into His divine image. John explains this perfectly in one of his epistles.

*1 John 3:2 Beloved, now we are children of God; and it has not yet been revealed what we shall be, but we know that **when He is revealed, we shall be like Him, for we shall see Him as He is.***

Once again, we see how Scripture very adequately interprets itself, while allowing personal biases to be set aside.

The Difference between the Sign and the Gift

There's one more area that can be confusing when it comes to speaking in tongues. We must understand that there are two different manifestations of tongues. There is the gift of tongues listed with the other gifts of the Spirit, and the tongue that comes with the baptism of the Holy Spirit. Paul explains the difference in his first letter to the Corinthians.

The Scripture reference that often causes the most confusion is the one that asks the rhetorical question, *"Do all speak with tongues?"* The obvious answer is, "No!"

1 Corinthians 12:29-30 Are all apostles? Are all prophets? Are all workers of miracles? [30]Do all have the gifts of healings? Do all speak with tongues? Do all interpret?

In the context of the above passage, Paul had just finished his teaching on the gifts of the Spirit and how members have different gifts to be used for strengthening the body of Christ. The gift of tongues he's referring to is the gift that is used when the Church comes together, which must be followed with an interpretation.

In chapter fourteen of 1 Corinthians, he addresses the issue of tongues, because the Corinthians were misusing the gift by all speaking in tongues when the church came together.

1 Corinthians 14:23 Therefore if the whole church comes together in one place, and all speak with tongues, and there come in those who are uninformed or unbelievers, will they not say that you are out of your mind?

Paul makes a clear distinction in this chapter between the use of tongues in your prayer time versus in the church. In the church, they must follow with an interpretation and in their own prayer life, he says, *"I thank my God I speak with tongues more than you all; yet in the church, I would rather speak five words with my understanding."*[247]

When referring to the gift of tongues in the Church, he says, *"Do all speak in tongues?"* When referring to the prayer language that comes with the baptism of the Holy Spirit, he says, *"I would that you all speak in tongues."*

How to Receive the Baptism of the Holy Spirit

Now that we've seen how the baptism of the Holy Spirit is for today and evidenced with speaking in tongues just as it was for the first disciples of Jesus, we should receive it. Jesus said, all those who believe in Him would speak in tongues and out of their innermost beings would flow rivers of living water. We are to be conduits of the blessings of God. As His ambassadors, we are to go forth, fervently in the power of His Spirit, ministering His purposes with passion. No matter what our calling in life is, the baptism of the Holy Spirit is necessary to keep us in tune with all that God desires to do in and through us.

The First Step is to Believe

One of the reasons I've been so laborious in this chapter is so that you are convinced in your hearts that the baptism of the Holy Spirit is for you. Abraham, who is the father of our faith received the promises of the Father because he was convinced that what God had promised, He was able to perform.

For me, believing was an important step. I was brought up to think the baptism of the Holy Spirit was very different than what I have just shared. Because I had an open mind after coming out of the hippie culture, I wanted to know for myself why I should believe certain truths. As Paul commended the Bereans for searching the Scriptures for themselves, I approached the subject in the same manner. I spent about six months reading books and studying the Scriptures about the baptism of the Holy Spirit until I was convinced on the subject.

Now, God wants you to receive the promise of the Holy Spirit by being convinced so that He can perform on your behalf. Jesus said, *"Your Heavenly Father will give the Holy Spirit to those who ask Him."* You must believe and be thoroughly convinced that He will fill you with the oil of His Holy Spirit. As you ask Him to baptize you in the Holy Spirit,

---

[247] 1 Corinthians 14:18-19

He is faithful to honor His promise towards you just as He has for countless others.

The Second Step is to Ask, Seek, and Knock

Once you come to the place where you genuinely believe the baptism of the Holy Spirit is for you, then ask, seek and knock until you receive it. As you do, there will be a genuine hunger that begins to grip your soul until you receive it.

Luke 11:9 So I say to you, ask, and it will be given to you; seek, and you will find; knock, and it will be opened.

There must be a heart of faith with an expectation of receiving as you seek Him. The heart of the Father wants nothing more than to grant you your request as you come before Him with a pure heart of belief and trust. The next verses assure us of this as Jesus continues this conversation with His disciples.

Luke 11:10-13 If a son asks for bread from any father among you, will he give him a stone? Or if he asks for a fish, will he give him a serpent instead of a fish? [12]Or if he asks for an egg, will he give him a scorpion? [13]If you then, being evil, know how to give good gifts to your children, how much more will your Heavenly Father give the Holy Spirit to those who ask Him!

The Third Step is to Apply Action to Your Faith

Faith without works is dead. True faith will always involve some sort of action that shows you are fully convinced of what you believe. The effort required in receiving the baptism of the Holy Spirit is to open your mouth and begin to speak, but not in any language you know. It was as the early disciples began to speak that the Spirit gave them the utterance.

Acts 2:4 And they were all filled with the Holy Spirit and began to speak with other tongues, as the Spirit gave them utterance.

In summary, I believe God desires that we all receive the baptism of the Holy Spirit with the evidence of speaking in tongues. In doing so, we allow our lamps to have a continuous supply of oil that's necessary to be adequately prepared when the bridegroom comes for His bride. It's the oil that keeps the fire or the passion in our lives going strong and causes us to minister as flames of fire.

May God bless you as you press into all that He has for you. I close this chapter with another poem that expresses the Father's heart as you ponder how He desires to bless you with the presence of the Holy Spirit.

Come Holy Spirit

By Ken L. Birks © 2017 Straight Arrow Ministries

The Holy Spirit of God, free to all, comes with might and power.
The promise given is to all who are afar off, as many as are called.
As the disciples long ago, He comes with tongues of fire in this hour.
Out of our inner beings flow rivers of living water, to be enthralled.
As the Father delights in giving, the Spirit comes to all those called.

Come Holy Spirit as we seek, ask and knock for your presence.
Asking in faith, believing in Your promise, we come with expectation.
As we seek with whole hearts, fill our vessels with Your excellence.
From our innermost beings, pour forth a new language with conviction.
As living water pours forth, hearts are filled with prophetic purpose.

Come Holy Spirit, burn the chaff that holds us back from purity.
Leaving sin behind, mortal bodies are quickened, walking in morality.
Not allowing sin to reign, the Holy Spirit is given full access.
As hurtful ways are revealed, we see what keeps us from access.
As His Spirit burns within, the chaff burns to make way for newness.

Come Holy Spirit, give guidance as we walk in Your ways.
Lead us in paths of righteousness as we are lead to Your desires.
As Your Spirit leads us, in conformity to Your image, we gaze.
As we follow, lead us away from the enemy's tempting fires.
Greater are You than anything the enemy throws our ways.

Come Holy Spirit, teach us in the ways of the Father, so fine.
As the anointing teaches us all things pertaining to life, we dine.
In all that's been given, reveal all that's in His heart of hearts.
With Your teaching drops like dew; we yield to what the Spirit imparts.
As we're taught to number our days, we're given to Your purposes.

Come Holy Spirit, release Your gifts to encourage and strengthen.
As healing and miracles come forth, heal all as Jesus did.
As the prophetic realms come forth, reveal the Father's intentions.
With the gifts of tongues, speak forth mysteries in our spirits.
As discerning of spirits comes forth, reveal Satan's pretensions.

We give thanks for Your Spirit who works in us the works of Jesus.
You are the One we give glory to for all that's been given and done.

The Sanctifying Process
of the Lord

Chapter Twelve

As we look to all that God desires for our lives; we must consider what it means to be sanctified for the Lord's prophetic purposes. The meaning of sanctification is to be set apart unto God in holiness. God has set us apart for His prophetic purposes. We have a big part to play in all that He's about to do. As Paul wrote to Timothy, *"We have been saved and called with a holy calling, not according to our works, but according to His own purpose and grace which was given to us in Christ Jesus."*[248] We must embrace the sanctifying and cleansing process before He can use us adequately.

When we accepted Christ as our Lord and Savior, we stepped into His righteousness, which covers all our sin and shame.[249] The Father, now, only sees us through the righteousness of Jesus. He sees us as being perfected forever as the writer of the book of Hebrews expresses so adequately. However, the sanctification process is an ongoing experience as we work out our salvation in fear and trembling.[250]

Hebrews 10:14 For by one offering He has perfected forever those who are being sanctified.

Upon salvation, the work of Christ is completed in our lives, but the work of the Holy Spirit is just beginning. He has much work to do as He leads us inexorably towards total conformity to the image of Christ.

Romans 8:29 For Whom He foreknew, He also predestined to be conformed to the image of His Son, that He might be the firstborn among many brethren.

When we accepted Jesus Christ as our Lord and Savior, we entered into the Father's predestinated purposes—His prophetic purposes. We must now be vessels of honor if we are to be used by Him for all that

---

[248] 2 Timothy 1:9
[249] 2 Corinthians 5:21
[250] Philippians 2:12

He's planned for us. The only way to be used by Him in a manner that brings glory to His name is to continually yield our vessels to the sanctifying process of the Holy Spirit. Otherwise, our works are burned as dead works.

2 Timothy 2:20 But in a great house, there are not only vessels of gold and silver, but also wood and clay, some for honor and some for dishonor.

Essential Keys of the Sanctifying Process

One of the essential keys to our growth and maturity in the Lord happens as we understand and embrace how the sanctifying process works. It's through the sanctifying operation of the Lord that our ears are trained to discern the voice of the Lord as He guides and directs us to be all that we can be in Christ. As we yield to the Holy Spirit in this process, He conforms us to the image of Christ because this is the direction of the Father's predestinated purposes.

2 Corinthians 3:17-18 Now the Lord is the Spirit; and where the Spirit of the Lord is, there is liberty. [18]But we all, with unveiled face, beholding in a mirror the glory of the Lord, are being transformed into the same image from glory to glory, just as by the Spirit of the Lord.

Keeping our Eyes Rested on the Lord

A major key to staying in this process is to keep our eyes rested on the Lord.[251] As we behold His image in our thoughts, we're gradually changed into His image from glory to glory. By meditating on all of His wonderful attributes, the mind of Christ begins to take shape in us as old ways of thinking dissipate.[252] As we give ourselves to the study of His Word, His ways and thoughts become embedded in our hearts and spirits, transforming and renewing our minds with new perspectives on life.[253] All things become new as the old gives way to the newness that is now changing us.[254] With spiritual eyes opened to the wonders of His grace and Spirit, our minds are filled with new revelation and understanding.[255]

It's as we spend time meditating on the changes the Father desires to bring about that the Holy Spirit, who is our helper, helps us to formulate plans of action that keep us accountable to what His desires are.

---

251 Isaiah 26:3, Colossians 3:1-3
252 1 Corinthians 2:12,16
253 Romans 12:1-2
254 2 Corinthians 5:17
255 Ephesians 1:17-18

The Breath of God Must Touch our Lives

As we allow the breath of God to touch our lives, He teaches us to discern His gentle voice and promptings. With this, we experience new liberty in the Spirit, which causes us to lay hold and cling to the new life that is now setting our hearts on fire. The sanctifying process of the Lord then begins to take root as He molds and shapes us by the power of the Holy Spirit and the word of God.

Just as the early disciples allowed Jesus to breathe upon them, so must we. However, we must always keep in mind; we have an enemy who wants nothing more than to steal and destroy that which has begun to take root in our hearts.[256] As Paul wrote to the Galatians, *"Who has bewitched you? Are you so foolish? Having begun in the Spirit, are you now being made perfect by the flesh?"*[257] The enemy of our faith will do whatever he can to shift our attention away from relying on the Holy Spirit to relying on our own strength and legalistic measures.

When we try to perfect ourselves by any other means than allowing the Holy Spirit to do His work, we produce dead works. We cannot afford to get caught up in dead works, created by legalistic measures that will eventually be burned. We have been given the Holy Spirit to burn the chaff in our lives so that our works are pure and holy, undefined by impure motives and false pretenses.

Our goal is to become Christ's workmanship as we allow the Holy Spirit to produce in us genuine works that will be rewarded throughout eternity. These are pure works born out of a relationship with the Holy Spirit and God's Word which allow us to become vessels unto honor engaged in pure and holy works of righteousness.

> ***Ephesians 2:8-10*** *For by grace you have been saved through faith, and that not of yourselves; it is the gift of God, ⁹not of works, lest anyone should boast. ¹⁰For we are His workmanship, created in Christ Jesus for good works, which God prepared beforehand that we should walk in them.*

Sanctified by Fire

When John the Baptist came preaching his message of repentance, people began looking to him as the coming Messiah. However, his response as seen in the following Scripture passage helps us to

---

[256] John 10:10
[257] Galatians 3:1-3

understand the root of the sanctifying process. It's the fire of the Lord that begins to burn the chaff in our lives.

*Matthew 3:11-12 I indeed baptize you with water unto repentance, but He who is coming after me is mightier than I, whose sandals I am not worthy to carry. **He will baptize you with the Holy Spirit and fire.** [12]His winnowing fan is in His hand, and He will thoroughly clean out the threshing floor, and gather His wheat into the barn, but **He will burn up the chaff with unquenchable fire.***

When we are baptized in the Holy Spirit, the fire of God comes to refine us, burning our sinful chaff as we change from glory to glory. The fire or passion that comes from the Holy Spirit's baptism is what helps us to be free from the fire of judgment. The prophet, Isaiah mentions this as well in a portion of Scripture, when He speaks of the spirit of burning that causes the Branch of the Lord to be beautiful and glorious.

*Isaiah 4:3-4 And it shall come to pass that he who is left in Zion and remains in Jerusalem will be called holy—everyone who is recorded among the living in Jerusalem. [4]When the Lord has washed the filth of the daughters of Zion from her midst, by the spirit of judgment and by the **spirit of burning.***

One of the most significant areas of uncleanness that we must deal with are the lusts of the flesh. These are areas that continually war against who we are in Christ. As we purpose to walk in the Spirit, we won't succumb to them while the fire of God continually burns the chaff of ungodly desires from us.

Galatians 5:16-18 I say Then: Walk in the Spirit, and you shall not fulfill the lust of the flesh. [17]For the flesh lusts against the Spirit, and the Spirit against the flesh; and these are contrary to one another so that you do not do the things you wish. [18]But If you are led by the Spirit, you are not under the law.

Our part in the sanctification process is to yield to the Holy Spirit, who is the One who convicts of sin. As we respond to His gentle promptings in these areas, He gives us the victory we need, causing us to triumph over the lusts that war against the flesh.[258] As we put on the characteristics of the new man, the old nature begins to disappear. We find that our desires are now toward all that God is doing in us rather than being dictated by the lusts of the flesh and the cultural norms of the world.

The sanctifying process is vital to our new lives in Christ because the cultures of the world all lie under the sway or control of the enemy,

---

[258] 2 Corinthians 2:14

which leaves us vulnerable to his devices. It's the fire of God that comes from the sanctifying process that protects us.

1 John 5:19 *We know that we are of God, and the whole world lies under the sway of the wicked one.*

With the enemy's tentacles reaching into all spheres of our cultures, we quickly become numb to God's ways. When our hearts and minds are more set on cultural norms rather than heavenly realities, our spirits become numb to God's ways and purposes to which we are called. The norms of our cultures then begin to dictate to us what is right and wrong, resulting in numbness of our spirits to the work of the Holy Spirit. Even though the Holy Spirit is still there, He's stifled or quenched, and the work He's been commissioned to do doesn't get done.[259] When the Spirit is quenched, there's a tendency to fall back to the condition Paul was addressing the Galatians—*Are you so foolish? Having begun in the Spirit, are you now being made perfect by the flesh?* Unfortunately, this is the state of many Christians in today's Christianity, and this is what disqualifies them from being vessels unto honor, to whom the Lord desires to use for His prophetic purposes. By adapting to the cultural norms rather than kingdom principles, they become stuck in their sin, quenching the sanctifying process of the Holy Spirit.

To gain a more tangible picture of what the sanctifying process looks like, let's take a closer look at the passage of Scripture that speaks of being vessels unto honor which makes us useful for the master, and prepared for every good work.

2 Timothy 2:19-22 *Nevertheless the solid foundation of God stands: "The Lord knows those are His," and,* **"Let everyone who names the name of Christ depart from iniquity."** [20]*But in a great house there are not only vessels of gold and silver, but also wood and clay, some for honor and some for dishonor.* [21]**Therefore if anyone cleanses himself from the latter, he will be a vessel for honor, sanctified and useful for the master, prepared for every good work.** [22]*Flee also youthful lusts; but pursue righteousness, faith, love, and peace with those who call on the Lord with a pure heart.*

As seen in this passage, there is an active command to cleanse ourselves. Keep in mind, even though Jesus has washed and made us righteous by His works, the Holy Spirit is still working to sanctify us entirely. In our relationship with the Holy Spirit, we labor together with Him. As we yield to His work within us, we put off the old and put on

---

[259] 1 Thessalonians 5:19

the new. We are to clothe ourselves in the Lord Jesus Christ, making no provision for the flesh.[260] As we enter the process of cleansing ourselves, we become prepared and useful for the Master's work.

Putting Off and Putting On

In Paul's letter to the Ephesians, where he's encouraging them to be knit together by what every joint supplies to bring about the effectual working of the body of Christ, he speaks of the importance of putting off the old nature and putting on the new character that brings this to pass. In his letters to the Ephesians, Colossians, and Galatians, he deals with the character of the new man that is to be formed in every Christian who has come to know the Lord Jesus Christ and His saving grace and power. We see him making a transition from theological statements to practical precepts in Christ. After laying a firm doctrinal foundation on who Christ is, he turns his attention to how Christians should live their lives. He lays the foundation for effective change for the glory of God to inhabit our lives. As Christ quickens our bodies, we are to be different. We should reflect a new pattern of living.

If the body of Christ is to come into the fullness of the stature of Jesus Christ with every joint supplying what's needed for growth and maturity, it starts with individual responsibility. Each member is to put off their former conduct and put on the new man that God created according to His true righteousness and holiness.

> ***Ephesians 4:20-24*** *But you have not so learned Christ, [21] if indeed you have heard Him, and been taught by Him, as the truth is in Jesus: [22] that **you put off, concerning your former conduct, the old man** which grows corrupt according to the deceitful lusts, [23] and be renewed in the spirit of your mind, [24] and **that you put on the new man** which was created according to God, in true righteousness and holiness.*

The above passage continues to reveal what the sanctifying process entails. We are to die to our former lives that were once engulfed in sin and shame as God renews us according to His righteousness and holiness. When we become crucified with Christ, we no longer identify with our former self that was under the sway of the world. In Christ, He has crucified us to the world and its lusts.

> ***Galatians 2:20*** *"I have been **crucified with Christ**; it is no longer I who live, but Christ lives in me; and **the life which I now live in the flesh I live by faith in the Son of God,** who loved me and gave Himself for me.*

---

[260] Romans 14:13

Galatians 6:14 But God forbid that I should boast except in the cross of our Lord Jesus Christ, by whom the world has been crucified to me, and I to the world.

Putting to Death the Sins of the Past

Being crucified to the world means that we are now in the process of putting away or putting to death the sins of the past. We freely submit to the power of the Holy Spirit as He convicts us of the sin in our lives. We allow the Spirit of God total and free access to those areas that are stumbling blocks to us. As we do, the same Spirit that raised Jesus from the dead now quickens our mortal bodies to die to the sin that so easily besets us. We labor together with Him as He convicts and quickens.

Colossians 3:5-7 (NLT) So put to death the sinful, earthly things lurking within you. Have nothing to do with sexual sin, impurity, lust, and shameful desires. Don't be greedy for the good things of this life, for that is idolatry. ⁶God's terrible anger will come upon those who do such things. ⁷You used to do them when your life was still part of this world.

Paul makes it clear; there are a few things in the above passage that must be put off. He mentions greed, sexual sins, which includes sex outside of marriage, homosexuality, and all other forms of sexual immorality. Peter also includes impurity, which involves all types of pornography such as impure thoughts, mentioned by Jesus.[261] Paul then discusses lust, which would consist of all the areas mentioned in his letter to the Galatians such as adultery, fornication, uncleanness, lewdness, idolatry, sorcery, contentions, jealousies, hatred, outbursts of wrath, selfish ambitions, dissensions, heresies, envy, murders, drunkenness, revelries and the like.[262] He says those who practice these things will not inherit the kingdom of God. In other words, we are to be busy practicing righteousness, so that we don't practice sin.[263]

It's important to make a distinction between those who practice sin and those who occasionally stumble. Those who are genuinely seeking to walk in the Spirit may stumble now and then but will immediately repent and continue walking in the Spirit rather than wallowing in the sin.[264] They will quickly and boldly run into the arms of their faithful High Priest, Jesus, who sympathizes with them, as they confess and forsake their sin.[265]

---

[261] Matthew 5:28
[262] Galatians 5:19-21
[263] 1John 3:5-7
[264] Romans 8:1-2, 1 John 1:9
[265] Hebrews 4:14-16

A word of caution to all: God will not be mocked. He knows what's in our hearts. When our hearts are deceived, we find ourselves playing games with God; He knows the real condition of our hearts. We may fool those around us, but we will never fool God. One of the tactics of the enemy is to twist the Scriptures to his destructive ways. Twisting Scriptures to justify our sins will only lead to our demise.[266]

> *Galatians 6:7-8 Do not be deceived, God is not mocked, for whatever a man sows, that he will also reap. [8]For he who sows to his flesh will of the flesh reap corruption, but if he sows to the Spirit will of the Spirit reap everlasting life.*

> *2 Corinthians 7:1 Therefore, having these promises, beloved, let us cleanse ourselves from all filthiness of the flesh and spirit, perfecting holiness in the fear of God.*

When we fail to walk in the Spirit as God directs, we quench the Holy Spirit within us. As a result, we become unworthy vessels with our light significantly lacking to those who are still perishing in their sins. When our salt loses its flavor, we find ourselves not useful for the Master's purposes.[267] In fact, we become enemies of the cross rather than proponents of it.[268]

Aside from the works of the flesh in the areas mentioned above, Paul goes on to point out other areas that must be put to death.

> *Colossians 3:8-9 But now you yourselves are to put off all these: anger, wrath, malice, blasphemy, filthy language out of your mouth. [9]Do not lie to one another, since you have put off the old man with his deeds.*

The expression *"put off"* is a strong one calling for a complete putting off of all that pertains to the old life. We are to strip off completely the former habits which cling to us like an old garment and fling them away like an outward suit of clothes. The following practices are as follows:

Anger and Wrath: Associated with anger is wrath or vengeful rage. When anger boils up there is wrath.

> *Proverbs 29:11 A fool vents all his feelings, but a wise man holds them back.*

Malice: Anger and wrath are wrong, but malice is worse because it's more rooted and deliberate. It's anger heightened and settled.

Filthy Communication: This would involve swearing, coarse talking, and jesting. As Christians, our language should be pure and holy.

---

[266] 2 Peter 3:16
[267] Matthew 5:13
[268] Philippians 3:18-19

144

In today's Christianity, it seems swearing, cursing and coarse talking have become more and more acceptable. The F-bomb gets tossed around like it's a regular part of our vocabulary. It's still a vulgar word that expresses the epitome of what is meant by filthy communication. It's getting more difficult to detect the difference between unbelievers and believers. Satan must be having a good laugh over this as he sees Christians everywhere being seduced by his tactics in this area. Even though some Christian cultures are more accepting of vulgar language, God's word is unchangeable. It's still swearing, cursing and filthy communication that must be done away with if we are to be vessels unto honor.

Ephesians 4:29 Let no corrupt word proceed out of your mouth, but what is good for necessary edification, that it may impart grace to the hearers.

Lying: To lie is to issue a false statement or piece of information deliberately presented as being right—a falsehood. Lying is anything meant to deceive or give a wrong impression.

The passage below shows, when we fail to change as the Holy Spirit directs, our ministry to those who are perishing is lacking. Without change, it's very difficult to be useful vessels for the Master's work. We will produce dead works that will ultimately be burned.

2 Corinthians 4:1-3 Therefore, since we have this ministry, as we have received mercy, we do not lose heart. ²But we have renounced the hidden things of shame, not walking in craftiness nor handling the word of God deceitfully, but by manifestation of the truth commending ourselves to every man's conscience in the sight of God. ³But even if our gospel is veiled, it is veiled to those who are perishing,

Once we entirely renounce all our hidden areas of shame by repentance, we are available to be used as vessels of honor, who bring glory and honor to the name of Christ.

Putting on the New Nature

In this section, the focus is on those character traits that are an essential part of the new creation Christ is forming in us. Our goal as Christians is to have the negative characteristics and habit patterns that were formed in us by our sinful, and fallen nature transformed into the Christ-like attributes of the new man or nature that are a part of God's divine nature.

Colossians 3:9-10 (NLT) Don't lie to each other, for you have stripped off your old evil nature and all its wicked deeds. ¹⁰In its place you have clothed yourselves with a brand-new nature that is continually being renewed as you learn more and more about Christ, who created this new nature within you.

It's important to realize that an active response to God's will always involve constant change. The character traits that we are looking at are traits that should be a part of all our lives in varying degrees. We need to understand that Christ desires to develop these character traits to their full potential in us as we are changed from glory to glory in His image.

The new man is created in true righteousness and holiness, meaning that if Christ is indeed a part of our lives, we will walk in His righteousness. As we do so, we take on His divine nature.

Ephesians 4:23-24 *and be renewed in the spirit of your mind, [24]and that you put on the new man which was created according to God, in true righteousness and holiness.*

2 Peter 1:4 *by which have been given to us exceedingly great and precious promises, that through these you may be partakers of the divine nature, having escaped the corruption that is in the world through lust.*

Conversion and sanctification are designed to necessitate a definite break with the corruption caused by sin. When we come to know God through Christ, we not only escape the corruption of sin but are renewed as the Holy Spirit restores the Father's divine nature within us.

The provision of the divine nature through repentance from sin and faith in Jesus Christ and the power of the Holy Spirit belong to the divine sovereignty of the Lord. However, the application and the fulfillment of these is the human responsibility of every believer. The seeds of these character traits come with being born again by God's Spirit,[269] but the full development of His divine nature is our responsibility as we labor together with Him. The Bible says, *"We are to put on the new man."*

God has given believers all things that pertain to life and godliness. However, it's the believers' responsibility to take what God has given and use it for the glory of God.

Colossians 3:12-15 *(NLT) Since God chose you to be the holy people whom he loves, you must clothe yourselves with tenderhearted mercy, kindness, humility, gentleness, and patience. [13]You must make allowance for each other's faults and forgive the person who offends you. Remember, the Lord forgave you, so you must forgive others. [14]And the most important piece of clothing you must wear is love. Love is what binds us all together in perfect harmony. [15]And let the peace that comes*

---

[269] 1 Peter 1:23

from Christ rule in your hearts. For as members of one body you are all called to live in peace. And always be thankful.

The characteristics mentioned above are essential in every one of us if we are to grow into balanced, mature Christians with the power and anointing of God flowing through us. They enable others to receive the gifts and callings in our lives, keep us from becoming wild tares in the kingdom of God, and keep us on course for all that God desires for us. With that in mind, let's take a quick look at them.

Brief Descriptions of the Above Character Traits

Tender Mercies: This involves heartfelt compassion expressed with tenderness. Because God comforts us through His mercy, we can comfort those who are in need as well.[270]

Kindness: To be kind has to do with being of a friendly nature, a person who is generous, hospitable, good and warmhearted. Kindness is often exhibited in acts that are shown with consideration, sympathy, and understanding towards others. A kind person is very courteous and thoughtful towards others.

Humbleness of Mind or Humility: The humble person is aware of their shortcomings so that they don't exalt themselves above others. It also has to do with showing an attitude of deferential respect. You are satisfied to be lowly and unpretentious.

Pride comes in all shapes and sizes. Some put themselves on a pedestal from which they judge the faults of everyone else. Others are so self-effacing that they cannot take their eyes off themselves and their inadequacies. A poor self-image is not humility. Still, others swing like a pendulum from one extreme to the other. Paul exhorts us not to exalt nor belittle ourselves but to think with sober judgment.[271] We are to be clothed with humility because God resists the proud.

1 Peter 5:5-6 Likewise you younger people, submit yourselves to your elders. Yes, all of you be submissive to one another, and be clothed with humility, for "God resists the proud, but gives grace to the humble." [6]Therefore humble yourselves under the mighty hand of God that He may exalt you in due time.

Meekness: A meek person is able to contain their strength under control and has to do with consideration for others and a willingness to

---

[270] 2 Corinthians 1:3-4
[271] Romans 12:3

waive their rights. It's essential to keep in mind that neither meekness nor gentleness is to be confused with weakness.

The meek are those people who humble themselves before God because they acknowledge their utter dependence upon Him. As a result, they are gentle in their dealings with others. You can be tender and soft with people because you have given control of your life to God and you don't have to "win" all the time.

> *2 Timothy 2:24 (NLT) The Lord's servants must not quarrel but must be kind to everyone. They must be able to teach effectively and be patient with difficult people.*

Forbearing and Forgiving: To forgive is to exercise forbearance. It means to endure, bear with, put up with one another. Tolerance and forgiveness are qualities of humility with patience in action. The forbearing person will remain calm whatever the provocation and will keep clear of severe reactions. The forgiving person must go even further by wiping the slate clean from their hearts, including all bitterness and irritation. If we expect forbearance and forgiveness from God, we must be able to forbear and forgive others as well. Tolerance and forgiveness go hand in hand.

> *Mark 11:25-26 (NLT) But when you are praying, first forgive anyone you are holding a grudge against, so that your Father in heaven will forgive your sins, too." 26 (NKJV) "But if you do not forgive, neither will your Father in heaven forgive your trespasses."*

> *Luke 17:3-4 (NLT) I am warning you! If another believer sins, rebuke him; then if he repents, forgive him. 4Even if he wrongs you seven times a day and each time turns again and asks forgiveness, forgive him."*

No matter how much others sin against you must be willing to forgive. We must continually be willing to forgive others as Christ has forgiven us.

Love: To love is to allow the glue that holds everything together act as the crowning grace of the new nature to come forth in the beauty that God intended for our lives.[272] When you love as mentioned in the passage below, you are releasing God's grace over others.

> *1 Corinthians 13:4-8 Love suffers long and is kind; love does not envy; love does not parade itself, is not puffed up; 5does not behave rudely, does not seek its own, is not provoked, thinks no evil; 6does not rejoice in iniquity, but rejoices in the truth; 7bears all things, believes all things, hopes all things, endures all things. 8Love never fails. But whether there*

---

[272] Colossians 3:14

are prophecies, they will fail; whether there are tongues, they will cease; whether there is knowledge, it will vanish away.

Summary

Each of these character traits shows how we as Christians are to be clothed and are to behave in our dealings with others, particularly with fellow-believers. These character traits enable the body of Christ to come forth as one new man, fitted and framed together as a holy temple that will house the glory of God in the same way as Solomon's temple did. We are the living stones God is using to build His temple.

In Peter's second epistle, he mentions these same traits, adding self-control and perseverance to the mix. He also says we must give all diligence when adding these characteristics to our lives. He says, when we do, we will never fall.[273]

As I conclude this chapter, I would like to leave you with a thread of thought that has run through this entire section. And that is, there's a thin line between what the genuine works of the Lord are versus dead works. On the outside, they can look similar just as it's difficult to tell the difference between a tare and a strand of wheat. The main difference between a tare and strand of wheat is; when the wind blows, the grain bends over, while the tare stands straight. With us, the difference is the motive of the heart. When we bow in humility before God and others, we won't be standing up straight with our pride, trying to get the glory. If what we're doing is to be seen by men, or vying for position, or even trying to earn God's favor, then the motive is wrong.

We already have all of God's favor. There's nothing we can do to earn any more. Jesus has already given us everything we need that pertains to life and godliness. When He completed His work on the cross, His work in our lives was finished. What we do, is in response to what He's already done. We are His workmanship. The Holy Spirit who is alive and well in each of us still has much work to do in our sanctifying process. In yielding to Him, we are able to add all these characteristics to our lives. We are to labor together with Him as He moves inexorably towards the goal of conforming us into the image of Christ from glory to glory.

Paul expressed his relationship with the Holy Spirit, in his letter to the Colossians of how He labors together with the Holy Spirit to bring about God's intended purposes in and through Him. He said, *"Him we preach, warning every man and teaching every man in all wisdom, that*

---

[273] 2 Peter 1:5-11

we may present every man perfect in Christ Jesus. **To this end I also labor, striving according to His working which works in me mightily.** [274]

You might ask, "If the Holy Spirit is working mightily on our behalf, why aren't we being changed from glory to glory quickly?" The key is found in what Paul said. He said he labors and strives according to the intensity of the Holy Spirit who works mightily. If we are not working vigorously along with Him, we end up frustrating and quenching the grace of God as He desires to work with us. It's like a sluggard and a gung-ho person being yoked together to get something done. All they do is frustrate each other, and nothing much gets accomplished.

If we haven't learned to walk with the footmen, how are we ever going to run with the horsemen? [275] It's the violent ones who take the kingdom by force. [276] If we are going to be the flames of fire God has called us to, we will we need to get in sync with the Holy Spirit and the work He's doing in our lives. We must yield and work with Him as He uses us to fulfill His prophetic purposes.

---

[274] Colossians 1:27
[275] Jeremiah 12:5
[276] Matthew 11:12

The Sanctifying Process

by Ken L. Birks © 2018 Straight Arrow Ministries

One offering perfected forever; we're sealed.
Predestined to be conformed to His image, we yield.
Entering God's prophetic purposes, we arrive.
Ears trained to hear His voice, He directs, we thrive.
The work of Christ finished, the Spirit's work drives.

Vessels of Honor, we seek to be as He purifies.
With unquenchable fire, the chaff burns away.
Walking in the Spirit, fleshly lusts disappear.
The process ensures, keeping our eyes on His visage.
Change comes, glory to glory, beholding His image.

Having begun in the Spirit, the enemy subverts.
Shifting our attention to legalism, Satan beguiles.
Testing the Word to protect, we're aware of Satan's wiles.
God's works are birthed, immersed in His workmanship.
From glory to glory, the process continues to equip.

With spiritual eyes opened, His wonders never cease.
Submitting His Word, His thoughts are embedded.
With minds filled with insight, newness is exceeded.
Yielding, new nature comes forth, replacing oldness.
Submitting to God's ways, the enemy leaves.

Pressing on, we stretch forward to things ahead.
Forgetting the past, we press forward in destiny.
From glory to glory, the prize within sight, we tread.
As vessels of honor, we engage in prophetic purposes.
Pressing on, we live by this rule as we are lead.

Hearts Fully Committed To God's Purposes

Chapter Thirteen

As we look further into what's needed in partnering together with the Father in His prophetic purposes, we must consider what it means to be wholly committed to the purposes of God. After all, this is one of the primary reasons God saved and called us.

*2 Timothy 1:8-9 Therefore do not be ashamed of the testimony of our Lord, nor of me His prisoner, but share with me in the sufferings for the gospel according to the power of God, ⁹who **has saved us and called us with a holy calling**, not according to our works, but **according to His own purpose and grace** which was given to us in Christ Jesus before time began.*

It takes hearts fully committed to God's purposes to keep the oil of His Holy Spirit continually flowing into our lives. This is a major part of keeping our lamps lit as we wait for our bridegroom. It doesn't matter what our station in life is, we're all called according to His purpose and grace. Whether we are full-time ministers, people in the marketplace, homemakers, construction workers, migrant workers, police, firemen, librarians, students, blue-collar workers, or professionals, we're all called to work out His purpose in our lives.

Do you know what your purpose in life is? If not, spend some time meditating on how you fit into God's purposes in your harvest field. Look around and see where you fit in and how God wants to use you with the gifts, He gave you. You might discover what your purpose is.

Counting the Cost

After experiencing salvation, there's usually a time when we count the cost of what it means for God to consecrate us for His purposes. We then make a firm decision to follow Him wholeheartedly after tasting of

His goodness. Consecrating our lives to Christ is what brings us into being true disciples of Jesus Christ.[277]

Luke 14:27-30 And whoever does not bear his cross and come after Me cannot be my disciple. [28]For which of you, intending to build a tower, does not sit down first and count the cost, whether he has enough to finish it— [29]lest after he has laid the foundation, and is not able to finish, all who see it begin to mock him, [30]saying, "This man began to build and was not able to finish?"

Once we are consecrated and accept the cost, God works on our behalf to conform us to His will.

Philippians 2:13 For it is God who works in you both to will and to do for His good pleasure.

Getting involved with God's purposes is what keeps us going as He works in us both to will and to do for a His good pleasure. When our hearts are fully consecrated to Him, He works on our behalf to bring us into an agreement with His sovereign purposes. This is what enables His sovereignty to meet with our free will and what prepares us to be totally in sync with Him and His sovereign purposes. God is so concerned about this that He's continually searching the earth for those individuals whose hearts are fully committed to Him in this manner.

Psalm 14:2 The Lord looks down from heaven upon the children of men, to see if there are any who understand, who seek God.

2 Chronicles 16:9 For the eyes of the Lord run to and fro throughout the whole earth, to show Himself strong on behalf of those whose heart is loyal to Him.

Those who seek God whole-heartedly are people like David, who served the purposes of God for His generation.[278] They're like Paul, who was able to say at the end of his life, *"I have fought the good fight and have finished the race."*[279] Will this be your testimony at the end of your life? Or will you be one of those who didn't count the cost and finish what was started? The choice is yours. No one can make it for you. There will be many who will have excuses just as those who made excuses to Jesus. But as Jesus said, *"Let the dead bury their dead, you come follow me."*[280]

---

[277] 1 Peter 2:1-3
[278] Acts 13:36
[279] 2 Timothy 4:7
[280] Matthew 8:22

Think of all the people who benefitted from kingdom blessings because David and Paul served His purposes for their generations. Think of all the people who will benefit from the blessings of the kingdom because we chose to consecrate our hearts to God for His purposes in our generation. This is a big part of counting the cost of what it means to be sanctified wholeheartedly. We must not only count the cost of what it means to be fully committed but also what it means not to be fully engaged. We are to be like the sons of Issachar, who understood their times and knew what to do. May the Lord show Himself strong to us as we fully surrender to Him.

What Being Fully Committed Entails

Now that we understand there's a cost involved in being fully committed, we must look at what that price entails. There are some essential attitudes and characteristics that need to be developed if we are to fulfill God's purposes for our lives. These are attitudes and qualities we must be in the process of diligently adding to our faith. As a result, we perfectly position ourselves to be vessels unto honor.

We Believe in the Promises of God

Just as Abraham believed in the promises of God and it was accounted unto him as righteousness, so must we.[281] Hearts fully committed unto God and his purposes must believe that God will perform on their behalf as He's promised. As seen below, when we believe God for His promises, it produces His glory through us as vessels unto honor.

> **2 Corinthians 1:20** *For all the promises of God in Him are Yes, and in Him Amen, to the glory of God through us.*

Caleb is a great example. When he went before Joshua concerning the land promised him, He reminded him of how he had fully followed the Lord by believing in the promise to take the land. He equated fully following the Lord with believing in His promises.

> **Joshua 14:7-9** *I was forty years old when Moses the servant of the Lord sent me from Kadesh Barnea to explore the land. And I brought him back a report according to my convictions, but my fellow Israelites who went up with me made the hearts of the people melt in fear. **I, however, followed the Lord my God wholeheartedly.** So on that day, Moses swore to me, 'The land on which your feet have walked will be your*

---

[281] Romans 4:20-22

*inheritance and that of your children forever **because you have followed the Lord my God wholeheartedly.'***

When we believe in the promises of God and His ability to perform on our behalf, we gain the ability to go forth with passion, fervency, and zeal fulfilling His word. We are able to engage the enemy, knowing we have total victory over him. We are fearless as we trample over him with all the power and authority given to us by Jesus.

Luke 10:19 *Behold, I give you the authority to trample on serpents and scorpions, and over all the power of the enemy, and nothing shall by any means hurt you.*

It's through believing in the promises of God that we become partakers of the divine nature of God, which enables us to be all that God has purposed for us. Without believing in His precious promises, we'll never be able to follow Him wholeheartedly. We must believe!

2 Peter 1:2-4 *Grace and peace be multiplied to you in the knowledge of God and Jesus our Lord, [3]as His divine power has given to us all things that pertain to life and godliness, through the knowledge of Him who called us by glory and virtue, [4]by which have been given to us **exceedingly great and precious promises, that through these you may be partakers of the divine nature,** having escaped the corruption that is in the world through lust.*

Overall Lifestyles are an Example of Living Sacrifices

As born again, Spirit-filled believers, who have a destiny to fulfill, we are to present ourselves unto God as living sacrifices. At the outset, this doesn't sound very exciting, but the truth is, it takes a sacrificial life to enjoy the excitement that comes from being a kingdom-minded person.

Romans 12:1-2 *I beseech you, therefore, brethren, by the mercies of God, that you present your bodies a living sacrifice, holy, acceptable to God, which is your reasonable service. [2]And do not be conformed to this world, but be transformed by the renewing of your mind, that you may prove what is that good and acceptable and perfect will of God.*

As Paul continues in this letter to the Romans, he goes on to explain how the gifts of the Spirit are to pour out of those who have presented themselves as living sacrifices.[282] He then shares what it means to behave like a Christian. We must love without hypocrisy, abhor evil, and cling to what is right. We are also to be kindly affectionate, in honor giving

---

[282] Romans 12:3-8

preference to others. We are not to lag in diligence, being fervent, rejoicing in hope, being.

All the above attitudes and characteristics go against the conformity and pattern of the world and are what put us in a position to accurately to discern God's will and purpose for our lives. By presenting ourselves as living sacrifices, God renews our minds according to His purposes, which now become the filter for all that we say and do. As it says, this is our reasonable service for all that Christ has done for us. It's an exchanged life—His life working in us as we give ourselves sacrificially to Him.

We're not Entangled with the Affairs of the World

Our God is a jealous God as it says in the Book of James. He doesn't like it when we become too friendly with the world. In fact, He considers us enemies when we do so.

James 4:4-5 Adulterers and adulteresses! Do you not know that friendship with the world is enmity with God? Whoever therefore wants to be a friend of the world makes himself an enemy of God. ⁵Or do you think that the Scripture says in vain, "The Spirit who dwells in us yearns in jealousy"?

Because we're in this world but not of it, we're going to be touched by worldly things in one degree or another. It's when they interfere with our passion and calling that they become snares to us. When we become more passionate about worldly pursuits than seeking God and His kingdom, we are in danger of committing spiritual adultery. They then become idols and snares to us. If we lack passion towards God and his kingdom, we should ask ourselves, "What has stolen our passion?" This why the apostle John told us explicitly not to love the things of the world in his epistle.

1 John 2:15-17 Do not Love the world or the things of the world. If anyone loves the world, the love of the Father is not in Him. ¹⁶For all that is in the world; the lust of the flesh, the lust of the eyes, and the pride of life; is not of the Father but is of the world. ¹⁷And the world is passing away, and the lust of it; but He who does the will of God abides forever.

As people who have a passion and desire to be a part of all that God is doing, we can't afford to be tainted by the world. As soldiers of this great army, God is preparing; we can't afford to entangle ourselves with the affairs of the world. They're nothing more than spiritual affairs that lead us into spiritual adultery.

2 Timothy 2:1-4 You, therefore, my son, be strong in the grace that is in Christ Jesus. ²And the things you have heard from me among many witnesses, commit these to faithful men who will be able to teach others also. ³You, therefore, must endure hardship as a good soldier of Jesus Christ. **⁴No one engaged in warfare entangled himself with the affairs of this life that he may please him who enlisted him as a soldier.**

You will find, if you are not giving yourself to the purposes of God, your desires and affections will fall back to the world to the point where you are too entangled to adequately serve God and His purposes even if you wanted to. You will no longer be considered a useful vessel. You will need to get untangled before you can, once again, become a useful vessel.

Decisions in Life Take on a New Perspective

When your life is governed by a heart wholly committed to God and His purposes, your decisions and choices will be made from a kingdom perspective. You will base your choices in life on God's overall mission and destiny rather than your own selfish ambitions and desires for the moment. In other words, you are seeking first the kingdom of God in all things. By submitting your choices to God, you discover His blessings freely flow as He pours into you all things that pertain unto life and godliness. Because you have now sought Him with a whole heart, you submit to God, even the most mundane things as well as the major decisions of your life as you acknowledge Him in all your ways.

Matthew 6:33 But seek first the kingdom of God and His righteousness, and all these things will be added unto you.

Leading up to the above passage, Jesus exhorted His disciples not to worry about food, clothing or shelter.[283] As long as they sought the kingdom of God first, the Heavenly Father would take care of their needs. Seeking Jesus and His kingdom first is a primary attribute of kingdom people who desire to be used by God. When our lives are so weighed down by trying to make ends meet, we have very little time for the prophetic purposes of God. We must trust in His ability to take care of us as we give ourselves to tending to the Father's business.

Proverbs 19:21 (NIV) Many are the plans in a man's heart, but it is the Lord's purpose that prevails.

A person whose heart is committed entirely to the Lord will acknowledge God in all their ways, which is to submit ideas, plans, and

---

[283] Matthew 6:24-34

other things of importance unto Him. This is a wholehearted commitment.

Proverbs 3:5-6 *(NIV) Trust in the Lord with all your heart and lean not on your own understanding; in all your ways submit to him, and he will make your paths straight.*

Submission implies submitting to God and His ways continually as well as the opinions of others at times. In our relationship with the Lord, we must always keep in mind that His thoughts and ways are much higher than ours. He sees our lives from an eternal perspective that has already seen our future. He knows what's ahead and plans our ways accordingly. As we freely submit our ways unto Him, He's able to direct our steps accordingly. The more submitted we are, the more of His grace and excellence we will experience. We are also to clothe ourselves in humility as we submit to one another.

1 Peter 5:6 *Therefore humble yourselves under the mighty hand of God, that He may exalt you in due time.*

Not My Will, But God's Will in Times of Testing

We all go through seasons of testing when we find ourselves in the wilderness, so to speak. It's during these seasons the rubber hits the road. Jesus sets the example for all of us. During the most significant trial of His faith, He cried out, *"Take this cup away from Me; nevertheless, not what I will, but what You will."*[284] Not our will but His will should be the cry of our hearts during seasons of testing. Our response to trials and testings are what reveal the actual state of our hearts. It's during the trials of faith that we clearly see our level of commitment.

As Moses was leading the children of Israel through the wilderness on their way to the Promised Land, he explained the reason and purpose for going through the desert.

Deuteronomy 8:2-3 *And you shall remember that the Lord your God led you all the way these forty years in the wilderness, to humble you, and test you, to know what was in your heart, whether you would keep His commandments or not. ³So He humbled you, allowed you to hunger, and fed you with manna which you did not know nor did your fathers know, that He might make you know that man shall not live by bread alone, but man lives by every word that proceeds from the mouth of the Lord.*

As seen in the above passage, wilderness periods are for our benefit. They allow God to humble and strip away the pride in our lives. They

---

[284] Mark 14:36

reveal what's really in our hearts. It's during wilderness seasons that the self-deception we've been under peels away. We are able to see where we stand in relation to His standard of righteousness. Wilderness periods also help us to grow in faith as we experience His unusual provision. We come to depend on His word that proceeds from Him rather than our means of survival.

Without seasons in the wilderness, we would lack the necessary means to be all that God has called us to. Therefore James, the Lord's brother wrote, *"Count it all joy when you fall into various trials, knowing that the testing of your faith produces patience. But let patience have its perfect work, that you may be perfect and complete, lacking nothing."* [285]

Job is another premiere example of what it means to accept the trials and testings that come our way. He probably experienced more hardships than most of us will ever experience. He passed his tests of faith with flying colors because he treasured God's word more precious than his necessary food. His testimony is as follows:

> *Job 23:8-12 Look, I go forward, but He is not there, and backward, but I cannot perceive Him; [9]When He works on the left hand, I cannot behold Him; when He turns to the right hand, I cannot see Him. [10]But He knows the way I take; when He has tested me, I shall come forth as gold. [11]My foot has held fast to His steps; I have kept His way and not turned aside. [12]I have not departed from the commandments of His lips; I have treasured the words of His mouth more than my necessary food.*

This is a prophetic picture of what it's like to experience the dark nights of the soul we all enter at times. Just as Jesus cried out in the dark night of His soul, *"My God why have you forsaken me,"* we too will experience those moments when it appears that God has forsaken us. It's in our dark moments when we must walk by faith and not by sight, weighing the eternal weight of His glory in comparison to our momentary light affliction. [286] We must treasure His words more than our necessary food by putting one foot in front of the other while holding fast to His steps. As we come out of the darkness, an added dimension of faith comes our way as we go from faith to faith. [287]

May God bless and keep you as you hold fast to His steps while crying out, "Not my will, but His will."

---

[285] James 1:2-4
[286] 1 Corinthians 4:16-18
[287] Romans 1:17

Walk Circumspectly, Redeeming the Time

We are urged to be circumspect in all our ways with an understanding of God's will and purpose. We are to be like the sons of Issachar, who knew how to respond to their times and seasons. It's essential to have an ear to the ground so that we understand what prophetic season we are in.

Those who wholeheartedly seek God are given revelation and understanding of how He's working during a particular season. God doesn't do anything, without first revealing it to His prophets or those who have prophetic ears to hear.[288] As Jesus said on many occasions, *"He who has ears to hear, let him hear!"*

> **Ephesians 5:15-17** *See that you walk circumspectly, not as fools (foolish virgins) but as wise, (wise virgins) redeeming the time because the days are evil. Therefore, do not be unwise, but understand what the will of the Lord is.[289]*

The word circumspect is from the Greek word, *"akribos"* and means diligent or perfect. The Merriam Webster Dictionary defines it as careful to consider all circumstances and possible consequences: Prudent.

With this definition in mind, we must now apply it to all that God desires to do in and through us as we enter His prophetic purposes for our generation. We must be wise in all our dealings in life. We are to redeem our time by not squandering it away on worthless pursuits and things. It's as we turn our hearts from useless things that we are revived in God's purposes.

> **Psalm 119:37** *Turn my eyes from looking at worthless things and revive me in Your way.*

As we set our hearts, upon understanding what the will of the Lord is, which entails diligently seeking Him with all our hearts, we are revived in our destiny and purpose. It doesn't matter what our station is in life. Wherever the Lord has planted us, that's our field of harvest where we are to put our hands to the plow, while not looking back.[290] If you are a stay at home mom, tending your little ones, that's your field to plow in. If you are in the marketplace that's your field of harvest to understand what the will of the Lord is in all that you encounter; the list goes on.

No matter what our field of harvest is, we can't afford to squander our opportunities by being involved in trivial pursuits. We are to be like

---

[288] Amos 3:7
[289] Parentheses added by me
[290] Luke 9:62

the virtuous woman of Proverbs, who is a type of the bride of Christ. She was diligent in all her pursuits, as she willingly worked with her hands.

Fervency Level is Maintained Under all Circumstances

We must also consider the consequences when we don't follow hard after the Lord. No matter what season we are in, we must maintain our level of fervency. It's easy to be fervent when everything is going well. The hard question is, how do we respond to the seasons when nothing is going right? From the list, Paul gave in his letter to the Romans; he mentioned that we are not to lag in diligence, but rather to be fervent in our spirits.[291] Keep in mind, Paul's appeal to the Colossians as well, when he said, *"To this end I also labor, striving according to His working which works in me mightily."* [292] Paul went through many seasons that weren't all that pleasant, yet during the worst of them, he kept his level of fervency high. After almost being stoned to death on one occasion, he urged the disciples to continue in the faith, saying, *"We must through many tribulations enter the kingdom of God."* [293]

Our seasons of discomfort, probably, won't come close to what Paul experienced, yet we seem to give up so quickly. Amid trials and hardships, we tend to revert to worldly things to comfort our souls instead of remaining fervent in the spirit. As Paul wrote to young Timothy, we must endure hardships as good soldiers of Jesus Christ.[294] Those who are violent in their faith, no matter what their circumstances are the ones who will take the kingdom by force.[295]

The kingdom of God has been suffering violent attacks from the enemy of our faith in every arena of society known to humanity. It's time for God's people to rise in the midst all the turmoil and destruction Satan has caused. We are to take the kingdom by force with a fervency and zeal that will quell the enemy's devices. For this to happen, we must be fervent in the spirit under all circumstances. Let us be like Paul and strive according to His working which works mightily in us.

> *Ephesians 1:19-20 And what is the exceeding greatness of His power toward us who believe, according to the working of His mighty power [20]which He worked in Christ when He raised Him from the dead and seated Him at His right hand in the heavenly places.*

---

[291] Romans 12:11
[292] Colossians 1;29
[293] Acts 14:22
[294] 2 Timothy 2:3
[295] Matthew 11:12

People whose hearts are fully committed to God's purposes will rise in fervency to the challenge of being all that they can be in Christ with His power working in them mightily. May God bless you mightily as you rise to the challenge!

There's a Genuine Delight in Giving to God's Purposes

The giving our treasures or finances reveals the actual condition of our hearts and how committed we are to God's purposes in the earth. If we're praying, *"Your kingdom comes to earth as it is in heaven,"* we should be willing to give of our treasures to help finance it. Jesus advised us strongly about this as seen in the following passage.

Matthew 6:19-21 "Do not lay up for yourselves treasures on earth, where moth and rust destroy and where thieves break in and steal; [20]but lay up for yourselves treasures in Heaven, where neither moth nor rust destroys and where thieves do not break in and steal. [21]For where your treasure is, there your heart will also be."

David is an excellent example of someone who was so devoted to God's purposes that he gave over and above what he had initially intended. He had a genuine delight in giving to his Lord.

1 Chronicles 29:3 "Moreover, because I have set my affection on the house of my God, I have given to the house of my God, over and above all that I have prepared for the holy house, my own special treasure of gold and silver."

Notice that it says that David first set his affection on the house of the Lord. Setting his affection on God's house is what caused him to give so freely and generously. When we see the Church as a living entity rather than a building or an institution, we are able to set our affection and love upon it to a greater degree. God is looking for those who will set their affection on the house that Jesus is building, His Church. It's as we set our hearts on the house of the Lord that our hearts are entirely committed to His purposes in the earth.

One of the reasons the church is suffering so much in our day and age is that people don't understand what it means to have a real love for the Church Jesus is building. Many see it as an institution, where they come to be entertained and blessed. Their hearts are filled with a consumer mentality that wants to receive without giving, whereas Jesus said it is more blessed to give than to receive.[296] For where your treasure is, there will be your heart.[297]

Those who sow sparingly will not have much stored for future kingdom endeavors. They will find themselves without the necessary means to do what God may be asking them to do. To those who give generously, the Heavenly Father will fill their future with abundance to do whatever comes their way. Those who cast their bread upon the waters will find it in due time.[298] The truth is, we can't out-give God. No matter what season of life we're in, whether abasing or abounding, we are to give out of our abundance and poverty.[299] Giving out of our abundance and poverty is what continually puts us in position to be conduits of blessing prepared for every good work. The Lord can use us in all circumstances because we have learned to trust in His provision no matter what our state of being is.

> **Ecclesiastes 11:6** *in the morning sow your seed, and in the evening do not withhold your hand; for you do not know which will prosper, either this or that, or whether both alike will be good.*

> **2 Corinthians 9: 6-8** *But this I say: He who sows sparingly will also reap sparingly, and he who sows bountifully will also reap bountifully. [7]So let each one give as he purposes in his heart, not grudgingly or of necessity; for God loves a cheerful giver. [8]And God is able to make all grace abound toward you, that **you always** having all sufficiency in all things, **may have an abundance for every good work.***

The people who give abundantly, give out of hearts committed entirely and consecrated to God and His purposes. They'll always find themselves in position as vessels of honor, sanctified and useful for the Master, prepared for every good work.[300]

May God bless you mightily as you sow bountifully with joy into His kingdom purposes with hearts wholly committed to Him.

The following poem summarizes poetically what this chapter has been about.

---

[296] Acts 20:35
[297] Matthew 6:21
[298] Ecclesiastes 11:1-4
[299] Philippians 4:11-12
[300] 2 Timothy 2:21

Hearts Freely and Totally Committed

By Ken L. Birks © 2018 Straight Arrow Ministries

Saved according to God's purposes we're drawn.
Filled with excitement and wonder, we respond
With hearts engaged, we come with expectation.
Having tasted of His goodness, we commit to Him.
With hearts filled with hunger, we ask for more.

What is it that's required, we ask?
Hearts freely and totally committed; He responds.
What does that entail and what's the cost, we ask?
Hearts committed as living sacrifices; He responds.
With hearts filled with questions, we count the cost.

Looking down, He searches for those who seek.
Will we be those whom He finds, we wonder?
As we count the cost and fully commit, He finds.
Now ready to fully discover what's ahead, we engage.
With hearts fully set on His purposes, we rejoice.

With hearts fully engaged, we discover His gifts.
We learn to behave like Christians, walking in obedience.
We learn to be fervent in spirit, rejoicing in hope.
We learn to be patient in tribulation, counting it all joy.
We are sensitive to the needs of others, clinging to goodness.

No longer slaves to sin, we're untangled from worldly affairs.
With our decisions now based on kingdom realities, we rejoice.
No longer my will, but His will, we freely give generously.
Walking circumspectly, time is redeemed for His desires.
Freely and totally committed, we bask in His goodness.

Waiting on the Lord

Chapter Fourteen

As we continue to process all that is involved in making ourselves ready to be a part of the five wise virgin class of Christians, who become the bride of Christ, we must consider what it means to wait on the Lord. It's those who have learned how to properly wait on the Lord who mount up with the wings of an eagle to be preserved and protected in the wilderness during the great tribulation.

Isaiah 40:31 But those who wait on the Lord shall renew their strength; they shall mount up with the wings like eagles, they shall run and not be weary, they shall walk and not faint.

Revelation 12:14 But the woman was given two wings of a great eagle, that she might fly into the wilderness her place, where she is nourished for a time and times and a half a time, from the presence of the serpent.

Waiting on the Lord is essential in keeping our lamps full of oil so that we are ready to be taken away to the bridal chamber to await the coming of our bridegroom at His Second coming.

Waiting on the Lord encompasses prayer and much more. It's a life governed by the ongoing presence and work of the Holy Spirit. It's choosing to walk in step with all that the Father reveals to us through the Holy Spirit and His Son, Jesus Christ.

1 Corinthians 2:9-12 But as it is written: "Eye has not seen, nor ear heard, Nor have entered into the heart of man the things God has prepared for those who love Him." [10]But God has revealed them to us through His Spirit. For His Spirit searches all things, yes, the deep things of God. [11]For what man knows the things of a man except the spirit of man which is in Him? Even so, no one knows the things of God except the Spirit of God. [12]Now we have received, not the spirit of the world, but the Spirit who is from God, that we might know the things that have been freely given to us by God.

As seen in the passage above, waiting on the Lord involves embracing with a heart of expectation all that God has freely given to us, which includes all things, even the deep stuff. He's given us the mind of Christ

167

so that we may know these things.[301] We have the same mentality that Christ possessed when He was on earth.

What's Involved in Waiting on the Lord?

Many of us are still operating from our carnal minds and perspectives, rather than allowing ourselves to be spiritually minded. The Holy Spirit must transform our minds before we can wait on the Lord in a manner that fills us with supernatural strength and supernatural abilities. We see this again in Peter's second epistle.

> *2 Peter 1:2-4 Grace and peace be multiplied to you in the knowledge of God and of Jesus our Lord, ³as His divine power has given to us all things that pertain to life and godliness, through the knowledge of Him who called us by glory and virtue, ⁴by which have been given to exceedingly great and precious promises, that through these **you may be partakers of the divine nature**, having escaped the corruption that is in the world through lust.*

In Paul's letter to the church at Ephesus, he, once again, shares this thought of being filled with the revelation and knowledge of Christ or the divine nature of God. Getting our minds renewed with the Father's divine nature is one of the reasons the Holy Spirit has been given—so that He can fill us with new perspectives that bring us into the exceeding greatness of His power and divine abilities.

> *Ephesians 1:17-20 That the God of our Lord Jesus Christ, the Father of Glory, may give you the spirit of wisdom and revelation in the knowledge of Him, ¹⁸the eyes of your understanding being enlightened; that you may know the hope of His calling, what are the riches of the glory of His inheritance of the saints, ¹⁹and what is the exceeding greatness of His power toward us, according to the working of His mighty power ²⁰which He worked in Christ when He raised Him from the dead and seated Him at His right hand in the heavenly places.*

Believing and Confessing

Let me ask you a question. On a daily basis, are you experiencing the exceeding greatness of the power of the Holy Spirit—the same power that raised Christ from the dead? Probably not. I know I'm not. It's His will and desire towards all of us. We may experience it in varying degrees at times, but for the most part, we're still lacking. Why is that? Could it be that we don't fully believe to the point we're fully convinced

---

[301] 1 Corinthians 2:16

in the same manner that Abraham was? He was entirely convinced, without wavering at the promise through unbelief of what God had promised. He believed God was able to perform on his behalf.[302] Being fully convinced is the kind of faith we must possess if we are to fulfill what it means to wait on the Lord.

Paul also walked in the faith of Abraham. His confession of faith was based on what he believed rather than the doubts and uncertainties that may have risen in his heart from time to time. His confession was, *"And since we have the same spirit of faith, according to what is written, 'I believed, and therefore I spoke,' we also believe and therefore speak."*[303]

When faith is based on the covenant promises God has given to us through His word rather than a list of failed experiences, we grow from faith to faith. We must speak and confess according to His word rather than our experiences. His word says He has given us all things that pertain to life and godliness. We must believe and therefore speak as Paul did. When we believe and speak according to God's ability and sufficiency rather than our sufficiency's, faith is released.

What is it that God has called you to do? It's through the communication or the sharing of our faith that it becomes effective. As we share or confess to others the acknowledgment of every good thing we have in Christ Jesus, we grow and mature in our faith and calling. Instead of communicating with others all the negatives of life, we must change our pattern of communication to those things we believe, have, and are in Christ.

Philemon 1:6 *that the sharing of your faith may become effective by the acknowledgment of every good thing which is in you in Christ Jesus.*

Acknowledging God in all our Ways

Waiting on the Lord involves acknowledging God in all our ways as we put our complete trust in Him. To recognize Him in all our ways, means we submit to Him in everything.

Proverbs 3:5-6 *Trust in the Lord with all your heart and lean not on your own understanding. ⁶In all your ways acknowledge Him (submit to Him – NIV), and He shall direct your paths. (He will make your paths straight – NIV)*

To recognize and submit to the Lord in all our ways involves those things we do every day, over and over. It's when we learn not to lean on

---

[302] Romans 4:20-22
[303] 2 Corinthians 4:13

our own understanding with the simple stuff that His divine nature becomes a part of how we think and respond.

In Peter's first epistle, he said we must gird up the loins of our minds and be sober.[304] We must learn to think and respond soberly in all that we do. As we do, when the significant trials of life hit us, our minds will be adequately trained and conditioned to respond in ways that glorify our Father in heaven. As a result, our paths are continually directed into His perfect will for our lives. It's when we fail to submit our paths unto Him that our way forward becomes a crooked path leading us into places that are not part of the Father's will and purpose for our lives.

Jesus is a perfect example of what it means to acknowledge God in all our ways, without leaning on our own understanding. There are many examples of how vital waiting on His Heavenly Father was to Jesus. One example is when Jesus called His disciples to Him after spending all night in prayer. He then chose His twelve apostles.[305]

Another example was the healing of Peter's mother-in-law when the whole city gathered at His door as He healed many who were sick and cast out many demons. Following this extraordinary time of ministry, He rose up very early the next morning to find a place of seclusion, where He could be alone with His Father. His disciples, wondering where He had disappeared to, sought Him out and found Him in prayer. They wanted Him to come back and continue ministering to the people because they were all waiting for Him.[306] Instead of staying to minister and leaning on His own understanding, which would've been the most logical thing to do, He was ready to move on after taking the time to wait on His Father. His reply to them was, *"Let us go into the next towns that I may preach there also because for this purpose I have come forth."*

Just as Jesus renewed His purpose and mission after spending time in prayer, waiting on His Father, it should be with us. So often we go about our days without having our purpose renewed. It's as we spend time in the word and prayer each day that God often reminds us of our purpose and mission for the day.

Hearing God's Voice and Praying Without Ceasing

Our relationship with God is a two-way conversation. Jesus said, His sheep hear his voice.[307] God desires to speak to us as much as we need to talk to Him. In short, waiting on God is as much about listening to the

---

[304] 1 Peter 1:13
[305] Luke 6:12-13
[306] Mark 1:29-38
[307] John 10:27

voice of the Holy Spirit as it's about presenting our petitions to the Lord. The life of Jesus shows us how His time in prayer included both aspects while waiting on the Father for specific instructions and ministry. Jesus also had extended seasons of prayer. We must have these extended seasons of waiting on the Lord as well so that we receive the direction and wisdom we need for our pilgrimage.

We are also urged to pray without ceasing.[308] What does that mean? Obviously, we need to spend time in prayer communicating to Him our needs, concerns, and intercession but it also involves listening to the various ways in which the Holy Spirit speaks to us. The Holy Spirit speaks to us in many ways, such as dreams, visions, circumstances, through the word, prophecy, and even the audible voice at times. Praying without ceasing includes our petitions and all the ways the Holy Spirit speaks as we keep our minds and hearts stayed on Him. Perfect peace comes to those who keep their hearts and minds stayed on the Lord.[309]

As we wait on the Lord, we must continually process and meditate on all the ways mentioned above. The more we begin to step out in faith, no matter how slight the tug may be, the more we become in tune with the way in which the Holy Spirit speaks to our spirits. His voice is a still small voice, barely detectable at times.[310] When God began to speak to Samuel and Elijah with a still small voice, they had to respond before they could hear the fullness of the message the Lord had for them.[311]

Too often our minds and hearts are so cluttered with worthless things; it's difficult to detect the still small voice of God. We must train our hearts and gird up the loins of our minds to hear the Shepherd of our souls as He speaks. As we understand and respond in faith, we grow from faith to faith. With our strength in God renewed, we mount up with the wings of an eagle to soar to new heights in Him as we find ourselves seated in heavenly places and seeing our lives from His perspective.[312]

Our Ministry to God and Others

The final aspect I want to mention concerning waiting on God is our ministry to Him and those around us. Just as a waiter or waitress in a restaurant waits on tables, so it is as we wait on the Lord.

1 Peter 4:9-11 Be hospitable to one another without grumbling. [10]As each one has received a gift, minister it to one another, as good stewards

---

[308] 1 Thessalonians 5:17
[309] Isaiah 26:3
[310] I Kings 19:11-12
[311] 1 Samuel 3:1-21, 1 Kings 19:13-18
[312] Ephesians 2:6

of the manifold grace of God. [11] If anyone speaks, let him speak as the oracles of God. If anyone ministers, let him do it with the ability which God supplies, that in all things God may be glorified through Jesus Christ, to whom belong the glory and the dominion forever and ever. Amen.

God has given to each one of us gifts that come forth from His great treasure house. Our part is to discover the gifts that have been freely given to us so that we can faithfully impart to others what we have received. As we are attentive to the needs and concerns of others in the same way a waitress or a waiter is when they are waiting on tables, we are able to put all our selfish ambitions aside to be entirely devoted to those we are ministering to. As we esteem their needs more important than ours, the purity of our gifting in God comes forth as His oracles and ability. His divine ability will flow uninterrupted as we apply ourselves as conduits of His manifold grace.

Waiting on God in the manner of serving others is integral in bringing the body of Christ into the fullness of the stature of Jesus Christ. As we are faithful to allow the blessings of God to flow freely in all things from one vessel to another, God is glorified. His body then experiences His strength and nourishment flowing through all the joints, which causes the practical working of His body with every part doing their share. This is what causes the body to grow as we determine to speak the truth in love to one another as oracles of God.[313]

May God's blessings mightily take hold of all our lives as we press into being all that He has ordained us to be.

---

[313] Ephesians 4:15-16

Waiting on the Lord

by Ken L. Birks © 2018 Straight Arrow Ministries

Waiting on the Lord, our lamps are kept fully lit.
With strength and vitality, we press on to outwit.
Into spiritual realms unknown, He takes us, fully abandoned.
Mounting up with the wings of an eagle, we don't faint.
Governed by the Spirit, we're free to soar without constraint.

With hearts of expectation, we embrace all that is decreed.
As the Spirit searches the Father's heart, we're replenished.
With the divine nature imparted, perspectives in life change.
As we wait on the Lord, He generously pours into our hearts.
With the mind of Christ, exceeding greatness is known in all parts.

As we believe and confess, faith arises to meet expectations.
Acknowledging God in all our ways, He directs our aspirations.
Fully convinced of His promises, we wait on Him who performs.
Trusting in Him, we wait as He brings to pass our desires.
Submitting our souls, paths are made straight for what He requires.

With an ear to His voice, we listen and wait as He instructs.
In presenting our prayers and petitions, He listens and conducts.
Praying without ceasing, our minds are stayed on Him.
With a still small voice, He whispers in our ears, His secrets.
Responding to His whispering, we go from faith to faith as zealots.

As we wait on Him, gifts arrive for serving and ministry.
Being attentive to the needs of others, we wait in symmetry.
With selfish ambitions set aside, we minister, accordingly.
In serving and waiting on others, grace flows in new dimensions.
Ready to soar to new heights, we wait on Him who strengthens.

Your Place and Function of Ministry

Chapter Fifteen

The Father desires to give each of us our very own seat at His table. He fills His table with excellent spiritual foods that contains everything we could possibly need in this life—all things that pertain unto life and godliness.[314] It's from this seat that we are nourished and encouraged to go forth fulfilling the Father's prophetic purposes. However, it's our responsibility to discover which seat belongs to us. Because He's intimately acquainted with our ways, He's fashioned our place to fit perfectly with who He has created us to be. David's testimony below gives us this understanding and hope.

> *Psalm 139:3,14-16 You comprehend my path and my lying down and are acquainted with all my ways. [14]I will praise You, for I am fearfully and wonderfully made; marvelous are your works, and my soul knows this very well. [15]My frame was not hidden from You when I was made in secret and skillfully wrought in the lowest parts of the earth. [16]***Your eyes saw my substance, being yet unformed, and in Your book, they all were written, the days fashioned for me when as yet there were none of them.*** [17]How precious are your thoughts to me, O God!*

The above passage is a powerful statement of God's plans and purposes concerning His involvement with us. As stated earlier in the book, when we are born again, we are saved according to His purposes. We then enter His predestinated plans for our lives, even though we always have a free will to do whatever we want. When we choose to die on a daily basis, we walk according to the plans and purposes that are written in His book.

When we are stubborn and fail to submit to His plans, we are unable to partake of the blessings that come from being willing and obedient.[315] Thankfully, God is a God of mercy and forgiveness, which causes our crooked ways to be straightened as we repent and return to His predestinated purposes.

---

[314] 2 Peter 1:3
[315] Isaiah 1:18-19

We have seen throughout this book, the Father's will is to make us flames of fire, who are to go forth fulfilling His prophetic purposes on the earth. As we consider all that is needed in partnering with the Holy Spirit, we must recognize the importance of discovering our gifts, talents, and passion that fit into the place of ministry the Father has carved out for us. Spiritual gifts are part of the keys to the kingdom that allow us to be all that God has destined for us. The Psalmist wrote, *"We were skillfully brought forth to fit into God's divine plans. All of our days were fashioned by Him while our substance was being formed in the womb."* [316] He gives us spiritual gifts to make this so.

Those who have learned to wait on the Lord as discussed in the previous chapter will come into alignment with the plans and purposes to which they were created. God looks down from heaven above and sees those who understand how they were created and designed for His plans and purposes.[317] It takes all kinds of individuals with their distinctive gifts, personalities, innate abilities, and positions in life to bring His prophetic purposes into play. A mother at home, raising her children or a construction worker is just as strategically involved as a person in the marketplace or an ordained minister, who is in full-time ministry. We are to live as called no matter what our station in life is.[318] If we are to be used by God for His purposes, we must be faithful to where He has strategically planted us.

It would be challenging to be useful vessels of honor without an understanding of how we fit into the whole of God's plans and purposes. As the prophecy of Joel mentioned, we are to walk in step with who God created us to be without pushing or shoving as we allow Him to fit and frame us together with one another. Walking in step with God and others can only be accomplished by knowing who we are in Christ as we operate in our gifts and callings. In doing so, we're appropriately placed and positioned where He's positioned us.

1 Corinthians 12:18 But now God has set the members, each one of them, in the body as He pleased.

Knowing that God has placed us as it has pleased Him, helps us to accept our placement in the body of Christ. It's God who establishes and puts us in positions of ministry. Remember, it's the saints who do the work of the ministry, not just those who are in ordained positions. Because God is intimately acquainted with all our ways, He knows

---

[316] Psalm 139:13-16 Paraphrased by me
[317] 1 Chronicles 16;9
[318] 1 Corinthians 7:17

exactly where we should be and how we are to function. It's our responsibility to discover who we are in Christ, what our gifts and ministries are, and how we fit into the scheme of the whole. As we ultimately surrender and submit to His will and purpose in humility, we discover what our gifts and callings are, which enables us to know our positions and purpose.

The Father desires to send us forth with His zeal passionately burning within us, but first, we must be in our designated positions. Otherwise, we won't be connected to the whole as we should with His anointing uninterrupted. When we're knitted and framed together with each part doing its share, the body will come into the fullness of the stature of Christ, fulfilling all the prophetic purposes before the Second coming of our Lord and Savior.[319]

Innate Abilities and Placement in the Body

As you begin to ponder what your position in life is, and how you are to be fitted and framed into the body of Christ, there are things to be considered. First, what are your talents or innate abilities? Make a list of all those things that you do well at—those things that come easily to you. When God created you, He gave you some innate abilities. Keep in mind that God always has a purpose in mind when He does something. As seen in the opening passage of Scripture to this chapter, God fearfully and wonderfully creates each one of us.

Movement of God Changes During Seasons of Life

Throughout our lives, we continually discover our innate abilities. As we approach different seasons in life, the movement of God changes, which often requires new skills that are yet to be determined. When we are genuinely walking with God and submitting to His ways, these capabilities seem to appear unannounced as you stand in wonder, thinking, "Where did that come from?" I'm convinced God prepares us for every new season that comes our way as we are faithful to wait on Him without leaning on our understanding.

Because we belong to God, we are His workmanship. He knows all things, past, present, and future as He prepares us for all the good works that will come forth from our new seasons. He will take things from your past and mesh them together with the future.

---

[319] Ephesians 4:13,16, 2:21

Ephesians 2:10 For we are His workmanship, created in Christ Jesus for good works, which God prepared beforehand so that we should walk in them.

As I have entered semi-retirement with new seasons coming upon me, I have experienced new innate abilities that have been lying dormant within me. What you're now reading is my third book. Before my first book, I had no idea that I had a talent for writing. I remember exactly how it happened. As I was waiting on the Lord in my usual way, the Lord prompted me with a gentle urge to write my life story. I immediately got my computer out and began to write. I was surprised at how comfortable and enjoyable it was. What was even more surprising was that I was able to recall and remember in detail events that had transpired over 40 years ago.[320]

The reality is, we all have creative abilities that are still unlocked. They're waiting to unfold. If we ignore them, we'll miss out on vital pieces that are needed to unlock the future that awaits us. They're talents that need to be integrated as we move forward in the grace of God for all that He has called us to be. It's been said, *"There is a gold mine hidden in every life."*[321] It's our responsibility to dig for the gold that's hidden away. No one can do it for us.

In writing my second book, I discovered all the study I'd put into over the past 40 years as a pastor and Bible teacher; God wanted to unearth in writing. God was now adding a new dimension to the innate abilities or talents He had given me to express the passion that consumes me.[322] My primary position in the body of Christ as a teacher remains, but the methods and movement of God in communicating the gift have changed.

In this past year and a half, I've begun writing biblical devotional poetry. Again, this came out of nowhere. One morning during my regular devotional time, I was watching the squirrels running and playing on our neighbor's rooftop. I heard the gentle whisper of the Lord say, "Why don't you write a poem about it." The poem was titled, "Looking out my Window."[323] Up until then, I'd never given a thought to writing poetry but decided to obey and begin writing. Again, I was amazed at how easy and enjoyable it was. Since then I have written over 50 biblical

---

[320] The Adventures of Space and Hobo can be found at the following website: www.booksbyken.com

[321] Quote from E.W. Kenyon

[322] The Journey – Discovering the Invisible Path can be found at the following website: www.booksbyken

[323] http://straitarrow.net/devotional-poetry/window.htm

devotional poems. After completing this book, I will be writing a devotional book based on those poems.[324] One of the things I love about this ability is that I'm able to submit my poetry to all kinds of online poetry groups, especially those which are secular. I have one secular group where I am referred to as the pastor of the group. It's an excellent opportunity to allow the light of the gospel to shine in some dark places. Most of these groups have thousands of followers with some over 100,000. I also love the idea of taking biblical concepts and presenting them in a concise manner that communicates God's will and purpose.

I still have much to learn about writing, but knowing God continually prepares us for every new season, brings much peace, contentment, and fulfillment when the circumstances of our lives change dramatically.

Spiritual Gifts and Divine Abilities

Not only do we have innate abilities given to us by our Creator, but we also have supernatural abilities He gives as spiritual gifts. The spiritual gifts we receive also help to define our place in the body of Christ.

Spiritual gifts are for manifesting Christ's presence with power in our domain of activity as seen in the following passage of Scripture.

*1 Corinthians 12:4-7 There are diversities of gifts, but the same spirit. [5]There are differences of ministries, but the same Lord, [6]and there are diversities of activities, but it is the same God who **works** in all. [7]But the **manifestation** of the Spirit is given to each one for the profit of all.*

In the above passage, the word "works" means active operation, effectual, powerful, to be active, efficient, fervent, and to be mighty in showing forth. The word "manifestation" means to make visible, clear and known. The actual meaning according to Vine's Greek Dictionary is to uncover, lay bare or reveal.

With these two definitions in mind, we can see it's God's desire for us to be fervent and mighty in showing forth and making His power visible through the gifts of the Spirit. As members of His body, we are to be zealous, active, effectual, efficient and powerful in manifesting the gifts of the Spirit for the benefit of the body as a whole.

In 1 Corinthians 12 and Romans 12, Paul lists most of the gifts of the Spirit. My purpose here is not to list and define all the gifts, but rather to make you aware that they are freely available to you. There are many books available to you about spiritual gifts. I would encourage you to

---

[324] You can find all 40 poems at the following website:
www.straitarrow.net/devotional-poetry

avail yourself of them for further understanding. I have a whole chapter dedicated to discovering your spiritual gifts in my book, "The Journey — Discovering the Invisible Path." You can purchase it through Amazon, Barnes and Noble, iBooks, and other media outlets.

God Releases His Power through Spiritual Gifts

Through the gifts of the Spirit, God releases His power. Just as the world needed to see displays of God's power throughout the ages, it's equally important today. Today's world is in as much decay and degeneration as it has been at any time in history. It needs to experience an impressive display of God's power and anointing. Otherwise, it's going to be carried away by the tide of violence and wickedness that is currently sweeping through nations of the world. The church—the body of Christ, is to be the pillar and ground of all truth—a city set on a hill with its lights brightly shining for all to see.[325]

It's up to us as His body to rise and be all that God has ordained in this critical hour of the church's destiny. Without the gifts of the Spirit operating in our lives, it will never happen. However, there's hope because God is in the process of positioning each of us to be a part of the end time anointing that will sweep the world as we allow His gifts to emerge in our lives. [326]

We are to Desire Spiritual Gifts

Ephesians 4:7 But to each one of us grace was given according to the measure of Christ's gift.

The manifestation of the Spirit, through the gifts, is freely given to us for the profit of all. We are encouraged strongly to desire spiritual gifts.[327] We are all given a measure of the Spirit that was in Christ with a measure of faith to go along with it. Having then gifts differing according to the grace given to us, we are to use them as the following passages of Scripture so adequately encourage us to do.

*Romans 12:5-6 so we, being many, are one body in Christ, and individually members of one another. Having then gifts differing according to the grace that is given to us, **let us use them.***

1 Peter 4:10 As each one has received a gift, minister it to one another, as good stewards of the manifold grace of God.

---

[325] 2 Timothy 3:15 & Matthew 5:14
[326] 1 Corinthians 4:20
[327] 1 Corinthians 14:1

Notice that it says, *"As each one has received a gift according to the grace given to us, we are to use them by ministering one to another."* We are good stewards of the manifold grace of God when we take to heart the admonition to discover and develop the gift or gifts freely given to us. As we do, we make contributions to the whole, which will have an effect on the world around us.

The gifts of God come much more natural to us than the fruit of the Spirit because they're freely given to us. The character of God must be worked in our lives as it confronts our will, which can be stubborn at times. We should not be afraid to ask God for whatever gifts we like. He says, *"Earnestly desire the best gifts."*[328] What are the best gifts? They're the ones that are designed to fit your passion. The Father delights in giving us gifts, so It's quite right to ask for more than one gift. Once we pray and ask the Father for the gift, we should have a heart of expectancy to receive.

Practice is Essential

As you receive, you must begin to practice the gifts as Paul told the Romans in his letter to them. He said, *"Let us use them."* We should look for every opportunity to use the spiritual gifts we have desired. The two gifts I operate in the most are prophecy and teaching. As a young Christian, I looked for every opportunity I could find to be used in those gifts. As a result, I have become very proficient in them.

Our spiritual gifts are needed to help the body come to the stature of the fullness of Christ. As we're faithful to minister to one another, we add dimensions of faith to those whom we are serving, as well as our own. As we're committed to doing so, we add to the increase and growth of the body.

May God bless you and use you mightily as the manifestation of His Spirit becomes visible to those to whom you minister.

Servanthood and Placement in the Body

One of the most critical ways of discovering our place of ministry is found through serving. It's one of the keys to the kingdom that enables us to determine our placement. In any given expression of the body of Christ, there are numerous places to serve. We are all called to be servants, no matter what our gifts and talents are. Servanthood offers us the opportunities to express the gifts He's freely given. If you already

---

[328] 1 Corinthians 12:31

know what your spiritual gift is, look for places where you can use your gift. Otherwise, look for a ministry that you feel passionate about.

As we get involved in serving in various ministry opportunities, we experience God working in and through us as He gives us the grace to do multiple tasks and ministry purposes. We begin to sense our calling and purpose and where we're best fitted. Serving and Ministry take us into a deeper relationship with Jesus Christ as the Holy Spirit communicates to us the Father's heart and desire in all that we do. As the Holy Spirit leads us to greater revelations of grace, work, and ministry the Father has for us, He shows us our place at His table.

May the blessing of God be in your life as you prepare to be a useful vessel in the Father's house by discovering your place and ministry at the Father's table.

Dining at the Father's Table

by Ken L. Birks © 2018 Straight Arrow Ministries

Unformed, our days are fashioned when they were nonexistent.
Filled with questions, we search for answers concerning existence.
With exquisite spiritual food set, the Father invites us to His table.
As we come in His presence to dine, we ponder where to recline.
He fills us with answers to the mysteries of life as we dine.

Finding our place, nourished and encouraged, hearts are set free.
Responding in faith to His invitation, we exult with glee.
Saved according to His purposes, we go forth with free will.
Embracing the cross with death to self, we fully embrace His will.
Like flames of fire, He empowers us to minister to fulfill.

With discovery, His gifts bring us to deeper levels of perceptions.
Intimately acquainted with our ways, the Father positions.
In the place fashioned by Him, He knows what gifts are needed.
He seats us accordingly as we're fitted and framed into place.
From our chosen place at the table, He sends us in His grace.

As seasons come and go, gifts continue to unlock the future.
Creative abilities once locked are unlocked as ministries evolve.
As we continue to dine with Him, He abundantly supplies.
No longer worried what the future holds, we go forth in His love.
Oh, what a pleasure to continually dine at the Father's table.

Embracing the Fear of God

Chapter Sixteen

In this section, the discussion has been about the essential elements of our faith that are needed in our preparation to be a part of all that God is doing that must be fulfilled before Jesus returns. These are the characteristics that will make us useful vessels as we serve the prophetic purposes of God for our generation as David and others throughout biblical history have done.

Another essential aspect we must discuss is that of embracing the fear of the Lord. As quoted in the book of Proverbs, *"The fear of God is the beginning of wisdom."* If we are to be wise in the ways of God, it begins by embracing the fear of the Lord.

Psalm 90:11-12 (NIV) If only we knew the power of your anger! Your wrath is as great as the fear that is your due. Teach us to number our days, that we may gain a heart of wisdom

Proverbs 9:10 The fear of the Lord is the beginning of wisdom, and the knowledge of the Holy is understanding.

Notice in the above Scripture, a direct correlation is made between the fear of the Lord and the knowledge of the Holy, which brings understanding. The fear of the Lord is designed to bring us into deeper realms of intimacy with our Lord and Savior. Without the intimacy that comes from fearing God, our bridegroom won't know us in the way He desires. Therefore, we must embrace the fear of God with all our hearts.

There is much to say concerning the fear of the Lord throughout the Bible. Moses said we are required by God to fear Him and walk in His ways.[329] David said God is to be greatly feared in the congregation of His saints.[330] Solomon said the whole duty of man is to fear God and keep His commandments.[331] Isaiah said we are to sanctify the Lord and let Him be our fear.[332] Jesus said we are to fear Him who can destroy our

---

[329] Deuteronomy 10:12
[330] Psalm 89:7
[331] Ecclesiastes 12:13
[332] Isaiah 8:13

185

soul in Hell.[333] Paul said we are to work out our salvation in fear and trembling. Peter said we are to pass our time of sojourning in fear.[334] The writer of the book of Hebrews said it's a fearful thing to fall into the hands of a living God.[335]

With all these great heroes of our faith including Jesus exhorting us to fear God, it's a wonder we don't consistently hear this message from pulpits throughout the world. It's a message Satan doesn't want us to understand. It seems all we're hearing is the message of the goodness of God. Paul spoke of the goodness and the severity of God. When the goodness of God is preached and taught without equal time to the severity of God, there's a significant absence in the knowledge of the Holy which leads to licentiousness—a lack of restraint that produces lewd and lawless behavior.

> **Jude 1:4** *For certain men have crept in unnoticed, who long ago were marked out for this condemnation, ungodly men, who turn the grace of our God into licentiousness and deny the only Lord God and our Lord Jesus Christ.*

Vines Expository dictionary defines licentiousness or lasciviousness as excess, the absence of restraint, indecency, and wantonness. Webster's dictionary defines it as lewd and lawless behavior. Other words to describe this behavior are debauched, promiscuous, carnal, lustful, indecent, obscene and smutty. This is what happens when one takes the grace of God and uses it as a license to sin.

> **Romans 6:1-2** *what shall we say then? Shall we continue in sin that grace may abound? ²Certainly not! How shall we who died to sin live any longer in it?*

Licentious behavior is what will lead to those of the unwise virgin class accepting the mark of the beast during the great tribulation period, thus blaspheming the Holy Spirit and being eternally damned to hell forever. It's the fear of the Lord with a knowledge of the Holy that gives us the understanding that prevents this from ever happening.

The fear of the Lord is designed to keep us from sinning and turning the grace of God into licentious behavior as Moses warned the children of Israel.

---

[333] Matthew 10:28
[334] 1 Peter 1:17
[335] Hebrews 10:31

Exodus 20:20 Moses said to the people, "Do not be afraid. God has come to test you so that the fear of God will be with you to keep you from sinning."

What is the Fear of the Lord?

As we have seen, the fear of God is the beginning of wisdom, but what does that involve? To begin with, it involves having awesome respect and awe for who God is in His sovereignty, majesty, and power. However, it also entails much more as we consider how it affects our walk with Him. It's something that needs to be embraced with all our hearts, minds, and souls as we seek to be all that God has called us to be.

The fear of God found in the Old Testament Scriptures is derived from two Hebrew words — *"Yir'ah and 'Yare."* These two words mean to tremble at His presence with fear, dread and terror as we stand in awe of a God, who placed the sand as a boundary for the sea, though the waves roar, and are unable to pass over it.

Jeremiah 5:22 "Do you not fear Me? Says the Lord. 'Will you not tremble at my presence, Who have placed the sand as the bound of the sea, by a perpetual decree, that it cannot pass beyond it? And though its waves toss to and fro, yet they cannot prevail; though they roar, yet they cannot pass over it.'"

In this passage, the prophet is rebuking the people of Israel for not standing in an awesome reverence and fear of God that should cause them to tremble at His presence because of His unlimited and creative power. David said something very similar as seen in the following passage.

Psalm 2:11-12 Serve the Lord with fear and rejoice with trembling. [12]Kiss the Son, lest, lest He be angry, and you perish in the way when His wrath is kindled but a little. Blessed be all those who put their trust in Him.

In today's Christian culture, the fear of God is often watered down when it comes to trembling in His presence. It settles for a sense of awe and respect, but the fear of God goes beyond that. We tend to leave out His severe side. The truth of the matter is, we must embrace His severe side and tremble before a God, who has the power to cast our souls into hell for eternity. The writer of the Book of Hebrews bears this thought out as well in the following passage.

Hebrews 12:28-29 Therefore, since we are receiving a kingdom which cannot be shaken, let us have grace, by which we may serve God acceptably with reverence and godly fear. [29]*For our God is a consuming fire.*

It would be impossible to fully appreciate the good news of the gospel of Jesus Christ without a comprehensive understanding of all that the fear of God entails. We must fully consider the dread and terror of the Lord as well as having an awesome sense of reverence and respect for who He is. We must see Him as perfectly holy and righteous in His severity and goodness as He becomes involved with us as we work out our salvation in fear and trembling.

> **Philippians 2:12-13** *Therefore, my beloved, as you have always obeyed, not as in my presence only, but now much more in my absence, work out your own salvation with fear and trembling;* [13]*for it is God who works in you both to will and do for it is His good pleasure.*

We are urged to tremble at God's word, which would mean having high regard for it. It's as we take the time to read and commit to applying the truths contained therein that we experience more of an intimate understanding of who He is and what He desires from us.

The amazing thing from the above passage is that it's God who works in us to change our will to embrace Him in fear and trembling. This is what helps our free will to be connected to His sovereign purposes. His sovereignty meets with our free will to get the job done.

Fearing God Embraces His Ongoing Presence

God is always watching us, even when His presence is not sensed. He continually examines every thought and motive, as well as the words and actions that pass before Him. When we're continually aware of His ongoing presence, we are much more careful with our secret thoughts, words, and actions, knowing that everything eventually comes to light. We must take all of this into account as we sojourn in fear.

> **Proverbs 5:21** *(NIV) For your ways are in full view of the Lord, and he examines all your paths.*

> **Luke 8:17** *For nothing is secret that will not be revealed, nor anything hidden that will not be known and come to light.*

> **Matthew 12:35-37** *A good man out of the good treasure of his heart brings forth good things and an evil man out of the evil treasure brings forth evil things.* [36]*But I say to you that for every idle word men may speak; they will give an account of it in the day of judgment.* [37]*For by your words you will be justified, and by your words, you will be condemned.*

The above passages should bring soberness to us as we realize God hears all our secret thoughts and knows the motives of our hearts towards Him and others. We are instinctively concerned about what others think of us. However, we should be more concerned about what pleases our Father in heaven as He evaluates our thoughts, words, actions, attitudes, and motives.

Luke 12:3 Therefore whatever you have spoken in the dark will be heard in the light, and what you have spoken in the ear in inner rooms will be proclaimed on housetops.

The Fear of the Lord Embraces God's Hatred of Sin

God has shown throughout the Old and New Testaments His hatred for sin. He sees sin as something that goes against the grain of all that He has destined for those who follow Him. God sees the destruction it causes. It's sin that gives birth to all the evil in the world, which causes the breakdown of cultures, resulting in the decay of all that He created. Therefore, He expects us to have a hatred for sin and evil in the same way that He does.

Proverbs 8:13 The fear of the Lord is to hate evil; pride and arrogance and the evil way.

Psalm 97:10 You who love the Lord, hate evil! He preserves them out of the hand of the wicked.

Romans 12:9 Let love be without hypocrisy. Abhor that which is evil. Cling to that which is good.

God's desire towards us is that we would fear Him by hating sin and evil so that we can live in harmony with His standard of righteousness. In this way, we can honor Him in all that we do.

It's important to keep in mind as Niki Gumbel reminds us, "God's hatred is not like ours: it contains no element of spite, pettiness or hypocrisy – but it is the reaction of the altogether holy and loving God to sin. His anger is his loving and holy hostility to evil."[336]

To Fear God is to Embrace His Discipline

Once we are saved and born again, it doesn't take very long to realize we still have foolish and sinful ways God needs to deal with. God has ways of dealing with them through His discipline by bringing these areas to the forefront of our lives.

---

[336] Quote from Niki Gumbel, author of Bible in one Year 2019.

Hebrews 12:5-8 And have you forgotten the exhortation which speaks to you as sons: My son do not despise the chastening of the Lord, nor be discouraged when you are rebuked by Him; ^{6}for whom the Lord loves, He chastens, and scourges every son whom He receives. ^{7}If you endure chastening, God deals with you as sons; for what son is there whom a father does not chasten.

God's chastening comes in various ways. It may be through His gentle voice revealing areas in our lives He desires to be changed. His chastening could also come through adverse circumstances that occur because of reaping what we've sown. Chastening could come from a brother or sister in the Lord, pointing out something that is destructive to our well-being or it may be someone over you in the Lord, pointing out something that is not only hurtful to you, but to those around you. Nevertheless, we all need to open our hearts and spirits to the examination of the Lord by giving Him permission to correct us.

We should be like David who said, *"Search me, O God, and know my heart; try me and know my anxieties and see if there is any wicked or hurtful way in me."*[337] When we are proactive with our faults as David was, we eliminate hardship and chastening by the Lord. This is the most significant way to embrace the fear of the Lord in chastening. It's also a much faster process with our growth in the Lord.

The Reality of Hell and the Lake of Fire

Romans 11:22 Therefore consider the goodness and the severity of God: on those who fell, severity; but toward you, goodness, if you continue in His goodness. Otherwise, you will also be cut off.

I often refer to the goodness and the severity of God as the two guardrails of life. When we lose sight of God's goodness, it has the potential of producing a recklessness in us that could cause us to crash hard. Because God is faithful and merciful, He has put the guardrail of His severity in place to keep us from going over the edge and crashing into the abyss below. To fall into the hands of a living God is the fear of God.

Jesus spoke of it when He said, *"Do not fear those who kill the body but cannot kill the soul. But rather fear Him who can destroy both the soul and body in Hell."*[338]

---

[337] Psalm 139:23-24
[338] Matthew 10:28

I understand how the fear of the Lord is awesome respect and reverence for God, but it also entails what Jesus spoke when He said, *"Fear Him, who "can destroy the soul and body in Hell."*[339] With this comes the necessity of a healthy Biblical understanding of the meaning of Hell is and who's going there.

The Reality of Hell

There is much to say in both the Old and New Testaments concerning Hell and the Lake of Fire. The Bible teaches that life continues after the physical death of the body. God created man with a natural, physical body and an eternal soul. The soul of man consists of who we are. It's the center of our mind, will, and emotions. The Bible teaches that life is eternal. Because the soul is immortal, we will either spend eternity in Heaven or Hell.

> **Daniel 12:2** *And many of those who sleep in the dust of the earth shall awake, some to everlasting life, some to shame and everlasting contempt.*

God created Hell for the devil and his demons to inhabit. It's such an awful place that Jesus said it would be better to cut off your hand or gouge out your eye rather than go there. There will be crying and total darkness in Hell—a lake made of unquenchable fire and brimstone with intense pain and agony.

> **Mark 9:43** *And if your hand makes you sin, cut it off. It is better for you to enter into life maimed than having two hands, to go to hell, into the fire that shall never be quenched.*

> **Mark 9:45** *And if your foot makes you sin, cut it off. It is better for you to enter life lame than having two feet, to be cast into hell, into the fire that shall never be quenched.*

It's true that people can partially experience hell on earth. Those who live in rebellion against God and His ways do experience, to a small degree, some of the things that those in Hell are suffering. This experience is, however, only a slight foretaste of the miseries that the occupants of hell will experience forever.

Hell will be a place of intense torment, pain, and weeping described as a furnace of fire where there will be wailing and gnashing of teeth.[340] "Jesus told the story of the "Rich Man and Lazarus," which illustrates to

---

[340] Matthew 13:42 & 50

us the intensity of the pain that will exist in Hell. The rich man tormented in the flame did not wish this place of torment upon anyone.[341] He cried out saying, *"Father, Abraham, have mercy on me, and send Lazarus that he may dip the tip of his finger in water and cool my tongue; for I am tormented in this flame."*[342]

I've heard people say at various times they would rather be partying in Hell with their friends than walking in gardens with their enemies. What an absurd statement! If they only realized how ridiculous it is. There will be no partying going on in Hell, just extreme loneliness, blackness, and darkness forever as the Bible describes it.[343] Now is the day of salvation that will save you from this terrible existence throughout eternity.

Bible teacher, Kevin Conner is quoted as saying, *"Hell will be an awful place, separated from the presence of God, the rejected Lamb, the holy angels, and the redeemed. There will be no light, life, peace, joy, righteousness, nor salvation. Only darkness and torment of conscience will be there for those who rejected and despised God's grace."*[344]

The critical thing to keep in mind is that Jesus did not come to condemn the world. He came to save the world from this awful place of torment.

> ***John 3:17-19*** *For God did not send His Son into the world to condemn the world, but that the world through Him might be saved. He who believes in Him is not condemned, but he who does not believe is condemned already because he has not believed in the name of the only begotten Son of God. And this is the condemnation, that the light has come into the world, and men loved darkness rather than light because their deeds were evil.*

> ***2 Peter 3:9-11*** *The Lord is not slack concerning His promise, as some count slackness, but is longsuffering toward us, not willing that any should perish but that all should come to repentance.*

Lots of People will End up in Hell

Among those who come from every background, race, society, religion, and culture, will be those who the Bible describes as:

- Those who do not know God - *2Thessalonians 1:8*
- Those who don't obey the Gospel - *2Thessalonians 1:8*

---

[341] Luke 16:19-28
[342] Luke 16:24
[343] Jude 1:13
[344] The Foundations of Christian Doctrine - Kevin Conner

- Sinners and hypocrites - *Isaiah 33:14*
- Those who practice lawlessness – *Matthew 13:41*
- Cowardly, unbelieving, abominable, murders, sorcerers, sexually immoral, idolaters, and all liars - *Revelation 21:8*
- Adulterers, thieves, homosexuals, covetous people, drunkards, and extortioners - *1Corinthians 6:9-10*

The Bible says the road to Hell is wide, and the road to heaven is narrow. Which road are you traveling on? *"Do not be deceived, God is not mocked; for whatever a man sows, that he will also reap."[345]*

Are We Secure in our Salvation?

You may be thinking, "I'm secure in my salvation. I can never lose it." If that's what you believe, this next section may be somewhat challenging for you. I would encourage you to read and ponder it. Allow the Scriptures to speak for themselves without trying to interpret them through any school of thought. Our loyalty needs to be to God's Word, not to schools of thought.

Personally, I do not believe a person goes through continuous cycles of being saved and lost repeatedly. Therefore, I do not think because a person is in a backslidden condition, they have necessarily lost their salvation, but I do believe there is a point where you can become so deceived in your backsliding that you eventually disown Christ by no longer believing. At this point, you fulfill the Scriptures that speak of disowning Christ.

Notice in the following passages: Christ cannot disown you, unless you, first, disown Him. Keep in mind; you cannot be disowned by Christ unless you are first owned by Him.

Matthew 10:33 *(NIV) But whoever disowns me before others, I will disown before my Father in heaven.*

2 Timothy 2:12 *(NIV) If we endure, we will also reign with him; if we disown him, he will also disown us.*

You may think you could never get to the place where you could disown Christ. The problem with that kind of thinking is, once you begin the slippery slope of backsliding, you further open yourself up to Satan's devices and deception to a higher degree. You have no idea where deception could lead you. Jesus speaks of a strong delusion that is

---

[345] Galatians 6:7

coming upon the world before His second coming. He says, *"If it were possible even the elect would be deceived."[346]* Paul speaks of a great falling away before the coming of Christ—a time when many will disown Christ.

A great deception is coming. To keep from being deceived, we will need both guardrails in place—the goodness and the severity of God. Those whose hearts are cold towards the Lord through their backsliding wouldn't have a chance. The enemy is already lurking around looking for those to whom he can devour. A backslider is easy pickings for him.

There will be a Great Falling Away

Paul speaks of a great falling away.[347] Those who fall away are those who have defected from the truth of the Christian faith. To fall away implies a strong rebellion or revolt that happens before the Second Coming of Christ. The point is, there will be people who will fall into this category. They are the ones who disown Christ.

Is it Possible to Fall Away Never to be Saved Again?

There is a point where the once saved believers are entirely reprobate in their minds and actions. The writer of the Book of Hebrews addresses this issue in the following passage. However, the stipulations shown below reveal that it's only a mature believer who can commit this sin.

> **Hebrews 6:4-9** *For it is impossible for those who were once enlightened, and have tasted the heavenly gift, and have become partakers of the Holy Spirit, and have tasted the good word of God and the powers of the age to come, if they fall away, to renew them again to repentance, since they crucify again for themselves the Son of God and put Him to an open shame.*

This passage shows, very clearly, there is a point where a Christian has backslidden so far that they can't come back. The Greek word for "fall away" is *"parapipto,"* which means to fall aside or to apostatize.[348]

These Christian believers were once:

- Enlightened - *John 1:6-12*
- Tasted of the Heavenly Gift - *John 3:16 & Romans 6:23*
- Made Partakers of the Holy Spirit - *Acts 19:2*
- Tasted of the Good Word of God - *Hebrews 5:12-14*

---

[346] Matthew 24:24
[347] 2 Thessalonians 2:3
[348] Strong's Greek Dictionary Concordance #3895

- Tasted of the Powers of the World to Come - *Acts 1:8*

These people have given up their birthright in the same way that Esau did. Giving up one's birthright is when backsliding leads to the extreme position of disowning Christ as Paul warned Timothy.[349] John refers to disowning Christ as the sin that leads unto death.[350] The writer of the Book of Hebrews refers to it as "willful sin" in a later chapter about the person who has trodden under foot the Son of God and insulted the Holy Spirit.[351] Jesus referred to it when He spoke of the individual who blasphemes the Holy Spirit and commits the unpardonable sin.

Mark 3:29 (NIV) But whoever blasphemes against the Holy Spirit will never be forgiven; they are guilty of an eternal sin.

The words "fall away" describe the person's willful and independent position. It means to walk alongside or out of the will of God with no intention of returning to God's way—total apostasy. There is an open renunciation of Jesus Christ and a gathering together with the enemies of Christ.

There Is a Point where God Cuts off those who Disown Him

If God did not spare natural Israel when they committed apostasy, what makes us think that He will save us if we fall away? We must continue in the goodness and severity of God. Otherwise, we, too, will be cut off.

Romans 11:21 For if God did not spare the natural branches, He may not spare you either.

The writer of the Book of Hebrews gives us a strong warning about drawing back unto perdition by letting us know that it's a fearful thing to fall into the hands of the living God. He takes no pleasure in those who draw back. We see this again in chapter ten.

Hebrews 10:31,38-39 It is a fearful thing to fall into the hands of the living God. ³⁸Now the just shall live by faith; but if anyone draws back, my soul has no pleasure in him." ³⁹But we are not of those who draw back to perdition but of those who believe to the saving of the soul.

When the above passage speaks of those who "draw back unto perdition" or waste and destruction, it's a possibility, or it would not have

---

[349] 2Timothy 2:12
[350] 1 John 5:16
[351] Hebrews 10:26-31

been written to warn us. The word perdition indicates loss of well-being, not of being. The destruction then is everlasting without annihilation.

*Hebrews 10:26-27 If we sin willfully after we have received the knowledge of the truth, there no longer remains a sacrifice of sins, but a **certain** fearful expectation of judgment, and fiery indignation which will devour the adversaries.*

Some would like to say this is referring to a person who continually rejects Jesus after they are convicted many times. It's just not so, as we see in the following Scriptures.

Hebrews 10:29-31 Of how much worse punishment, do you suppose, will be thought worthy who has trampled the Son of God underfoot, counted the blood of the covenant by which he was sanctified a common thing, and insulted the Spirit of grace? [30]For we know Him who said, "Vengeance is Mine," says the Lord, And again "The Lord will judge His people." [31]It is a fearful thing to fall into the hands of the living God."

This person:

- **Was sanctified by the blood of Jesus:** To be sanctified means to be set apart from the world unto God.
- **Has trodden underfoot the Son of God:** To trample underfoot the person of Jesus and all that He is and has done is to count Him as refuse. Trodding underfoot the Son of God is an act of utter contempt for Christ.
- **Has counted the blood of Jesus as unholy:** To value the precious, sinless blood of Jesus as that of a pig or unclean thing.
- **Has done despite unto the Spirit of Grace:** He insults the Holy Spirit, who he had received by God's grace by insulting all the work of the Spirit he had been a partaker of, such as salvation, baptism, healing, gifts, fruit, etc. To insult the Holy Spirit is to blaspheme Him for which there is no forgiveness.

As we have seen, to "fall away" consists of total renunciation or disowning of Christ and Christianity. However, we must keep in mind; backsliding is where the process begins. Once a person starts to backslide, they open themselves up to greater deception from Satan. Our enemy is a devouring lion, who goes after those who are weak in the faith. Don't be fooled! He will come after you with everything he has. As you begin the downward spiral of backsliding, his goal is for you to commit apostasy. That's why I'm afraid to backslide. I understand I have fallen into the hands of a living God.

I don't believe anyone knows where this cut-off point is. We are not the judge nor could we because we don't have all the facts in each case. Even if we did, we would not have the wisdom to analyze them. God is the righteous judge, and there is a point where God says, "No more—that's it!"

Judgment Awaits those who Blaspheme the Holy Spirit

The entire second chapter of Peter's second epistle describes believers who go back and become apostate.

2 Peter 2:20-21 For if, after they have escaped the pollutions of the world through the knowledge of the Lord and Savior Jesus Christ, they are again entangled in them and overcome, the latter end is worse for them than the beginning. [21] For it would have been better for them not to have known the way of righteousness, than having known it, to turn from the holy commandment delivered to them.

We must give serious consideration to this passage. It says, *"It would have been better for them not to have known the way of righteousness."* How could it possibly be better not to have known the way of righteousness? Could it be because they have committed the unpardonable sin and eternal judgment is what awaits them? There's no opportunity for them to turn back to the Lord. Those who disown Him are done!

Hebrews 10:26-27 If we sin willfully after we have received the knowledge of the truth, there no longer remains a sacrifice of sins, [27] but a certain fearful expectation of judgment, and fiery indignation which will devour the adversaries.

2 Peter 3:17 You, therefore, beloved, since you know these things beforehand, beware lest you also fall from your own steadfastness, being led away with the error of the wicked.

As seen from the testimony of Scripture, there is an agreement that it's possible to lose your salvation. I have been purposely laborious so that you can see for yourself how the Scriptures on this subject agree with one another. As you take this to heart, you will have built a stronghold of righteousness as a strong guardrail to keep you safe and secure.

Be assured, as you stay close to the guardrail of God's goodness with a heart of thanksgiving you will be safe and secure. If not, the guardrail of the severity of God is there to stop you from your foolishness and from falling into the abyss. As you take the time to build both guardrails by getting these Scriptures and principles embedded in your heart, you will be safe and secure throughout your journey in the Lord. As you are careful to build your guardrails, you will experience eternal security!

Psalm 107:43 *Whoever is wise will observe these things, and they will understand the lovingkindness of the Lord.*

As we are faithful to observe everything regarding what it means to fear God, we will be a part of the wise virgin class, prepared as useful vessels, who bring glory and honor to our Lord and Savior, the Lord Jesus Christ. The fear of the Lord is a significant piece of our wedding garments as we make ourselves ready to be a part of His glorious bride without spot or wrinkle.

One last thought: Fear God and enjoy the company of His angels as they encamp around you and protect you from all that is evil.

Psalm 34:7 *The angel of the Lord encamps all around those who fear Him and delivers them.*

Embracing the Fear of the Lord

by Ken L. Birks © 2018 Straight Arrow Ministries

Coming to the Father, we stand in awe of all that He is.
To all who pass by, He is greatly to be feared and revered.
In His goodness and severity, we learn from Him.
Trembling at His word, wisdom and knowledge are imparted.
In the congregation of the saints, He is to be feared.

As Moses said, we are to fear God and walk in His ways.
As Isaiah said, we are to let Him be our fear.
As Jesus said, fear Him who can destroy your soul in Hell.
As Peter said, pass the time of sojourning in fear.
It's a fearful thing to fall into the hands of a living God.

As we fear God, perfect love casts out all fear.
As we tremble at His Word, He blesses beyond measure.
Working out salvation in fear and trembling, He works.
In His severity, He is perfectly righteous in all His ways.
As He examines, our ways are in full view of Him.

As we stand before Him, we embrace His discipline.
With every secret thought, we know He's watching.
As we stand in righteousness, we hate sin and evil.
In fear, we recognize the reality of Hell.
In fear, we understand He cuts off those who disown.

To those who fear Him, His lovingkindness is understood.
To those who fear Him, Angels encamp around them.
To those who fear Him, He preserves from corruption.
To those who fear Him, His intimacy is enjoyed.
To those who fear Him, He restores and sets free.

Rightly Dividing
The Word of Truth

Chapter Seventeen

We're living in an era in which the prophets, along with Jesus, the apostles of Christ, and the apostle Paul have spoken extensively. In all probability, we're living in the time that Jesus described as the coming birth pangs—an era of time in which the masses are under a deceptive cloud of darkness that's invading every nook and cranny of our world. The master deceiver is busily at work casting spells of darkness and deception as the whole world lies in his sway.[352] As deception takes root, truth falls in the streets.[353] This deception and siege is just part of the birth pangs that Jesus mentioned.

*Matthew 24:4-8 And Jesus answered and said to them: "**Take heed that no one deceives you.** ⁵For many will come in My Name, saying, 'I am the Christ,' and will deceive many. ⁶And you will hear of wars and rumors of wars. See that you are not troubled; for all these things must come to pass, but the end is not yet. ⁷For nation will rise against nation, and kingdom against kingdom. And there will be famines, pestilence, and earthquakes in various places. ⁸All these are the beginning of sorrows. (birth pangs NASB)*

The Pillars of Truth Must be Restored

With our world under siege by the enemy of our faith, is this not a time for the Church to arise with her pillars of truth in place?

1 Timothy 3:15 But if I am delayed, I write so that you may know how you ought to conduct yourself in the house of God, which is the church of the living God, the pillar, and ground of the truth.

As the master deceiver is busily working casting spells of darkness and deception, the Church is not exempt. Satan has his false prophets, apostles, and teachers throughout the world spreading his lies and half-truths from the nations of the world's pulpits. The Church seems to be

---

[352] 1 John 5:19
[353] Isaiah 59:14

ignorant of Satan's methods. While the Church marches onward with a watered-down gospel that barely mentions the cross of Christ and the need for genuine repentance, it creates a vacuum in which the deceptive tactics and lies of Satan are becoming firmly entrenched in the Church of Jesus Christ.

Jesus warned us about the many false Christs and prophets that would arise to deceive the elect.[354] Paul said in his first epistle to Timothy, *"In latter times some will depart from the faith, giving heed to deceiving spirits and doctrines of demons."*[355] Paul also warned the time would come when people wouldn't endure sound doctrine by turning away from the truth. He said they would go after false teachers, who tickle their ears.[356] Peter mentions in his second epistle, a warning about deceptive teachers and doctrines, where he says the following:

*2 **Peter** 2:1-3a But there were also false prophets among the people, even as there will be false teachers among you, who will secretly bring in destructive heresies, even denying the Lord who bought them, and bring upon themselves swift destruction. ²And many will follow their destructive ways, because of whom the way of truth will be blasphemed. ³By covetousness they will exploit you with deceptive words.*

In our world today, false teaching is running rampant. With the advent of the internet, anyone can have a voice without any accountability whatsoever. It's the perfect tool for Satan and his cohorts to transform themselves into deceitful workers, who masquerade as apostles and teachers of Christ. As the apostle, Paul said, *"And no wonder! For Satan, himself transforms himself into an angel of light."*

As church attendance becomes less and less important with the advent of the internet and other forms of media, a great vacuum is being formed for Satan to unleash his seductive lies with the antichrist spirit gaining momentum across the globe. John, the beloved apostle, spoke of the antichrist spirit that is already in the world and how we are to exercise discernment.

*1 **John** 4:1-3 Beloved, do not believe every spirit, but test the spirits, whether they are of God; because many false prophets have gone out into the world. ²By this you know the Spirit of God: Every spirit that confesses that Jesus Christ has come in the flesh is of God, ³and every spirit that does not confess that Jesus Christ has come in the flesh is not*

---

[354] Matthew 24:24-25
[355] 1 Timothy 4:1
[356] 2 Timothy 4:3-4

of God. And this is the Antichrist, which you have heard was coming and is now already in the world.

Now is the time for godly leaders to be raised up, who will be bold as lions and unafraid to preach and teach the whole counsel of God's word in an uncompromising manner. It's time for them to rightly divide the word of truth in such a way that the pillars of truth are fully restored. The truth of God's word must replace the lies and tactics of the enemy that have caused His truth to be nonexistent in the world He created. The Church Jesus is building is designed to have the truth of God's word flowing forth from it into the streets of our world rather than the lies and deceitful tactics of the enemy.

The Church of Jesus Christ must quit abdicating the authority given to it and rise up with authority it has in Christ. Jesus is coming back for a glorified Church of which the authority of hell won't have any effect.[357] The Church Jesus is building will be the pillar and ground of the truth just as He was and is.[358] Unfortunately, Satan understands this more than the Church does. He's in the process of taking full advantage of the lack of discernment that is currently sweeping through the ranks of God's people. He uses innocent people who are caught up in their own wisdom rather than the foolishness of Christ. In their wisdom, they preach and teach from perspectives that feed the consumerism and self-indulgent mentality of the masses. It's time for the Church to take heed to the words of Jeremiah, the prophet.

Jeremiah 5:30-31 *An astonishing and horrible thing has been committed in the land:* *[31] The prophets prophesy falsely, and the priests rule by their own power, and My people love to have it so. But what will you do in the end?*

The above passage describes the Church in today's world as it pays little attention to the admonition Paul gave Timothy to divide the word of truth rightly. Thankfully, God is raising up godly ministers who will rightly divide the word of truth to lead His people back to building a Church that will be the pillar and ground of all truth.

There is a strong need for the word of truth to be rightly divided without twisting or wresting the Scriptures to appease the multitudes with words that tickle their ears. It's time for godly leaders to believe that all Scripture was inspired by God, which is to be used for instruction in righteousness and profitable for doctrine. They must rise up and

---

[357] Matthew 16:18
[358] 1 Timothy 2:15

declare the whole counsel of the word of God without fear of consequences.[359] Just as Jesus and the apostles of Christ preached and taught the word, uncompromisingly, so must we in a day of darkness and gloom when sin is exalted as righteousness. Godly leaders must stand up and proclaim the whole counsel of God's word with boldness without the fear of losing the crowd's acceptance.

Two Aspects of Feeding the Sheep

When Jesus spoke to Peter after His resurrection and asked him three times whether he loved him or not, He used two different Greek words for tending and feeding the sheep.[360] As Jesus challenged Peter to feed the sheep, the two Greek words He used for the word *"feed"* were *bosko and poimaino.* In a spiritual sense, *bosko* implies the feeding or preaching and teaching the whole counsel of God uncompromisingly.[361] *Poimaino* involves tending and care.[362]

Paul said he was innocent of the blood of all men by not being afraid to declare the whole counsel of God. He knew perfectly well what would happen when the word wasn't declared with authority. He was aware of the savageness of Satan, and how he comes in, not sparing the flock. He, therefore, warned the Ephesian elders to shepherd the church of God, through the whole counsel of God's word.

> *Acts 20:26-29 Therefore I testify to you this day that I am innocent of the blood of all men. [27]For I have not shunned to declare to you the whole counsel of God. [28]Therefore take heed to yourselves and to the flock of God, among which the Holy Spirit has made you overseers, to shepherd the church of God, which He purchased with His own blood. [29]For I know this, that after my departure savage wolves will come in among you, not sparing the flock.*

Just as Jesus often spoke in a way that people were offended by the purity of the word that came forth from his lips, so must the teachers and preachers do today. If we are to continue to build the Church Jesus purchased with His blood, we must build on the foundation of our Chief Cornerstone, Jesus Christ. There is no other foundation.[363]

---

[359] 2 Timothy 3:16, Acts 20:27-28
[360] John 21-15-17
[361] Strong's #1006 — Verb — βόσκω, bosko — bos'-ko
[362] Strong's #4165 — Verb — ποιμαίνω, poimaino — poy-mah'ee-no
[363] 1 Corinthians 3:11

Teachers will Incur a Stricter Judgment

James, the Lord's brother warned us that those who become teachers of God's word would incur a stricter judgment. I'm not sure what that fully entails, but it's enough to put the fear of God into me concerning what I teach. It compels me to be diligent in presenting myself approved to God, a worker who does not need to be ashamed, rightly dividing the word of truth.[364]

James 3:1 My brethren, let not many of you become teachers, knowing that we shall receive a stricter judgment.

One of Satan's favorite ploys is to twist the Scriptures in such a way that God's people get left in the wake of confusion and unbelief. Peter wrote, speaking of the coming of the Day of the Lord, in which the heavens would pass away with a great noise, and the elements would melt with fervent heat that those who are unlearned and unstable would twist the Scriptures to their destruction. Considering this, we are to consider what manner of persons we should be in holy conduct and godliness.[365]

2 Peter 3:14-17 Therefore, beloved, looking forward to these things, be diligent to be found by Him in peace, without spot and blameless; 15and consider that the longsuffering of our Lord is salvation—as also our beloved brother Paul, according to the wisdom given to him, has written to you, 16as also in all his epistles, speaking in them of these things, in which are some things hard to understand, which untaught and unstable people twist to their own destruction, as they also do the rest of the Scriptures. 17You therefore, beloved, since you know this beforehand, beware lest you fall from your own steadfastness, being led away with the error of the wicked.

We must understand that Satan knows and understands how to use the Scriptures for his own purposes. With Jesus, he tried twisting the Scriptures in such a way to tempt him. However, Jesus defeated Satan because He was well immersed in the Scriptures and knew how to use them in wielding the sword. As ministers of God's word, we must know how to wield the sword of the Spirit as well. When we compromise the authority, we have in the word of God by twisting the Scriptures to our advantage, we give into Satan's ploys and give him a foothold in the Church Jesus is building. We must learn to shepherd the Church Jesus is

---

[364] 2 Timothy 2:15
[365] 2 Peter 3:7-11

building by maintaining integrity to the word of God in all matters. It's the word that is quicker and sharper than any two-edged sword.[366] Therefore, we have a God-given responsibility to wield it in such a way that it brings glory and honor unto the name of the Lord Jesus Christ.

Principles for Rightly Dividing the Word of Truth

As Paul wrote to young Timothy, we are to divide the word of truth rightly. Rightly dividing the word of truth doesn't just happen. There are a few principles that are necessary for it to happen that must be engaged by those who seek to uncover the buried treasure that lies between the covers of this great book known as the Bible.

2 Timothy 2:15 Be diligent to present yourself approved to God, a worker who does not need to be ashamed, rightly dividing the word of truth.

Must Believe God Inspired all Scripture

A major foundational stone of our faith is to believe that God inspired all Scripture. If we don't believe this, then, we are in doubt concerning the death and resurrection of Christ upon whom our salvation rests. It's the first and foremost principle of how to rightly divide the word of truth. It's what makes us complete in God and equips us for every good work as seen in the following passage of Scripture.

2 Timothy 3:16-17 All Scripture is given by the inspiration of God and is profitable for doctrine, for reproof, for correction, for the instruction in righteousness, [17]that the man of God may be complete, thoroughly equipped for every good work.

We do not have the prerogative to pick and choose which Scriptures are inspired by God and which aren't. If this were so, there would be no foundation on which to build and interpret doctrine. It's absolutely necessary that all doctrine is based on the fact that all Scripture was inspired by God. If you don't believe this, then we have nothing further to discuss. The conversation ends there because prophecy never came by the will of man, but by Holy men of God who spoke as God moved on them by the Holy Spirit.[367]

If we are to engage in the prophetic purposes God has for our generation, we must embrace the divine inspiration of Scriptures with all our hearts. We must be fully persuaded and convinced of the authenticity of Scripture, which enables us to be devoted to the truths contained

---

[366] Hebrews 4:12
[367] 2 Peter 1:21

therein. It's from the Scriptures we receive further revelation and understanding of the times we are living in and what God has prepared for us.

Hebrews 4:12 For the word of God is living and powerful, and sharper than any two-edged sword, piercing even to the division of soul and spirit, and of joints and marrow, and is a discerner of the thoughts and intents of the heart.

As the Holy Spirit breathes on the Scriptures, they become alive in our hearts discerning the thoughts and intents of our hearts. In other words, it allows our thoughts to come into alignment with God's thoughts, enabling our minds to plan our ways[368] and discern doctrinal truths.

Be Fully-Immersed in the Foundational Principles

Before a house is built, it must have a sure foundation. In His word, God has referred to His people as a spiritual house and a temple.[369] If we are to be all that God has purposed for our lives, we must have a strong spiritual foundation. Jesus shared about this when He spoke of building on the rock. He made a distinction between those who build on sand and those whose houses are built on the rock. He said the foolish build on the sand with no foundation, while the wise build on a firm foundation of rock.[370]

Peter says we are to desire the pure milk of the word that we may grow thereby.[371] The writer of the book of Hebrews identifies the milk of the word as the elementary principles of Christ that must be in our lives before; we are permitted to go on to maturity.[372] In other words, we must have a spiritual building permit before we can move forward in our understanding and revelation of God's word. The foundational stones of God's word are a necessity before moving forward into deeper spiritual truths and realms. Otherwise, we will produce nothing but dead works, which amount to nothing more than wood, hay or stubble with a house built on sand.[373]

We all know the story of the big bad wolf and the three pigs. Well, the big bad wolf is here, and he's blowing with all his might. Many are

---

[368] Proverbs 16:3,9

[369] 2 Peter 2:5, 1 Corinthians 6:19, Ephesians 2:19-22

[370] Matthew 7:24-27

[371] 1 Peter 1-3

[372] Hebrews 5:12-13, 6:1-3

[373] 1 Corinthians 3:12-16

being set up through false teaching, only to have their spiritual homes blown to pieces by the enemy of our faith. Will you be one of them? As Paul said, *"For I know this, that after my departure savage wolves will come in among you, not sparing the flock."*[374] We are to be skillful in the word of righteousness. This is what prepares us for the enemy's devices.

> *Hebrews 5:12-14 For though by this time you ought to be teachers, you need someone to teach you again the first principles of the oracles of God; and you have come to need milk and not solid food. [13] **For everyone who partakes only of milk is unskillful in the word of righteousness, for he is a babe.** [14] But solid food belongs to those who are of full age, that is those who by reason of use have their senses exercised to discern both good and evil.*

What the writer is saying here is, until you have become skilled in the first principles, you will not be able to divide the word of truth rightly. Becoming skilled only happens to those who have immersed themselves in the elementary principles of Christ. They're then able to chew on the meat of God's word. The next section in Hebrews identifies what those principles are.

> *Hebrews 6:1-3 Therefore, leaving the discussion of the elementary principles of Christ, let us go on to perfection, not laying again the foundation of repentance from dead works and of faith towards God, [2] of the doctrine of baptisms, of laying on of hands, of resurrection of the dead, and of eternal judgment. [3] And this we will do if God Permits.*[375]

The prophet, Isaiah says something very similar. He spoke of the knowledge that comes to those who are weaned from the milk.

> *Isaiah 28:9-10 Whom shall he teach knowledge? And whom will he make to understand the message? Those just weaned from milk? Those just drawn from the breasts? [10] For precept must be upon precept, line upon line, line upon line, here a little, there a little."*

Those of the wise virgin class are those who take the time to immerse themselves in the elementary principles of Christ, building a sure foundation that will weather whatever storms come their way. Those who build on sand will be swallowed up in the great falling away, having fallen into the traps of the enemy! As Paul so aptly says, *"For no other*

---

[374] Acts 20:29

[375] Please note: Complete teachings on all these subjects are available from the following sources: www.kenbirks.com/bible-studies
www.straitarrow.net/bible-studies/, www.kenbirks.com/perspectives-both/

foundation can anyone lay than that which is laid, which is Jesus Christ."[376]

If our understanding of the elementary principles of Christ is incorrect, it will affect our ability to rightly divide the heavier truths of God's word. We will be hindered from discovering the divine harmony of the revelation of His word. The pieces of the puzzle won't fit together to paint a complete picture.

Must Believe there's a Divine Harmony of Revelation

If we believe that all Scripture is inspired by God, then we must also believe in the divine harmony of revelation that comes forth from Scripture. Holy men of God spoke as God moved on them by the Holy Spirit as Peter appropriately wrote. Therefore, we must believe that God spoke with continuity throughout the Bible. Scripture will interpret Scripture.

> **2 Peter 1:20-21** *Knowing this first, that no prophecy of Scripture is of any private interpretation, [21]for prophecy never came by the will of man, but holy men of God spoke as they were moved by the Holy Spirit.*

If we are to believe in the divine harmony of the Scriptures, it will entail that we believe all doctrines stand in agreement with one another. They must fit together in divine harmony without contradicting one another. Just as Paul exhorted Timothy to take heed to doctrine,[377] we must do the same. In other words, we must be careful about how we treat it.

We must be honest and forthright in our understanding of the Scriptures without bias. There must be more of a loyalty to the purity of God's word than to the various streams of thought in which we were trained to think. We must continually examine our doctrinal beliefs as we entertain new thought patterns. The Bereans were considered nobler because they did not readily accept what Paul was saying. They studied the Scriptures for themselves to make sure what he was saying was true.[378] We should do the same.

The Holy Spirit Teaches us

We have the greatest teacher in the universe at our disposal, the Holy Spirit. He is our anointed teacher to guide us through the Scriptures. We have the same Holy Spirit within us as the holy men and prophets of old

---

[376] 1 Corinthians 3:11
[377] 1 Timothy 4:16
[378] Acts17:11 KJV

had. He is in each of us to teach us as we allow Him to open the Scriptures to our understanding. It's the Holy Spirit who searches the heart of the Father to reveal things unto us.[379] The Father desires for all of us to have the spirit of revelation so that He can teach us.[380]

1 John 2:20, 27 But you have an anointing from the Holy One, and you know all things. [27]But the anointing which you have received from Him abides in you, and you do not need that anyone teach you; but as the same anointing teaches you concerning all things, and is true, and just as it has taught you, you will abide in Him.

God has designed His word and His Spirit to partner together in all things, including how we interpret doctrine. For example, on the day of Pentecost when the Holy Spirit came upon the early believers as a mighty rushing wind with tongues of fire, Peter relied on the Scriptures to interpret what was happening.[381] Jesus often referred to the Scriptures as He explained how the Father was working in and through Him as seen in the following passage.

Luke 4:17-19,21 And He was handed the book of the prophet Isaiah. And when He had opened the book, He found the place where it was written: [18]"The Spirit of the Lord is upon Me to preach the gospel to the poor; He has sent Me to heal the broken-hearted, to proclaim liberty to the captives and recovery of sight to the blind, to set at Liberty those who are oppressed; [19]to proclaim the acceptable year of the Lord." [21]And He began to say to them, "Today this Scripture is fulfilled in your hearing." (see also the passages in the footnote)[382]

The apostles of Christ referred to the Scriptures on many occasions as they were developing doctrine and interpreting experiences that were coming their way. For example, when they needed someone to take Judas' place, they relied on Scripture for direction.[383] Paul often referred to the Scriptures when making doctrinal points as well. Let us not forget, as Paul wrote, *"All Scripture is profitable for doctrine."*[384] One of the most important aspects of our faith in Christ is based on a Scripture he referred to from the Old Testament.

---

[379] 1 Corinthians 2:7-11
[380] Ephesians 1:17-18
[381] Acts 2:16-21
[382] Matthew 21:13, 26:24, 31, Mark 7:6, Luke 24:46
[383] Acts 1:20
[384] 2 Timothy 3:16

*Romans 1:16-17 For I am not ashamed of the gospel of Christ, for it is the power of God to salvation for everyone who believes, for the Jew first and for the Greek. [17]**For in it the righteousness of God is revealed from faith to faith; as it is written, "The just shall live by faith."**[385]*

Even though the Holy Spirit teaches us as the beloved apostle John stated, does that mean we don't need anointed teachers to teach us as well? Absolutely not! We are to not only glean from the anointed teachers, the Father places in our midst but also to be like the Bereans. They not only received the word with all readiness but searched the Scriptures for themselves to make sure what they were hearing was true.[386] They were learning how to divide the truth rightly.

I have often told my Bible students, "Don't believe something just because I told you, study it for yourself so that you will own it." It's when we study to show ourselves approved as a workman, who does not need to be ashamed that we own the truth. It gets woven into the fiber of our being. Studying for ourselves is what gives us the spiritual authority that is needed to come against the lies and deception of the enemy.

God Often Speaks in Riddles and Mysteries

As we seek to understand all that God reveals to us through His word, it's important to know that the Bible is full of mysteries, dark sayings, and riddles. We are to discover and search them out before we can properly understand all that the Father has contained in His will and purpose for our lives and the Church.

Romans 16:25 Now to Him who is able to establish you according to my gospel and the preaching of Jesus Christ, according to the revelation of the mystery kept secret since the world began.

Ephesians 1:7, 9-10 In Him we have redemption… [9]having made known to us the mystery of His will, according to His good pleasure which He purposed in Himself, [10]that in the dispensation of the fullness of the times He might gather together in one all things in Christ, both which are in heaven and which are on earth—in Him.

The Father desires to reveal the mystery of His will to us as we rightly divide His word of truth. However, His truths are concealed so that only those who have ears to hear can hear and interpret His word.

---

[385] Habakkuk 2:4
[386] Acts 17:11

Proverbs 1:5-6 *A wise man will hear and increase in learning, and a man of understanding will attain to wise counsel, to understand a proverb and an enigma, the words of the wise and their riddles.*

Proverbs 25:2 *It is The glory of God to conceal a matter, but the glory of kings to search out a matter.*

Throughout the writings of Paul, he refers to the gospel as God's mystery in Christ that was hidden for ages but has now been revealed in us.[387] Jesus often spoke in parables so that only those who had ears to hear could understand the mysteries of the kingdom.[388] Paul also spoke of certain truths that were mysteries such as the Godhead, the second coming, the Church as a bride, the mystery of godliness and more.[389]

The book of Revelation says the mystery of God will be finished in the days of the sounding of the seventh trumpet.[390] When we arise to meet Jesus in the clouds, all mysteries will be solved. We will be known as He is. That which is perfect will be complete. However, there are still many mysteries to be revealed before He returns.

It's in the study of the Scriptures with the aid of the Holy Spirit that we're led from one clue to another as the mysteries of His word are unfolded and opened to our spiritual understanding. By allowing Scripture to interpret Scripture the great mysteries and riddles concealed in God's word get solved.

The Bible is a gigantic puzzle with many pieces that must be interlocked together to fully understand and solve the mysteries contained therein. As with any puzzle, the pieces must interlock together before the complete picture is seen. The Bible is no different. There are many pieces to the mysteries contained therein that must be interlocked together before the complete picture of who God is and what His purposes are in heaven and earth. Some of the pieces are quite simple and interlock easily while others are somewhat nebulous and difficult to find how they fit in with the whole. With the aid of the Holy Spirit, He helps us fit all the pieces together in divine harmony.

Over the years, I have put together many jigsaw puzzles. I have always found that putting the border pieces together first is very helpful. Once the border pieces are all put together, it's much easier to assemble the remaining pieces of the puzzle. I have a six-year-old granddaughter who loves to put puzzles together. I often spend time with her putting

---

[387] Colossians 1:26-27, 2:2,
[388] Luke 8:10, Mark 4:11
[389] Romans 11:25, 16:25, 1 Corinthians 4:1,15:51, Ephesians 5:32, 1 Timothy 3:9, 16
[390] Revelation 10:7

them together. I have found that she likes to pick out her favorite part of the puzzle by looking at the box. She will begin to find the pieces that belong to the picture she sees. While she's doing that, I find myself putting the border together while she's working on a cluster that will fit in at some point. Once the border is together, and her cluster is complete, we must then find the pieces that interlock the border to the cluster. To find these pieces is the more difficult part because they're not as obvious. They're pieces which are more of a mixture of the two parts being joined together. Sometimes we'll have a couple of clusters we are working on that must be fitted and joined together at some point. Again, the pieces that join the clusters are a mixture of the two.

The Bible is very similar to a jigsaw puzzle. It has many mysteries that must be fitted together in divine harmony to see the whole picture. The border pieces are those pieces that are straightforward and easily understood and interpreted. They are obvious to their meaning. When trying to determine the mind of God in any given subject, it is best to start with the border pieces. With the border pieces in place, it's much easier to fit various clusters of thought into the whole. You will find those Scriptures that are somewhat nebulous and difficult to understand will easily join together the clusters of thought with those pieces that obvious and straight forward.

The problem in determining true doctrine is that we have many clusters of thought that don't fit together in harmony with one another. As stated, many Scriptures are vague in their meaning. When we try to build on that which is indefinite rather than that which is precise and easily understood, we end up with a distortion of the truth. When you build on that which is straightforward and easily understood, you will eventually find the connecting pieces that allow the ambiguous Scriptures to be connected.

Submitting Thinking Processes to the Purity of God's Word

We all have strongholds of thinking that must be torn down and brought into the captivity of Christ.[391] It requires a willing heart to break down old ways of thinking and processing before we can have open minds to fully receive all that God has for us from the purity of His word. We must be willing to cast down those arguments that exalt themselves against the knowledge of God. It's the purity of God's word that we must conform our thinking and be loyal to if we are to stop the deception that is in our lives and the Church.

---

[391] 2 Corinthians 10:5

Psalm 12:6 The words of the Lord are pure words, like silver, tried in a furnace of earth, purified seven times.

Psalm 119:140 Your word is very pure; therefore, Your servant loves it.

Proverbs 30:5 Every word of God is pure; He is a shield to those who put their trust in Him.

Doctrinal deception is a major area of concern when it comes to rightly dividing the word of truth. We've all come from various backgrounds of thinking in which we've been taught us to think. As a man thinks, so is he. The problem is, we become loyal to those ways rather than the purity of God's word. We may have certain doctrinal positions, simply because that's the way someone taught us. Sometimes our identity and security are so intertwined to a stream or denomination that we're afraid to embrace or even consider something other than what we've been taught. When we become more connected to a stream of consciousness rather than the Lord Jesus Christ and His word, we open ourselves up to deception and deceit. As Paul wrote, we must be transformed by the renewing of our minds, so that we can prove what the good and acceptable and perfect will of God is.[392]

If we are to be dedicated servants of God who desire to be vessels of honor whom the Lord uses for His prophetic purposes in our generation, we must conform our thinking to the purity of His word.

The Word Takes Precedence Over Experience

The word must take precedence over the Spirit because the word is pure and tested as seen in the aforementioned Scriptures. However, even though the Holy Spirit is perfect and pure, our experiences are subjective. When the Spirit's revelation enters our spirit, it's first pure and unadulterated. It then must pass through the doorways of our minds and be submitted to God's Word to remain pure. Without the purity of God's Word, His revelation is distilled through our un-sanctified thoughts and emotions and loses its purity.

If we allow our experiences to dictate doctrine, we become vulnerable to Satan's devices. When we base doctrine on spiritual experiences, there is no continuity. Everyone's experiences vary in various degrees depending on a person's emotions. We are not to think beyond the word.[393] In other words, our thoughts and emotions are to be subject to

---

[392] Romans 12:2
[393] 1 Corinthians 4:6

God's word, bringing every thought into its captivity. We are to test and prove all things.[394]

Many winds blow through the body of Christ—some good and some bad. We are to test all things by the word, holding fast to that which is true, while discarding that which is false. Some of the winds that come and go in the Church are based more on personal experiences than the purity of God's word. They're often referred to as extra-Biblical experiences. As a result, they become movements throughout the body of Christ, especially in the ranks of what is coined as "Charismatic Christianity." Don't get me wrong! I am also a Charismatic believer, but I'm also a strong believer in maintaining integrity to the purity of God's word, which has been already tested.

My spiritual father in the Lord, Dick Benjamin, coined a term that I think is quite good. He said, "Test the wind by the word." A major issue I have with some of my Charismatic brothers and sisters is that there doesn't seem to be much discernment when it comes to various winds blowing through the Church. There's ignorance to the fact that we have an enemy who loves to stir things up, causing all kinds of confusion and distrust amongst ourselves. Paul spoke of this when he said, *"We should no longer be children, tossed to and fro carried about with every wind of doctrine, by the trickery of men, in the cunning craftiness of deceitful plotting."*

Satan is a deceitful plotter and is aware of how gullible many Christians can be because of their lack of understanding and integrity when it comes to holding to the purity of God's word. Deceitfulness will only get worse as we come closer and closer to the second coming of Christ. Now is the time to re-examine what we believe and adhere to the purity of His word by rightly dividing it.

Many are still children in their understanding of God's word. Because the Church has focused so much on a consumerism and seeker mentality in the past few decades, God's people are quite illiterate when it comes to His word. They're easy pickings for Satan's deceitful plotting. As leaders and teachers, it's our responsibility to rightly divide the word of truth, so that they're not picked off by the enemy. We must abandon smoke and mirror theology and adhere to the purity of God's word.

Satan also understands the deceitfulness of the human heart and develops plans accordingly. The prophet Jeremiah said it best when he said, *"The heart is deceitful above all things, and desperately wicked;*

---

[394] 2 Corinthians 10:5, 1 Thessalonians 5:21

who can know it? I the Lord, search the heart, I test the mind, even to give every man according to his ways, according to the fruit of his doings. "[395]

If God in His sovereignty wants to knock me down and cause me to laugh, shake, bark like a dog, roar like a lion or whatever, that's His prerogative. But, it's my responsibility as to what I do with it. I don't have the right to try and duplicate something to others or start a movement if it's not clearly defined in His word. God will test our minds and give us according to our ways even if they're wrong. This is where the deception comes in. Just because God doesn't stop us, we tend to think He's putting His approval on it.

What often happens in Charismatic circles, is that a particular church may start to have what they deem as an outpouring of the Spirit, which attracts multitudes coming to their services. As a result, people from other parts of the country and even the world flock to them. They then go back to their churches and try to duplicate what they saw. Before you know it, another wind is blowing, and a movement gets launched with very little discernment. A movement needs to be thoroughly tested by the word in its infancy before it's released further. Otherwise, where do we draw the line in weirdness? Without drawing a line by testing the movement by the word, we swing the door wide open for Satan to come in with his deceptive ploys. Those who do contend for doctrinal purity and discernment often get accused of being legalistic.

Let's not forget; Satan can transform his ministers into false prophets and apostles who can perform signs and wonders. We are not to be ignorant of his devices. A movement or revival should take us further into God's prophetic purposes rather than being a spiritual playground.

A great example of how the word and Spirit work together for God's prophetic purposes to come forth is discovered on the day of Pentecost when the feast day of Pentecost was fully fulfilled. By rightly dividing the word of truth, Peter was able to define what was happening in the spiritual realm as the Holy Spirit suddenly came on them as a mighty rushing wind with tongues of fire. When the multitudes heard the sound and came together, they were confused, amazed, and perplexed, while others mocked saying, *"They are drunk and full of new wine."* [396]

Peter, full of the Holy Spirit and the word of God stood up and interpreted what was happening by allowing the Scriptures to interpret the prophetic event. He then began to quote from the prophet Joel concerning the outpouring of the Holy Spirit that was promised. Instead

---

[395] Jeremiah 17:9-10
[396] Acts 2:1-14

of this event being a spiritual playground with people perplexed and filled with confusion, he was able to identify the prophetic purpose that God through the Holy Spirit and His word fulfilled in their presence.[397] As a result, these early disciples went forth in their generation fulfilling the purposes of God just as David had done for his generation.

We still have many prophetic purposes and waves of revival yet ahead to be fulfilled before Jesus returns for His bride. Let us esteem His word by rightly dividing it. As we do, it will be a light unto our paths as we point the way for others to follow. Let us not leave a wake of perplexity, confusion and mocking behind us by not giving the word of God preference over how the Holy Spirit speaks and moves. We must allow our Holy Spirit inspired thoughts and experiences to be sanctified by the washing of His word.

May God bless you mightily as you go forth fulfilling His prophetic purposes for your lives and the kingdom of God. Allow His zeal to set you on fire as one of His flaming ministers filled with passion and zeal to take the kingdom by force.

---

[397] Acts 2:14-39

Rightly Dividing the Word of Truth

by Ken L. Birks © 2018 Straight Arrow Ministries

Beguiled by the enemy, truth in the streets disappears.
With seeds of deception sown, the Church cries out in tears.
As truth disappears, darkness settles across the globe.
Casting his spells of deception, the world lies in Satan's sway.
With false teaching running rampant, the enemy has his say.

Casting off the spells of darkness, the Church rises in relief.
Called to be the pillar and ground of all truth, she rises in belief.
Believing that all Scripture is inspired by God, she mends.
Called to divide the word of truth rightly, she makes amends.
In repentance, she returns to her foundation to rebuild.

With no other foundation to build upon, she rightly divides.
Immersing herself in the elementary principles, she presides.
Line upon line, here a little, there a little, she speaks with truth.
No longer caught in self-deception, she speaks truth in love.
With divine harmony of revelation in play, she comes alive.

Fully immersed in the unction of the Spirit, she teaches, reaffirmed.
With insight into riddles and mysteries, deeper truths are discerned.
With her thinking process submitted to the word, she rightly divides.
As the word takes precedence over the Spirit, in truth, she delivers
Knowing teachers receive a stricter judgment; she builds the pillars.

With the pillars of truth in place, light begins to dispel the darkness.
With the Father's glory rising upon His people, truth increases.
Not placating for the sake of relevancy, truth is restored in the streets.
As truth restores, light penetrates those once caught in hopelessness.
Without blinders, multitudes see the light, now penetrating the darkness.

Afterword

Throughout this book, my goal has been to reveal some of God's predestinated purposes that have both been fulfilled and unfulfilled. I have chosen to use the term "Prophetic Purposes" rather than "Predestinated Purposes." In actuality, they are predestinated purposes born out of the Father's foreknowledge. Speaking of Jesus, Peter points out in his Pentecost message that Jesus was delivered according to the predestinated purposes of the Father to be crucified.

Acts 2:23 *"Him, being delivered by the determined purpose and foreknowledge of God, you have taken by lawless hands, have crucified, and put to death.*

This book has been about the predestinated or prophetic purposes of God and how He fulfills them through His people as we go forth as His ministers of flaming fire. In the process, God must deal with the free will He has given to us. With that in mind, it's important to understand the difference between God's foreknowledge and His predestinated purposes and how they work together. All His predestinated purposes flow out of His foreknowledge. The most important event in the history of mankind was predestinated because of His foreknowledge. Peter mentions this in his Pentecost message as seen in the above Scripture.

Definition of Foreknowledge

"Fore" or "before" simply means God knows beforehand what the future holds. Because of the Father's omniscience, He knows the end from the beginning. He is the Alpha and the Omega. All that is to be known is known by Him

The Greek word for *"foreknow"* is *"proginosko."* which means "to know beforehand." The Greek word for *"foreknowledge"* is *"prognosis"* and means "a knowing beforehand."

Definition of Predestination

Predestination is to foreordain or determine an act or event. It's not simply foreknowledge of a future event, but rather making that event take place. It is predetermined to happen, and nothing can change it.

As seen throughout this book, God has made His prophetic purposes come to pass in spite of the weaknesses in His chosen instruments of righteousness. In His sovereignty, He was able to work with each of His instruments, who were chosen because of His omniscience or foreknowledge. He had complete confidence in them and knew they would make the right choices according to their free will. It's God who works on our behalf both to will and do His purposes. As we die daily to our desires and will, He works in us His will.

> ***Philippians 2:12-13*** *Therefore, my beloved, as you have always obeyed, not as in my presence only, but now work out your own salvation with fear and trembling:* *¹³* ***for it is God who works in you both to will and do for His good pleasure.***

As we faithfully submit our hearts in obedience to Him, we remove all roadblocks to what He is able to do in and through us as His ministers of flaming fire.

Whenever the Bible refers to predestination, it's always in reference to the events that God has predetermined to happen that are in accordance to his overall plans and purposes that have been marked out in advance according to His foreknowledge.

Noted Bible teacher, Kevin Conner describes predestination and foreknowledge in the following way: "The word *"predestinate"* is the Greek word *"Pro-orizo,"* and means *"to previously mark out a boundary line, to pre-determine, decide beforehand."* Compared with foreknowledge, predestination is used to refer to a determination made previous to it's actually coming to pass, and which carried with it the power to make it come to pass. Thus, it's an act of will that is only attributed to God Himself. We may say that foreknowledge is *"to know beforehand that certain things will happen,"* while predestination is *"to arrange or determine beforehand how they shall happen"* However, foreknowledge precedes predestination. God's foreknowledge did not stem from election or predestination. Election and predestination are founded in God's foreknowledge."[398]

It's important to understand when the Bible speaks of predestination; it's not in reference to our personal lives. It's after we receive salvation through the blood of Jesus Christ that we enter the predestinated purposes of God, the Father. As we submit to the on-working power of the Holy Spirit, God is able to work in us according to His plans and purposes. We always have choices. We must choose daily to die to self just as Paul did if we are to be used by God. Otherwise, our works are dead rather than being conformed to His workmanship in us.

---

[398] Quote by Kevin Conner, "The Foundations of Christian Doctrine," Pg. 250.

Prophetic Purposes and the Zeal of the Lord

The following Scripture verifies the fact that in a general sense, we are all predestinated to be conformed to the image of Christ, which is a major element in the predestinated purposes of God. According to 2 Corinthians 3:17-18, we are all being transformed from glory to glory into the image of Christ by the Holy Spirit, who is in our lives.

Romans 8:29 *For whom He foreknew, He also predestinated to be conformed to the image of His Son, that He might be the firstborn among many brethren.*

When the Holy Spirit enters our lives through salvation, He's been commissioned by the Father to bring us into conformity to His plans and purposes. This does not mean it automatically happens for us, as we have the power to quench His work in us through our disobedience and stubbornness. This is why we must die daily.

God, the Father, has much to do before the second coming of His Son, Jesus Christ comes to receive us unto Himself. May we allow the Holy Spirit to do what He has been commissioned to do by our Heavenly Father. We must allow our free wills to be submitted to His predestinated purposes, lest we become wild tares in the kingdom of God.

May God's blessing be upon us as we march forth in accordance with all that He has purposed for our lives. May His anointing fill our lamps as we wait patiently for Him. He will come to us like the latter rain, a mighty outpouring of His Spirit as we go forth like flames of fire to fulfill all that the prophets have foretold — His prophetic purposes.

Isaiah 65:2b *These are the ones I look on with favor: those who are humble and contrite in spirit, and who tremble at my word.*

BooksbyKen.com

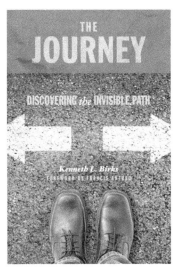

The Adventures of Space and Hobo tells the story of Ken's nomadic life after Vietnam. It explores the on-the-ground confusion and chaos of the Vietnam War and its effects on a generation, and those who served. Named "Space" by a new friend, Hobo, Ken and his traveling companion hit the road to partake of all the possibilities of that generation in search of adventure and uncharted experiences. The story takes us step by step along the path of the awakening of a lost soul, on his way to finding an understanding of himself, his path, and the meaning of his life.

The Journey gives you a glimpse into the path God has purposed for your life. Whether you're just starting out on your journey, anywhere in the middle, or you're detoured and have lost your way, this practical guide book will shine the light on the invisible path that not only leads to God's goodness and experiencing His kingdom within, but also to the greatest adventure of your life.

Quote from Francis Anfuso – Ken makes complex concepts simple and masterfully unpacks the Bible's greatest mysteries. He provides a sure foundation upon which to build a lifetime of insight."

For more information on either of these books and other materials by Ken Birks, please visit www.booksbyken.com

About the Author

Ken Birks is an ordained Pastor/Teacher in the Body of Christ. He has functioned as an elder, one of the staff pastors, and a Bible teacher at The Rock of Roseville in California for the past 20 years. He is presently semi-retired with a writing ministry and functions as a wedding officiant in the Sacramento region. Prior to this, Ken was the Senior Pastor of Golden Valley Christian Center, a Spirit-filled, non-denominational, church in Roseville for twelve years.

Ken attended and graduated from the Charismatic Bible College of Anchorage where he came into the relationship with Apostle Dick Benjamin, who was then the Sr. Pastor of Abbott Loop Christian Center (ALCC) in Anchorage, Alaska.

Aside from The Lord Jesus Christ, the core of Ken's spiritual being and the person he's become is a direct result from the influence and teaching he's received from Dick Benjamin for more than 25 years."

Other influences have been Bob Mumford from Life Changers and, in the past 18 years, Pastor Francis Anfuso of The Rock of Roseville.

Ken has been married to his wife, Lydia for 39 years, plus. They have two adult children and consider them their highest calling, along with the many teens and children whom they have been foster or surrogate parents to over the past 25 years.

Ken also has an internet ministry called "Sowing Seeds of Faith" located at kenbirks.com. Sowing Seeds of Faith reaches over 30,000 unique visitors a month with free Bible studies, devotional poetry, sermon outlines, audio, and video messages, podcasts, and other Bible study materials to help equip saints for the work of the ministry.

Workbooks & Other Materials

Biblical Perspectives Course

This course features lessons that are designed to give you a solid Biblical foundation in the elementary truths of God's Word. The lessons have three things in mind—building a doctrinal foundation, developing godly character, and helping you discover and find the destiny and purpose God has for your life. Please see the following website for more information and Lesson Titles:

www.kenbirks.com/perspectives-both/

More Biblical Perspectives Course

This course features lessons focused on three major areas of our Christian growth - doctrine, character, and destiny.

These lessons are designed to give you the Biblical understanding that will strengthen your Christian foundation and take you on a deeper walk with God.

Please see the following website for more information and lesson titles:

www.kenbirks.com/perspectives-both/

Small Group Lesson Guides

25 Lessons to help you discover Jesus in your midst during small group Bible studies.

Please see the following website for complete information and titles:

www.kenbirks.com/discipleship/lesson-guides.htm

References

Jim Feeney, Ph.D., Former Sr. Pastor and "Owner and Webmaster at Pentecostal Bible Studies and Free Pentecostal Sermon Central"

"I've known Pastor Ken Birks for several decades. He and I have worked in various ministerial capacities in the same family of churches. Ken is held in very high esteem among our many pastoral colleagues. He is a minister with a strong grasp of the Word of God, a broad variety of administrative skills, a heart for souls, a proven experiential familiarity with the gifts of the Holy Spirit, and an unwavering commitment to the work of the Lord. His wife, Lydia is likewise a dedicated servant of God. The two of them have been an exemplary couple in the Lord's work, and I have been honored to know them and see the lasting fruits of their labors since the 1970s."

John Dubler, Senior Pastor of Good Shepherd Bible Chapel

"Ken Birks is an extremely effective teacher of the Scriptures. He combines a healthy respect for the Word with enthusiasm and personal experiences that match what he is teaching. I strongly recommend him as a pastor, teacher, and elder. Ken is a man of unimpeachable integrity and his longevity in the Body of Christ as a pastor give credence to the message of hope and encouragement that he brings to all. Ken is available for speaking engagements within the United States and can be reached at ken@straitarrow.net

Websites

www.kenbirks.com – Sowing Seeds of Faith, Bible Studies and More

www.straitarrow.net – Bible Studies, Podcasts, Seminars, More

www.straitarrow.net/devotional-poetry – Biblical Devotional Poetry

www.straitarrow.net/Newsletters - Bi-Monthly Newsletters

www.booksbyken.com – How to order Ken's books and materials

www.sacramento-wedding-officiants.com – Wedding Officiating

Email: klbirks@gmail.com

Twitter: twitter.com/klbirks

Linkedin: www.linkedin.com/in/kenbirks